A First Course in Statistical Programming with R

This third edition of Braun and Murdoch's bestselling textbook now includes discussion of the use and design principles of the *tidyverse* packages in R, including expanded coverage of *ggplot2*. *R Markdown* is also discussed. The simulation chapter has been expanded to include an introduction to the Box–Müller and Metropolis–Hastings algorithms. New examples and exercises have been added throughout.

This is the only introduction you'll need to start programming in R, the computing standard for analyzing data. Co-written by a retired R Core Team member and an established R author, this book comes with real R code that complies with the standards of the language. Unlike other introductory books on the R system, this book emphasizes portable programming skills that apply to most computing languages and techniques used to develop more complex projects. Solutions, data sets, and any errata are available from the book's website www.statprogr.science. Worked examples—all from real applications—hundreds of exercises, and downloadable code, data sets, and solutions make a complete package for anyone working in or learning practical data science.

W. John Braun is Professor of Statistics at UBC's Okanagan campus. His research interests are in the modeling of environmental phenomena, such as wildfire, as well as statistical education, particularly as it relates to the R programming language.

Duncan J. Murdoch is a Professor Emeritus and was a member of the R Core Team of developers and co-president of the R Foundation. He is one of the developers of the rgl package for 3D visualization in R, and has also developed numerous other R packages.

A First Course in Statistical Programming with R

Third Edition

W. John Braun and Duncan J. Murdoch

CAMBRIDGE
UNIVERSITY PRESS

University Printing House, Cambridge CB2 8BS, United Kingdom

One Liberty Plaza, 20th Floor, New York, NY 10006, USA

477 Williamstown Road, Port Melbourne, VIC 3207, Australia

314–321, 3rd Floor, Plot 3, Splendor Forum, Jasola District Centre, New Delhi – 110025, India

79 Anson Road, #06–04/06, Singapore 079906

Cambridge University Press is part of the University of Cambridge.

It furthers the University's mission by disseminating knowledge in the pursuit of education, learning, and research at the highest international levels of excellence.

www.cambridge.org

Information on this title: www.cambridge.org/9781108995146

DOI: 10.1017/9781108993456

First published 2007

Second edition 2016

Third edition 2021

A catalogue record for this publication is available from the British Library.

ISBN 978-1-108-99514-6 Paperback

Contents

Expanded contents

Preface to the third edition

The R community continues to be active, with numerous conferences, user groups, and new packages appearing since we wrote the second edition of this text. In particular, use of the *tidyverse* style of R programming has exploded. In this edition we have included the new Chapter 5 on several *tidyverse* packages, and greatly expanded our coverage of `ggplot2` in Chapter 3 and the `magrittr` pipe operator in Chapter 4. We have also added a section on using R Markdown to Chapter 2.

But this text is about statistical computing *using* R, it's not just a manual on how to use R: so as with other parts of the book, we've written these new parts to emphasize and discuss the underlying ideas. If you work through this book you'll learn a lot about R, but we hope you'll also learn a lot of ideas that will apply to other computing languages and systems.

The later chapters on the more mathematical aspects of statistical computing have also been updated. Chapter 6 now includes expanded coverage of Markov chain Monte Carlo including the Metropolis–Hastings algorithm with an example using it in Bayesian inference.

This edition was built with R version 4.0.2, and once again `knitr` was crucial in putting together the manuscript. Some of the richness of the R environment is indicated by the list of packages and versions used in the production of this book, as shown in the table below. We thank the R Core group and the authors of all of those packages for their work in making R such a rich system. We also thank careful readers Woonchan Cho and Julian Stander for pointing out several errors in the previous edition. All the new errors are ours!

W. John Braun
Duncan Murdoch

October, 2020

Packages used to produce this book.

Package	Version	Package	Version	Package	Version	Package	Version
DBI	1.1.0	evaluate	0.14	leaflet	2.0.3	rgl	0.102.25
KernSmooth	2.23-17	fastmap	1.0.1	lifecycle	0.2.0	rlang	0.4.7
MPV	1.55	forcats	0.5.0	lpSolve	5.6.15	rvest	0.3.6
NLP	0.2-0	fs	1.5.0	lubridate	1.7.9	scales	1.1.1
R6	2.4.1	generics	0.0.2	magrittr	1.5	shiny	1.5.0
Rcpp	1.0.5	ggplot2	3.3.2	manipulateWidget	0.10.1	sos	2.0-0
assertthat	0.2.1	glue	1.4.2	microbenchmark	1.4-7	stringi	1.5.3
backports	1.1.10	grid	4.0.2	mime	0.9	stringr	1.4.0
blob	1.2.1	gtable	0.3.0	miniUI	0.1.1.1	tibble	3.0.3
brew	1.0-6	haven	2.3.1	modelr	0.1.8	tidyr	1.1.2
broom	0.7.1	highr	0.8	munsell	0.5.0	tidyselect	1.1.0
cellranger	1.1.0	hms	0.5.3	patchDVI	1.10.1	tidyverse	1.3.0
colorspace	1.4-1	htmltools	0.5.0	pillar	1.4.6	tools	4.0.2
compiler	4.0.2	htmlwidgets	1.5.2	pkgconfig	2.0.3	vctrs	0.3.4
crayon	1.3.4	httpuv	1.5.4	promises	1.1.1	webshot	0.5.2
crosstalk	1.1.0.1	httr	1.4.2	purrr	0.3.4	xfun	0.18
dbplyr	1.4.4	janeaustenr	0.1.5	quadprog	1.5-8	xml2	1.3.2
digest	0.6.25	jsonlite	1.7.1	readr	1.4.0	xtable	1.8-4
dplyr	1.0.2	later	1.1.0.1	readxl	1.3.1		
ellipsis	0.3.1	lattice	0.20-41	reprex	0.3.0		

Preface to the second edition

A lot of things have happened in the R community since we wrote the first edition of this text. Millions of new users have started to use R, and it is now the premier platform for data analytics. (In fact, the term "data analytics" hardly existed when we wrote the first edition.)

RStudio, a cross-platform integrated development environment for R, has had a large influence on the increase in popularity. In this edition we recommend RStudio as the platform for most new users, and have integrated simple RStudio instructions into the text. In fact, we have used RStudio and the `knitr` package in putting together the manuscript.

We have also added numerous examples and exercises, and cleaned up existing ones when they were unclear. Chapter 2 (Introduction to the R Language) has had extensive revision and reorganization. We have added short discussions of newer graphics systems to Chapter 3 (Programming Statistical Graphics). Reference material on some common error messages has been added to Chapter 4 (Programming with R), and a list of pseudo-random number generators as well as a more extensive discussion of Markov chain Monte Carlo is new in Chapter 5 (Simulation). In Chapter 6 (Computational Linear Algebra), some applications have been added to give students a better idea of why some of the matrix decompositions are so important.

Once again we have a lot of people to thank. Many students have used the first edition, and we are grateful for their comments and criticisms. Some anonymous reviewers also provided some helpful suggestions and pointers so that we could make improvements to the text. We hope our readers find this new edition as interesting and educational as we think it is.

W. John Braun
Duncan Murdoch

November, 2015

Preface to the first edition

This text began as notes for a course in statistical computing for second year actuarial and statistical students at the University of Western Ontario. Both authors are interested in statistical computing, both as support for our other research and for its own sake. However, we have found that our students were not learning the right sort of programming basics before they took our classes. At every level from undergraduate through Ph.D., we found that the students were not able to produce simple, reliable programs; that they didn't understand enough about numerical computation to understand how rounding error could influence their results, and that they didn't know how to begin a difficult computational project.

We looked into service courses from other departments, but we found that they emphasized languages and concepts that our students would not use again. Our students need to be comfortable with simple programming so that they can put together a simulation of a stochastic model; they also need to know enough about numerical analysis so that they can do numerical computations reliably. We were unable to find this mix in an existing course, so we designed our own.

We chose to base this text on R. R is an open source computing package which has seen a huge growth in popularity in the last few years. Being open source, it is easily obtainable by students and economical to install in our computing lab. One of us (Murdoch) is a member of the core R development team, and the other (Braun) is a co-author of a book on data analysis using R. These facts made it easy for us to choose R, but we are both strong believers in the idea that there are certain universals of programming, and in this text we try to emphasize those: it is not a manual about programming in R, it is a course in statistical programming that uses R.

Students starting this course are not assumed to have any programming experience or advanced statistical knowledge. They should be familiar with university-level calculus, and should have had exposure to a course in introductory probability, though that could be taken concurrently: the probabilistic concepts start in Chapter 5. (We include a concise appendix reviewing the probabilistic material.) We include some advanced topics in simulation, linear algebra, and optimization that an instructor may choose to skip in a one-semester course offering.

We have a lot of people to thank for their help in writing this book. The students in Statistical Sciences 259b have provided motivation and feedback, Lutong Zhou drafted several figures, Kristy Alexander, Yiwen Diao, Qiang Fu, and Yu Han went over the exercises and wrote up detailed solutions, and Diana Gillooly of Cambridge University Press, Prof. Brian Ripley of Oxford University, and some anonymous reviewers all provided helpful suggestions. And of course, this book could not exist without R, and R would be far less valuable without the contributions of the worldwide R community.

W. John Braun
Duncan Murdoch

February, 2007

1

Getting started

Welcome to the world of statistical programming. We will start in this chapter by giving you an idea of what statistical programming is all about. We will also tell you what to expect as you proceed through the rest of the book. The chapter will finish with some instructions about how to download and install R, the software package and language on which we base our programming examples, and RStudio, an "integrated development environment" (or "IDE") for R.

1.1 What is statistical programming?

Computer programming involves controlling computers, telling them what calculations to do, what to display, etc. Statistical programming is harder to define. One definition might be that it's the kind of computer programming statisticians do—but statisticians do all sorts of programming. Another would be that it's the kind of programming one does when one is doing statistics: but again, statistics involves a wide variety of computing tasks.

For example, statisticians are concerned with collecting and analyzing data, and some statisticians would be involved in setting up connections between computers and laboratory instruments: but we would not call that statistical programming. Statisticians often oversee data entry from questionnaires, and may set up programs to aid in detecting data entry errors. That *is* statistical programming, but it is quite specialized, and beyond the scope of this book.

Statistical programming involves doing computations to aid in statistical analysis. For example, data must be summarized and displayed. Models must be fit to data, and the results displayed. These tasks can be done in a number of different computer applications: Microsoft Excel, SAS, SPSS, R, Stata, etc. Using these applications is certainly statistical computing, and usually involves statistical programming, but it is not the focus of this book. In this book our aim is to provide a foundation for an understanding of how those applications work: what are the calculations they do, and how could you do them yourself.

Since graphs play an important role in statistical analysis, drawing graphics of one, two or higher dimensional data is an aspect of statistical programming.

An important part of statistical programming is stochastic simulation. Digital computers are naturally very good at exact, reproducible computations, but the real world is full of randomness. In stochastic simulation we program a computer to act as though it is producing random results, even though if we knew enough, the results would be exactly predictable.

Statistical programming is closely related to other forms of numerical programming. It involves optimization, and approximation of mathematical functions. Computational linear algebra plays a central role. There is less emphasis on differential equations than in physics or applied mathematics (though this is slowly changing). We tend to place more of an emphasis on the results and less on the analysis of the algorithms than in computer science.

1.2 | Outline of this book

This book is an introduction to statistical programming. It contains a lot of specific advice about the hows and whys of the subject. We will start with basic programming: how to tell a computer what to do. We do this using the open source R statistical package, so we will teach you R, but we will try not to *just* teach you R. We will emphasize those things that are common to many computing platforms.

Statisticians need to display data. We will show you how to construct statistical graphics. In doing this, we will learn a little bit about human vision, and how it motivates our choice of display.

In our introduction to programming, we will show how to control the flow of execution of a program. For example, we might wish to do repeated calculations as long as the input consists of positive integers, but then stop when an input value hits 0. Programming a computer requires basic logic, and we will touch on Boolean algebra, a formal way to manipulate logical statements. The best programs are thought through carefully *before* being implemented, and we will discuss how to break down complex problems into simple parts. When we are discussing programming, we will spend quite a lot of time discussing how to *get it right*: how to be sure that the computer program is calculating what you want it to calculate. We will talk about the importance of consistency and clarity in complex projects, using the example of the *tidyverse* project for data science.

One distinguishing characteristic of statistical programming is that it is concerned with randomness: random errors in data, and models that include stochastic components. We will discuss methods for simulating random values with specified characteristics, and show how random simulations are useful in a variety of problems.

Many statistical procedures are based on linear models. While discussion of linear regression and other linear models is beyond the scope of this book, we do discuss some of the background linear algebra, and how the computations it involves can be carried out. We also discuss the general problem of numerical optimization: finding the values which make a function as large or as small as possible.

Each chapter has a number of exercises which are at varying degrees of difficulty. Solutions to selected exercises can be found on the web at `www.statprogr.science`.

1.3 | The R package

This book uses R, which is an open source package for statistical computing. "Open source" has a number of different meanings; here the important one is that R is freely available, and its users are free to see how it is written, and to improve it. R is based on the computer language S, developed by John Chambers and others at Bell Laboratories in 1976. In 1993 Robert Gentleman and Ross Ihaka at the University of Auckland wanted to experiment with the language, so they developed an implementation, and named it R. They made it open source in 1995, and thousands of people around the world have contributed to its development.

1.4 | Why use a command line?

The R system is mainly command-driven, with the user typing in text and asking R to execute it. Nowadays most programs use interactive graphical user interfaces (menus, touchscreens, etc.) instead. So why did we choose such an old-fashioned way of doing things?

Menu-based interfaces are very convenient when applied to a limited set of commands, from a few to one or two hundred. However, a command-line interface is open ended. As we will show in this book, if you want to program a computer to do something that no one has done before, you can easily do it by breaking down the task into the parts that make it up, and then building up a program to carry it out. This may be possible in some menu-driven interfaces, but it is much easier in a command-driven interface.

Moreover, learning how to use one command-line interface will give you skills that carry over to others, and may even give you some insight into how a menu-driven interface is implemented. As statisticians, it is our belief that your goal should be understanding, and learning how to program at a command line will give you that at a fundamental level. Learning to use a menu-based program makes you dependent on the particular organization of that program.

There is no question that command-line interfaces require greater knowledge on the part of the user—you need to remember what to type to achieve a particular outcome. Fortunately, there is help. We recommend that you use the RStudio integrated development environment (IDE). IDEs were first developed in the 1970s to help programmers: they allow you to edit your program, to search for help, and to run it; when your first attempt doesn't work, they offer support for diagnosing and fixing errors. RStudio is an IDE for R programming, first released in 2011. It is produced by a Public Benefit Corporation[1] named RStudio, and is available for free use.

[1] Public Benefit Corporations are for-profit corporations whose corporate decisions must balance the interests of community, customers, employees, and shareholders.

1.5 | Font conventions

This book describes how to do computations in R. As we will see in the next chapter, this requires that the user types input, and R responds with text or graphs as output. To indicate the difference, we have typeset the user input and R output in a tinted box. The output is prefixed with ##. For example

```
This was typed by the user
```

```
## This is a response from R
```

In most cases other than this one and certain exercises, we will show the actual response from R corresponding to the preceding input.[2]

There are also situations where the code is purely illustrative and is not meant to be executed. (Many of those are not correct R code at all; others illustrate the syntax of R code in a general way.) In these situations we have typeset the code examples in an upright typewriter font. For example,

[2] We have used the `knitr` package so that R itself is computing the output. The computations in the text were done with R version 4.0.2 (2020-06-22).

```
f( some arguments )
```

1.6 | Installation of R and RStudio

R can be downloaded from `https://cloud.r-project.org`. Most users should download and install a *binary version*. This is a version that has been translated (by *compilers*) into machine language for execution on a particular type of computer with a particular operating system. R is designed to be very *portable*: it will run on Microsoft Windows, Linux, Solaris, macOS, and other operating systems, but different binary versions are required for each. In this book most of what we do would be the same on any system, but when we write system-specific instructions, we will assume that readers are using Microsoft Windows.

Installation on Microsoft Windows is straightforward. A binary version is available for Windows Vista or above from the web page `https://cloud.r-project.org/bin/windows/base`. Download the "setup program," a file with a name like `R-4.0.2-win.exe`. Clicking on this file will start an almost automatic installation of the R system. Though it is possible to customize the installation, the default responses will lead to a satisfactory installation in most situations, particularly for beginning users.

One of the default settings of the installation procedure is to create an R icon on your computer's desktop.

You should also install RStudio, after you have installed R. As with R, there are separate versions for different computing platforms, but they all look and act similarly. You should download the "Open Source Edition" of "RStudio Desktop" from www.rstudio.com, and follow the instructions to install it on your computer.

1.7 | Getting started in RStudio

Once you have installed R and RStudio, you will be ready to start statistical programming. We'll start with a quick tour of RStudio, and introduce more detail in later chapters.

When you are working in RStudio, you'll see a display something like Figure 1.1. (The first time you start it, you won't see all the content that is in the figure. After working with it for a while, you may have customized it to look quite different!) The display includes four *panes*. The top left pane is the *Source Pane*, or editor. You will type your program (or other document) there. You can have several open files in this pane; the tabs allow you to choose which is active. The bottom left pane is called the *Console Pane*.

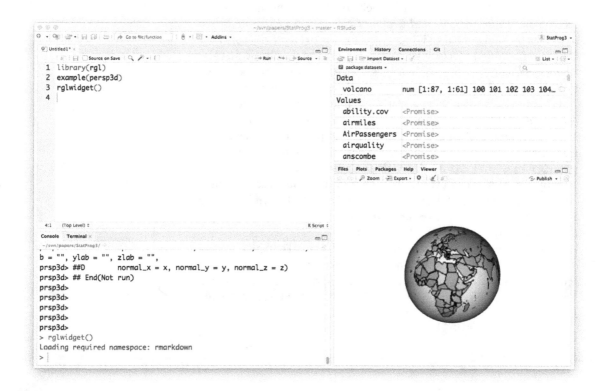

Fig. 1.1 A typical RStudio display.

This is where you communicate with R. You can type directly into this pane, but it is usually better to work within the editor pane, because that way you can easily correct mistakes and try again.

The two right-hand panes contain a variety of *tabs*. In the figure, the top pane is showing the *Environment Pane* (i.e. the workspace), and the bottom pane is showing a plot; we'll discuss these and the other tabs in later chapters. For now, you just need to know the following points:

- You should do most of your work in the editor, but you can occasionally type in the console.
- The console pane displays what R is doing.
- All of the panes can be resized and repositioned, so sometimes it may appear that you've lost one, but there's no need to worry: just find the header of the pane and click there with your mouse, and the pane will reappear. If the pane is there but the content isn't what you want, try clicking on the tabs at the top.

1.8 | Going further

This book introduces statistical programming with R, but doesn't come close to covering everything. Here are some further resources.

- There are many textbooks that will teach you more about statistics. We recommend *Data Analysis and Graphics Using R: An Example-Based Approach* by Maindonald and Braun and *Introductory Statistics with R* by Dalgaard for an introductory level presentation, and the classic *Modern Applied Statistics with S* by Venables and Ripley for more advanced material. *R for Data Science* by Grolemund and Wickham describes the "tidy" approach to data science that we will introduce in Chapter 5 and *Advanced R* by Wickham gives more detail about programming in R.
- There are many tools that use R in preparing printed documents. We particularly like `knitr`, which you can read about online at `https://yihui.name/knitr` or in the book *Dynamic Documents with R and knitr* by Xie. It provides a very rich system; for a simple subset (useful to write your assignments for class!), we describe R Markdown in Section 2.7.3. See `https://rmarkdown.rstudio.com/` for more details on this subset.
- R can also be used to prepare interactive web pages. The Shiny system displays output from R based on prepared scripts that are controlled in a browser. The user doesn't need to install R, but he or she can see R output. You can see an example and read more about Shiny at `https://shiny.rstudio.com`.

Introduction to the R language

Having installed the R and RStudio systems, you are now ready to begin to learn the art of statistical programming. The first step is to learn the *syntax* of the language that you will be programming in; you need to know the rules of the language. This chapter will give you an introduction to the syntax of R. Most of what we discuss here relates to what you would type into the R console or into the RStudio script window.

2.1 First steps

Having opened R or RStudio, you may begin entering and executing commands, usually interactively. Normally, you will use the Source Pane to type in your commands, but you may occasionally use the Console Pane directly. The greater-than sign (>) is the prompt symbol which appears in the Console Pane.

2.1.1 R can be used as a calculator

Anything that can be computed on the calculator app on your smartphone can be computed at the R prompt. The basic operations are + (add), - (subtract), * (multiply), and / (divide). For example, try

```
5504982/131071
```

Upon pressing the Enter key (or CTRL-Enter, or CMD-Enter, depending on your system), the result of the above division operation, 42, appears in the Console Pane, preceded by the command you executed, and prefixed by the number 1 in square brackets:

```
5504982/131071
## [1] 42
```

The [1] indicates that this is the first (and in this case only) result from the command. Many commands return multiple values, and each line of results will be labeled to aid the user in deciphering the output.

For example, the sequence of integers from 17 to 58 may be displayed as follows:

```
17:58
##  [1] 17 18 19 20 21 22 23 24 25 26 27 28 29 30 31 32 33 34 35 36 37 38
## [23] 39 40 41 42 43 44 45 46 47 48 49 50 51 52 53 54 55 56 57 58
```

The first line starts with the first return value, so is labeled `[1]`; the second line starts with the 23rd, so is labeled `[23]`.

Everything that you type after a # sign is assumed to be a comment and is ignored by R.

```
5:(2*3 + 10)    # the result is  the same as 5:16
##  [1]   5   6   7   8   9 10 11 12 13 14 15 16
(7:10) + pi       # pi is a stored constant
## [1] 10.14159 11.14159 12.14159 13.14159
```

Note the use of parentheses in the examples above. Parentheses are used to ensure that the operations (in this case, `:`, `*` and `+`) are carried out in the order that we desire. In the first case, parentheses were necessary to obtain the result we wanted to see. The following shows what happens when the parentheses are omitted:

```
5:2*3 + 10
## [1] 25 22 19 16
```

If you are surprised by this result, it would be a good exercise to break the calculation down into the three separate operations in order to determine exactly what R is doing.

The parentheses were not required in `(7:10) + pi`. We used them anyway, for two reasons. First, they can help others read and understand the code more quickly. Second, although R follows strict and consistent rules regarding order of operations, we believe it is too easy for a user to forget one or more of these rules. Therefore, we recommend using parentheses whenever you are unsure (or even in cases where you think you may be right).

R can also be used to compute powers with the ^ operator. For example,

```
3^4
## [1] 81
```

Modular arithmetic is also available. For example, you can compute the remainder after division of 31 by 7, i.e. 31 (mod 7):

```
31 %% 7
## [1] 3
```

and the integer part of a fraction as

```
31 %/% 7
## [1] 4
```

We can confirm that 31 is the sum of its remainder plus seven times the integer part of the fraction:

```
7*4 + 3
## [1] 31
```

2.1.2 Named storage

R has a workspace known as the *global environment* that can be used to store the results of calculations, and many other types of objects. For a first example, suppose we would like to store the result of the calculation `1.0025^30` for future use. (This might arise from a compound interest calculation based on an interest rate of 0.25% per year and a 30-year term.) We will assign this value to an object called `interest.30`. To do this, we type

```
interest.30 <- 1.0025^30
```

We tell R to make the assignment using an arrow that points to the left, created with the less-than sign (`<`) and the hyphen (`-`). R also supports using the equals sign (`=`) in place of the arrow in most circumstances, but we recommend using the arrow, as it makes clear that we are requesting an *action* (i.e. an assignment), rather than stating a *relation* (i.e. that `interest.30` is equal to `1.0025^30`), or making a permanent definition. Note that when you run this statement, no output appears: R has done what we asked, and is waiting for us to ask for something else.

You can see the results of this assignment by typing the name of our new object at the prompt:

```
interest.30
## [1] 1.077783
```

Think of this as just another calculation: R is calculating the result of the expression `interest.30`, and printing it. You can also use `interest.30` in further calculations if you wish. For example, you can calculate the bank balance after 30 years at 0.25% annual interest, if you start with an initial balance of $3000:

```
initialBalance <- 3000
finalBalance <- initialBalance * interest.30
finalBalance
## [1] 3233.35
```

Example 2.1

An individual wishes to take out a loan, today, of P at a monthly interest rate i. The loan is to be paid back in n monthly installments of size R, beginning one month from now. The problem is to calculate R.

Equating the present value P to the future (discounted) value of the n monthly payments R, we have

$$P = R(1+i)^{-1} + R(1+i)^{-2} + \cdots + R(1+i)^{-n}$$

or

$$P = R \sum_{j=1}^{n} (1+i)^{-j}.$$

Summing this geometric series and simplifying, we obtain

$$P = R \left(\frac{1 - (1+i)^{-n}}{i} \right).$$

This is the formula for the present value of an annuity. We can find R, given P, n and i as

$$R = P \frac{i}{1 - (1+i)^{-n}}.$$

In R, we define variables as follows: `principal` to hold the value of P, and `intRate` to hold the interest rate, and `n` to hold the number of payments. We will assign the resulting payment value to an object called `payment`.

Of course, we need some numerical values to work with, so we will suppose that the loan amount is $1500, the interest rate is 1% and the number of payments is 10. The required code is then

```
intRate <- 0.01
n <- 10
principal <- 1500
payment <- principal * intRate / (1 - (1 + intRate)^(-n))
payment

## [1] 158.3731
```

For this particular loan, the monthly payments are $158.37.

2.1.3 Quitting R

To quit your R session, run

```
q()
```

or choose `Quit Session...` from the `File` menu. You will then be asked whether to save an image of the current workspace, or not, or to cancel.

The workspace image contains a record of the computations you've done, and may contain some saved results. Hitting the Cancel option allows you to continue your current R session. We rarely save the current workspace image, but occasionally find it convenient to do so.

Note what happens if you omit the parentheses () when attempting to quit:

```
q

## function (save = "default", status = 0, runLast = TRUE)
## .Internal(quit(save, status, runLast))
## <bytecode: 0x7f9bc3498ee8>
## <environment: namespace:base>
```

This has happened because q is a *function* that is used to tell R to quit. Typing q by itself tells R to show us the (not very pleasant-looking) contents of the function q. By typing q(), we are telling R to *call* the function q. The action of this function is to quit R. *Everything* that R does is done through calls to functions, though sometimes those calls are hidden (as when we click on menus), or very basic (as when we call the multiplication function to multiply 14 times 3).

Recording your work

Rather than saving the workspace, we prefer to keep a record of the commands we entered, so that we can reproduce the workspace at a later date. The easiest way to do this in RStudio is to enter commands in the Source Pane, and run them from there. At the end of a session, save the final script for a permanent record of your work. In other systems a text editor and some form of cut and paste serve the same purpose.

Exercises

1 Calculate the remainder after dividing 31079 into 170166719.
2 Calculate the interest earned after 5 years on an investment of $2000, assuming an interest rate of 3% compounded annually.
3 Using one line of R code, calculate the interest earned on an investment of $2000, assuming an interest rate of 3% compounded annually, for terms of 1, 2, ..., 30 years.
4 Calculate the monthly payment required for a loan of $200,000, at a monthly interest rate of 0.003, based on 300 monthly payments, starting in one month's time.
5 Use R to calculate the area of a circle with radius 7 cm.
6 Using one line of R code, calculate the respective areas of the circles having radii $3, 4, \ldots, 100$.
7 In the expression 48:(14*3), are the brackets really necessary? What happens when you type 48:14*3?
8 Do you think there is a difference between 48:14^2 and 48:(14^2)? Try both calculations. Using one line of code, how would you obtain the squares of the numbers $48, 47, \ldots, 14$?

2.2 | Basic features of R

2.2.1 Functions

Most of the work in R is done through *functions*. For example, we saw that to quit R we can type q(). This tells R to *call* the function named q. The parentheses surround the *argument list*, which in this case contains nothing: we just want R to quit, and do not need to tell it how.

We also saw that q is defined as

```
q

## function (save = "default", status = 0, runLast = TRUE)
## .Internal(quit(save, status, runLast))
## <bytecode: 0x7f9bc3498ee8>
## <environment: namespace:base>
```

This shows that q is a function that has three *arguments*: save, status, and runLast. Each of those has a *default value*: "default", 0, and TRUE, respectively. What happens when we execute q() is that R calls the q function with the arguments set to their default values.

If we want to change the default values, we specify them when we call the function. Arguments are identified in the call by their position, or by specifying the name explicitly. For example, both

```
q("no")
q(save = "no")
```

tell R to call q with the first argument set to "no", i.e. to quit without saving the workspace. If we had given two arguments without names, they would apply to save and status. If we want to accept the defaults of the early parameters but change later ones, we give the name when calling the function, e.g.

```
q(runLast = FALSE)
```

or use commas to mark the missing arguments, e.g.

```
q( , , FALSE)
```

Note that we must use = to set arguments. If we had written q(runLast <- FALSE) it would be interpreted quite differently from q(runLast = FALSE). The arrow says to put the value FALSE into a variable named runLast. We then pass the result of that action (which is the value FALSE) as the first argument of q(). Since save is the first argument, it will act like q(save = FALSE), which is probably not what we wanted.

It is a good idea to use named arguments when calling a function which has many arguments or when using uncommon arguments, because it reduces the risk of specifying the wrong argument, and makes your code easier to read.

2.2.2 R is case-sensitive

Consider this:

```
x <- 1:10
MEAN(x)

## Error in MEAN(x): could not find function "MEAN"
```

Now try

```
MEAN <- mean
MEAN(x)

## [1] 5.5
```

The function `mean()` is built in to R. R considers `MEAN` to be a different function, because it is case-sensitive: `m` is different from `M`.

2.2.3 Listing the objects in the workspace

The calculations in the previous sections led to the creation of several simple R objects. These objects are stored in the current R workspace. A list of all objects in the current workspace can be printed to the screen using the `objects()` function:

```
objects()

## [1] "MEAN"          "finalBalance"   "initialBalance"
## [4] "intRate"       "interest.30"    "n"
## [7] "payment"       "principal"      "x"
```

A synonym for `objects()` is `ls()`. In RStudio the Environment Pane shows both the names and abbreviated displays of the objects' values.

Remember that if we quit our R session without saving the workspace image, then these objects will disappear. If we save the workspace image, then the workspace will be restored at our next R session.[1]

2.3 | Vectors in R

2.3.1 Numeric vectors

A numeric vector is a list of numbers. The `c()` function is used to collect things together into a vector. We can type

```
c(0, 7, 8)

## [1] 0 7 8
```

Again, we can assign this to a named object:

```
x <- c(0, 7, 8)   # now x is a 3-element vector
```

To see the contents of x, simply type

---

[1] This will be true if we start R from the same folder (working directory) as where we ended the previous R session. Normally this will be the case, but users are free to change the folder during a session using the menus or the `setwd()` function. Type `?setwd` to obtain help with this function.

```
x
```

```
## [1] 0 7 8
```

The : symbol can be used to create sequences of increasing (or decreasing) values. For example,

```
numbers5to20 <- 5:20
numbers5to20
```

```
## [1]  5  6  7  8  9 10 11 12 13 14 15 16 17 18 19 20
```

Vectors can be joined together (i.e. *concatenated*) with the c function. For example, note what happens when we type

```
c(numbers5to20, x)
```

```
## [1]  5  6  7  8  9 10 11 12 13 14 15 16 17 18 19 20  0  7  8
```

Here is another example of the use of the c() function.

```
some.numbers <- c(2, 3, 5, 7, 11, 13, 17, 19, 23, 29, 31, 37, 41,
    43, 47, 59, 67, 71, 73, 79, 83, 89, 97, 103, 107, 109, 113, 119)
```

If you type this in the R console (not in the RStudio Source Pane), R will prompt you with a + sign for the second line of input. RStudio doesn't add the prompt, but it will indent the second line. In both cases you are being told that the first line is incomplete: you have an open parenthesis which must be followed by a closing parenthesis in order to complete the command.

We can append numbers5to20 to the end of some.numbers, and then append the decreasing sequence from 4 to 1:

```
a.mess <- c(some.numbers, numbers5to20, 4:1)
a.mess
```

```
## [1]    2   3   5   7  11  13  17  19  23  29  31  37  41  43  47  59
## [17]   67  71  73  79  83  89  97 103 107 109 113 119   5   6   7   8
## [33]    9  10  11  12  13  14  15  16  17  18  19  20   4   3   2   1
```

Remember that the numbers printed in square brackets give the index of the element immediately to the right. Among other things, this helps us to identify the 22nd element of a.mess as 89: just count across from the 17th element, 67.

2.3.2 Extracting elements from vectors

A nicer way to display the 22nd element of a.mess is to use square brackets to extract just that element:

```
a.mess[22]
```

```
## [1] 89
```

We can extract more than one element at a time. For example, the third, sixth, and seventh elements of a.mess are

```
a.mess[c(3, 6, 7)]
## [1]  5 13 17
```

To get the third through seventh element of numbers5to20, type

```
numbers5to20[3:7]
## [1]  7  8  9 10 11
```

Negative indices can be used to avoid certain elements. For example, we can select all but the second and tenth elements of numbers5to20 as follows:

```
numbers5to20[-c(2,10)]
##  [1]  5  7  8  9 10 11 12 13 15 16 17 18 19 20
```

The third through eleventh elements of numbers5to20 can be avoided as follows:

```
numbers5to20[-(3:11)]
## [1]  5  6 16 17 18 19 20
```

Using a zero index returns nothing. This is not something that one would usually type, but it may be useful in more complicated expressions. For example, recall that x contains the vector $(0, 7, 8)$ so that

```
numbers5to20[x]
## [1] 11 12
```

Do not mix positive and negative indices. To see what happens, observe

```
x[c(-2, 3)]
## Error in x[c(-2, 3)]: only 0's may be mixed with negative subscripts
```

The problem is that it is not clear what is to be extracted: do we want the third element of x before or after removing the second one?

Always be careful to make sure that vector indices are integers. When fractional values are used, they will be truncated towards 0. Thus 0.6 becomes 0, as in

```
x[0.6]
## numeric(0)
```

The output numeric(0) indicates a numeric vector of length zero.

2.3.3 Vector arithmetic

Arithmetic can be done on R vectors. For example, we can multiply all elements of x by 3:

```
x * 3

## [1]  0 21 24
```

Note that the computation is performed elementwise. Addition, subtraction, and division by a constant have the same kind of effect. For example,

```
y <- x - 5
y

## [1] -5  2  3
```

For another example, consider taking the 3rd power of the elements of x:

```
x^3

## [1]   0 343 512
```

The above examples show how a binary arithmetic operator can be used with vectors and constants. In general, the binary operators also work element-by-element when applied to pairs of vectors. For example, we can compute $y_i^{x_i}$, for $i = 1, 2, 3$, i.e. $(y_1^{x_1}, y_2^{x_2}, y_3^{x_3})$, as follows:

```
y^x

## [1]    1  128 6561
```

When the vectors are different lengths, the shorter one is extended by *recycling*: values are repeated, starting at the beginning. For example, to see the pattern of remainders of the numbers 1 to 10 modulo 2 and 3, we need only give the 2:3 vector once:

```
c(1, 1, 2, 2, 3, 3, 4, 4, 5, 5, 6, 6, 7, 7, 8, 8, 9, 9,
  10, 10) %% 2:3

##  [1] 1 1 0 2 1 0 0 1 1 2 0 0 1 1 0 2 1 0 0 1
```

R will give a warning if the length of the longer vector is not a multiple of the length of the smaller one, because that is often a symptom of an error in the code. For example, if we wanted the remainders modulo 2, 3, and 4, this is the wrong way to do it:

```
c(1, 1, 2, 2, 3, 3, 4, 4, 5, 5, 6, 6, 7, 7, 8, 8, 9, 9, 10, 10) %% 2:4

## Warning in c(1, 1, 2, 2, 3, 3, 4, 4, 5, 5, 6, 6, 7, 7, 8,8,9,9,10,10)%%2:4:
## longer object length is not a multiple of shorter object length

##  [1] 1 1 2 0 0 3 0 1 1 1 0 2 1 1 0 0 0 1 0 1
```

(Do you see the error?)

2.3.4 Simple patterned vectors

We have seen the use of the `:` operator for producing simple sequences of integers. Patterned vectors can also be produced using the `seq()` function as well as the `rep()` function. For example, the sequence of odd numbers less than or equal to 21 can be obtained using

```
seq(1, 21, by = 2)
## [1]  1  3  5  7  9 11 13 15 17 19 21
```

Notice the use of `by = 2` here. The `seq()` function has several *optional parameters*, including one named `by`. If `by` is not specified, the default value of 1 will be used.

Repeated patterns are obtained using `rep()`. Consider the following examples:

```
rep(3, 12)                    # repeat the value 3, 12 times
## [1] 3 3 3 3 3 3 3 3 3 3 3 3
rep(seq(2, 20, by = 2), 2)   # repeat the pattern 2 4 ... 20, twice
## [1]  2  4  6  8 10 12 14 16 18 20  2  4  6  8 10 12 14 16 18 20
rep(c(1, 4), c(3, 2))        # repeat 1, 3 times and  4, twice
## [1] 1 1 1 4 4
rep(c(1, 4), each = 3)       # repeat each value 3 times
## [1] 1 1 1 4 4 4
rep(1:10, rep(2, 10))        # repeat each value twice
## [1]  1  1  2  2  3  3  4  4  5  5  6  6  7  7  8  8  9  9 10 10
```

2.3.5 Vectors with random patterns

The `sample()` function allows us to simulate things like the results of the repeated tossing of a 6-sided die.

```
sample(1:6, size = 8, replace = TRUE) # an imaginary die is tossed 8 times
## [1] 5 4 2 4 3 1 4 5
```

2.3.6 Character vectors

Scalars and vectors can be made up of strings of characters instead of numbers. All elements of a vector must be of the same type. For example,

```
colors <- c("red", "yellow", "blue")
more.colors <- c(colors, "green", "magenta", "cyan")
                        # this appended some new elements to colors
z <- c("red", "green", 1)  # an attempt to mix data types in a vector
```

To see the contents of `more.colors` and `z`, simply type

```
more.colors
## [1] "red"     "yellow" "blue"     "green"     "magenta" "cyan"
z                         # 1 has been converted to the character "1"
## [1] "red"    "green" "1"
```

There are two basic operations you might want to perform on character vectors. To take substrings, use `substr()`. It takes arguments `substr(x, start, stop)`, where `x` is a vector of character strings, and `start` and `stop` say which characters to keep. For example, to print the first two letters of each color use

```
substr(colors, 1, 2)
## [1] "re" "ye" "bl"
```

The `substring()` function is similar, but with slightly different definitions of the arguments: see the help page `?substring`.

The other basic operation is building up strings by concatenation within elements. Use the `paste()` function for this. For example,

```
paste(colors, "flowers")
## [1] "red flowers"     "yellow flowers" "blue flowers"
```

There are two optional parameters to `paste()`. The `sep` parameter controls what goes between the components being pasted together. We might not want the default space, for example:

```
paste("several ", colors, "s", sep = "")
## [1] "several reds"     "several yellows" "several blues"
```

The `paste0()` function is a shorthand way to set `sep = ""`:

```
paste0("several ", colors, "s")
## [1] "several reds"     "several yellows" "several blues"
```

The `collapse` parameter to `paste()` allows all the components of the resulting vector to be collapsed into a single string:

```
paste("I like", colors, collapse = ", ")
## [1] "I like red, I like yellow, I like blue"
```

2.3.7 Factors

Factors offer an alternative way to store character data. For example, a factor with four elements and having the two levels, `control` and `treatment` can be created using:

```
grp <- c("control", "treatment", "control", "treatment")
grp
## [1] "control"   "treatment" "control"   "treatment"

grp <- factor(grp)
grp
## [1] control   treatment control   treatment
## Levels: control treatment
```

Factors can be an efficient way of storing character data when there are repeats among the vector elements. This is because the levels of a factor are internally coded as integers. To see what the codes are for our factor, we can type

```
as.integer(grp)
## [1] 1 2 1 2
```

The labels for the levels are only stored once each, rather than being repeated. The codes are indices of the vector of levels:

```
levels(grp)
## [1] "control"   "treatment"
levels(grp)[as.integer(grp)]
## [1] "control"   "treatment" "control"   "treatment"
```

The levels() function can be used to change factor labels as well.[2] For example, suppose we wish to change the "control" label to "placebo". Since "control" is the first level, we change the first element of the levels(grp) vector:

```
levels(grp)[1] <- "placebo"
```

An important use for factors is to list all possible values, even if some are not present. For example,

```
sex <- factor(c("F", "F"), levels = c("F", "M"))
sex
## [1] F F
## Levels: F M
```

shows that there are two possible values for sex, but only one is present in our vector.

2.3.8 More on extracting elements from vectors
As for numeric vectors, square brackets [] are used to index factor and character vector elements. For example, the factor grp has four elements, so we can print out the third element by typing

[2] Actually the change is made by a different function with the strange name levels<-, but that is beyond the scope of this text.

```
grp[3]
## [1] placebo
## Levels: placebo treatment
```

We can access the second through fifth elements of `more.colors` as follows:

```
more.colors[2:5]
## [1] "yellow"  "blue"     "green"    "magenta"
```

2.3.9 Matrices and arrays

To arrange values into a matrix, we use the `matrix()` function:

```
m <- matrix(1:6, nrow = 2, ncol = 3)
m
##      [,1] [,2] [,3]
## [1,]    1    3    5
## [2,]    2    4    6
```

We can then access elements using two indices. For example, the value in the first row, second column is

```
m[1, 2]
## [1] 3
```

Somewhat confusingly, R also allows a matrix to be indexed as a vector, using just one value:

```
m[4]
## [1] 4
```

Here elements are selected in the order in which they are stored internally: down the first column, then down the second, and so on. This is known as *column-major* storage order. Some computer languages use *row-major* storage order, where values are stored in order from left to right across the first row, then left to right across the second, and so on.

Whole rows or columns of matrices may be selected by leaving one index blank:

```
m[1,]
## [1] 1 3 5
m[, 1]
## [1] 1 2
```

A more general way to store data is in an *array*. Arrays have multiple indices, and are created using the array function:

```
a <- array(1:24, c(3, 4, 2))
a

## , , 1
##
##      [,1] [,2] [,3] [,4]
## [1,]    1    4    7   10
## [2,]    2    5    8   11
## [3,]    3    6    9   12
##
## , , 2
##
##      [,1] [,2] [,3] [,4]
## [1,]   13   16   19   22
## [2,]   14   17   20   23
## [3,]   15   18   21   24
```

Notice that the dimensions were specified in a vector c(3, 4, 2). When inserting data, the first index varies fastest; when it has run through its full range, the second index changes, etc.

Exercises

1 Calculate the sum $\sum_{j=0}^{n} r^j$, where r has been assigned the value 1.08, and compare with $(1 - r^{n+1})/(1 - r)$, for $n = 10, 20, 30, 40$. Repeat for $r = 1.06$.

2 Referring to the above question, use the quick formula to compute $\sum_{j=0}^{n} r^j$, for $r = 1.08$, for all values of n between 1 and 100. Store the 100 values in a vector.

3 Calculate the sum $\sum_{j=1}^{n} j$ and compare with $n(n + 1)/2$, for $n = 100, 200, 400, 800$.

4 Referring to the above question, use the quick formula to compute $\sum_{j=1}^{n} j$ for all values of n between 1 and 100. Store the 100 values in a vector.

5 Calculate the sum $\sum_{j=1}^{n} j^2$ and compare with $n(n + 1)(2n + 1)/6$, for $n = 200, 400, 600, 800$.

6 Referring to the above question, use the quick formula to compute $\sum_{j=1}^{n} j^2$ for all values of n between 1 and 100. Store the 100 values in a vector.

7 Calculate the sum $\sum_{i=1}^{N} 1/i$, and compare with log(N) + 0.6, for $N = 500, 1000, 2000, 4000, 8000$.

8 Using rep() and seq() as needed, create the vectors

0 0 0 0 0 1 1 1 1 1 2 2 2 2 2 3 3 3 3 3 4 4 4 4 4

and

1 2 3 4 5 1 2 3 4 5 1 2 3 4 5 1 2 3 4 5 1 2 3 4 5

9 Using rep() and seq() as needed, create the vector

1 2 3 4 5 2 3 4 5 6 3 4 5 6 7 4 5 6 7 8 5 6 7 8 9

10 Create the vector

```
##  [1] 0 0 0 1 1 1 1 0 0 0 1 1 1 1 0 0 0 1 1 1 1 0 0 0 1 1 1 1 0 0
## [31] 0 1 1 1 1
```

and convert it to a factor. Identify the levels of the result, and then change the level labels to obtain the factor:

```
##  [1] Male    Male    Male    Female Female Female Female Male
##  [9] Male    Male    Female Female Female Female Male    Male
## [17] Male    Female Female Female Female Male    Male    Male
## [25] Female Female Female Female Male    Male    Male    Female
## [33] Female Female Female
## Levels: Male Female
```

11 Use the `more.colors` vector, `rep()` and `seq()` to create the vector

```
"red"     "yellow"  "blue"     "yellow"  "blue"     "green"
"blue"    "green"   "magenta" "green"   "magenta" "cyan"
```

12 Convert the character vector from the preceding exercise to a factor. What are the levels of the factor? Change the `"blue"` label to `"turquoise"`.

2.4 | Data storage in R

2.4.1 Approximate storage of numbers

One important distinction in computing is between exact and approximate results. Most of what we do in this book is aimed at approximate methods. It is possible in a computer to represent any rational number exactly, but it is more common to use approximate representations: usually *floating point representations*. These are a binary (base-two) variation on scientific notation. For example, we might write a number to four significant digits in scientific notation as 6.926×10^{-4}. This representation of a number could represent any true value between 0.00069255 and 0.00069265. Standard floating point representations on computers are similar, except that a power of 2 would be used rather than a power of 10, and the fraction would be written in binary notation. The number above would be written as $1.011_2 \times 2^{-11}$ if four binary digit precision was used. The subscript 2 in the mantissa 1.011_2 indicates that this number is shown in base 2; that is, it represents $1 \times 2^0 + 0 \times 2^{-1} + 1 \times 2^{-2} + 1 \times 2^{-3}$, or 1.375 in decimal notation.

However, 6.926×10^{-4} and $1.011_2 \times 2^{-11}$ are not identical. Four binary digits give less precision than four decimal digits: a range of values from approximately 0.000641 to 0.000702 would all get the same representation to four binary digit precision. In fact, 6.926×10^{-4} *cannot* be represented exactly in binary notation in a finite number of digits. The problem is similar to trying to represent 1/3 as a decimal: 0.3333 is a close approximation but is not exact. The standard precision in R is 53 binary digits, which is equivalent to about 15 or 16 decimal digits.

To illustrate, consider the fractions 5/4 and 4/5. In decimal notation these can be represented exactly as 1.25 and 0.8, respectively. In binary notation 5/4 is $1 + 1/4 = 1.01_2$. How do we determine the binary representation of 4/5? It is between 0 and 1, so we'd expect something of the form $0.b_1b_2b_3 \cdots$ where each b_i represents a "bit," i.e. a 0 or 1 digit. Multiplying by 2 moves all the bits left by one, i.e. $2 \times 4/5 = 1.6 = b_1.b_2b_3 \cdots$. Thus $b_1 = 1$, and $0.6 = 0.b_2b_3 \cdots$.

We can now multiply by 2 again to find $2 \times 0.6 = 1.2 = b_2.b_3 \cdots$, so $b_2 = 1$. Repeating twice more yields $b_3 = b_4 = 0$. (Try it!)

At this point we'll have the number 0.8 again, so the sequence of 4 bits will repeat indefinitely: in base 2, 4/5 is $0.110011001100 \cdots$. Since R only stores 53 bits, it won't be able to store 0.8 exactly. Some rounding error will occur in the storage.

We can observe the rounding error with the following experiment. With exact arithmetic, $(5/4) \times (4/5) = 1$, so $(5/4) \times (n \times 4/5)$ should be exactly n for any value of n. But if we try this calculation in R, we find

```
n <- 1:10
1.25 * (n * 0.8) - n
```

```
## [1] 0.000000e+00 0.000000e+00 4.440892e-16 0.000000e+00 0.000000e+00
## [6] 8.881784e-16 8.881784e-16 0.000000e+00 0.000000e+00 0.000000e+00
```

i.e. it is equal for some values, but not equal for $n = 3, 6,$ or 7. The errors are very small, but non-zero.

Rounding error tends to accumulate in most calculations, so usually a long series of calculations will result in larger errors than a short one. Some operations are particularly prone to rounding error: for example, subtraction of two nearly equal numbers, or (equivalently) addition of two numbers with nearly the same magnitude but opposite signs. Since the leading bits in the binary expansions of nearly equal numbers will match, they will cancel in subtraction, and the result will depend on what is stored in the later bits.

Example 2.2
Consider the standard formula for the sample variance of a sample $x_1, \ldots, x_n$:

$$s^2 = \frac{1}{n-1} \sum_{i=1}^{n} (x_i - \bar{x})^2,$$

where $\bar{x}$ is the sample mean, $(1/n) \sum x_i$. In R, s^2 is available as `var()`, and $\bar{x}$ is `mean()`. For example:

```
x <- 1:11
mean(x)
```

```
## [1] 6
```

```
var(x)
```

```
## [1] 11
```

```
sum( (x - mean(x))^2 ) / 10
```

```
## [1] 11
```

Because this formula requires calculation of $\bar{x}$ first and the sum of squared deviations second, it requires that all x_i values be kept in memory. Not too long ago memory was so expensive that it was advantageous to rewrite the formula as

$$s^2 = \frac{1}{n-1} \left(\sum_{i=1}^{n} x_i^2 - n\bar{x}^2 \right).$$

This is called the "one-pass formula," because we evaluate each x_i value just once, and accumulate the sums of x_i and of x_i^2. It gives the correct answer, both mathematically and in our example:

```
( sum(x^2) - 11 * mean(x)^2 ) / 10
```

```
## [1] 11
```

However, notice what happens if we add a large value A to each x_i. The sum $\sum_{i=1}^{n} x_i^2$ increases by approximately nA^2, and so does $n\bar{x}^2$. This doesn't change the variance, but it provides the conditions for a "catastrophic loss of precision" when we take the difference:

```
A <- 1.e10
x <- 1:11 + A
var(x)
```

```
## [1] 11
```

```
( sum(x^2) - 11 * mean(x)^2 ) / 10
```

```
## [1] 0
```

Since R gets the right answer, it clearly doesn't use the one-pass formula, and neither should you.

2.4.2 Exact storage of numbers

In the previous section we saw that R uses floating point storage for numbers, using a base 2 format that stores 53 bits of accuracy. It turns out that this format can store some fractions exactly: if the fraction can be written as $n/2^m$, where n and m are integers (not too large; m can be no bigger than about 1000, but n can be very large), R can store it exactly. The number 5/4 is in this form, but the number 4/5 is not, so only the former is stored exactly.

Floating point storage is not the only format that R uses. For whole numbers, it can use 32 bit integer storage. In this format, numbers are stored as binary versions of the integers 0 to $2^{32} - 1 = 4294967295$. Numbers that are bigger than $2^{31} - 1 = 2147483647$ are treated as negative values by subtracting 2^{32} from them, i.e. to find the stored value for a negative number, add 2^{32} to it.

Example 2.3

The number 11 can be stored as the binary value of 11, i.e. $0\ldots01011$, whereas -11 can be stored as the binary value of $2^{32} - 11 = 4294967285$, which turns out to be $1\ldots10101$. If you add these two numbers together, you get 2^{32}. Using only 32 bits for storage, this is identical to 0, which is what we'd hope to get for $11 + (-11)$.

How does R decide which storage format to use? Generally, it does what you (or whoever wrote the function you're using) tell it to do. If you want integer storage, append the letter L to the value: 11 means the floating point value, 11L means the integer value. Most R functions return floating point values, but a few (e.g. seq(), which is used in expressions like 1:10) return integer values. Generally you don't need to worry about this: values will be converted as needed.

What about 64 bit integers? Modern computers can handle 64 bits at a time, but in general, R can't. The reason is that R expects integer values to be a subset of floating point values. Any 32 bit integer can be stored exactly as a floating point value, but this is not true for all 64 bit integers.

2.4.3 Dates and times

Dates and times are among the most difficult types of data to work with on computers. The standard calendar is very complicated: months of different lengths, leap years every four years (with exceptions for whole centuries) and so on. When looking at dates over historical time periods, changes to the calendar (such as the switch from the Julian calendar to the modern Gregorian calendar that occurred in various countries between 1582 and 1923) affect the interpretation of dates.

Times are also messy, because there is often an unstated time zone (which may change for some dates due to daylight savings time), and some years have "leap seconds" added in order to keep standard clocks consistent with the rotation of the earth.

There have been several attempts to deal with this in R. The base package has the function strptime() to convert from strings (e.g. "2020-12-25", or "12/25/20") to an internal numerical representation, and format() to convert back for printing. The ISOdate() and ISOdatetime() functions are used when numerical values for the year, month, day, etc. are known. Other functions are available in the chron package.

2.4.4 Missing values and other special values

The missing value symbol is NA. Missing values often arise in real data, but they can also arise because of the way calculations are performed.

```
some.evens <- NULL      # creates a vector with no elements
some.evens[seq(2, 20, 2)] <- seq(2, 20, 2)
some.evens

## [1] NA  2 NA  4 NA  6 NA  8 NA 10 NA 12 NA 14 NA 16 NA 18 NA 20
```

What happened here is that we assigned values to elements $2, 4, \ldots, 20$ but never assigned anything to elements $1, 3, \ldots, 19$, so R uses NA to signal that the value is unknown.

Consider the following:

```
x <- c(0, 1, 2)
x / x

## [1] NaN   1   1
```

The NaN symbol denotes a value which is "not a number" which arises as a result of attempting to compute the indeterminate $0/0$. This symbol is sometimes used when a calculation does not make sense. In other cases, special values may be shown, or you may get an error or warning message.

```
1 / x

## [1] Inf 1.0 0.5
```

Here R has tried to evaluate $1/0$ and reports the infinite result as Inf.

When there may be missing values, the is.na() function should be used to detect them. For instance,

```
is.na(some.evens)

##  [1]  TRUE FALSE  TRUE FALSE  TRUE FALSE  TRUE FALSE  TRUE FALSE  TRUE
## [12] FALSE  TRUE FALSE  TRUE FALSE  TRUE FALSE  TRUE FALSE
```

(The result is a "logical vector." More on these in Section 2.8.) The ! symbol means "not," so we can locate the non-missing values in some.evens as follows:

```
!is.na(some.evens)

##  [1] FALSE  TRUE FALSE  TRUE FALSE  TRUE FALSE  TRUE FALSE  TRUE FALSE
## [12]  TRUE FALSE  TRUE FALSE  TRUE FALSE  TRUE FALSE  TRUE
```

We can then display the even numbers only:

```
some.evens[!is.na(some.evens)]

##  [1]  2  4  6  8 10 12 14 16 18 20
```

Here we have used *logical indexing*, which will be further discussed in Section 2.8.2.

Exercises

1 Assume 4 binary digit accuracy for the following computations.

  (a) Write out the binary representation for the approximate value of $6/7$.
  (b) Write out the binary representation for the approximate value of $1/7$.
  (c) Add the two binary representations obtained above, and convert back to the decimal representation.

(d) Compare the result of part (c) with the result from adding the binary representations of 6 and 1, followed by division by the binary representation of 7.

2 Can you explain these two results? (Hint: see Section 2.4.1.)

```
x <- c(0, 7, 8)
x[0.9999999999999999]

## numeric(0)

x[0.99999999999999999]

## [1] 0
```

3 In R, evaluate the expressions

$$2^{52} + k - 2^{52}$$

$$2^{53} + k - 2^{53}$$

$$2^{54} + k - 2^{54}$$

for the cases where $k = 1, 2, 3, 4$. Explain what you observe. What could be done to obtain results in R which are mathematically correct?

4 Explain why the following result is not a violation of Fermat's last theorem:

```
(3987^12 + 4365^12)^(1/12)

## [1] 4472
```

5 Note the output of

```
strptime("02/07/91", "%d/%m/%y")
```

and

```
strptime("02/07/11", "%d/%m/%y")
```

6 Note the output of

```
strptime("02/07/11", "%y/%m/%d")  - strptime("02/05/11", "%y/%m/%d")
```

7 Note the output of

```
format(strptime("8/9/10", "%d/%m/%y"), "%a %b %d %Y")
```

2.5 | Packages, libraries, and repositories

We have already mentioned several *packages*, i.e. base, knitr, and chron. In R, a package is a module containing functions, data, and documentation. R always contains the base packages (e.g. `base`, `stats`, `graphics`); these contain things that everyone will use. There are also contributed packages (e.g. `knitr` and `chron`); these are modules written by others to use in R.

When you start your R session, you will have some packages loaded and available for use, while others are stored on your computer in a *library*. To be sure a package is loaded, run code like

```
library(knitr)
```

To see which packages are loaded, run

```
search()
##  [1] ".GlobalEnv"        "package:knitr"      "package:stats"
##  [4] "package:graphics"  "package:grDevices"  "package:utils"
##  [7] "package:datasets"  "package:methods"    "Autoloads"
## [10] "package:base"
```

(Your list will likely be different from ours.) This list also indicates the search order: a package can only contain one function of any given name, but the same name may be used in another package. When you use that function, R will choose it from the first package in the search list. If you want to force a function to be chosen from a particular package, prefix the name of the function with the name of the package and `::`, e.g.

```
stats::median(x)
```

Thousands of contributed packages are available, though you may have only a few dozen installed on your computer. If you try to use one that isn't already there, you will receive an error message:

```
library(notInstalled)
## Error in library(notInstalled): there is no package called 'notInstalled'
```

This means that the package doesn't exist on your computer, but it might be available in a *repository* online. The biggest repository of R packages is known as CRAN. To install a package from CRAN, you can run a command like

```
install.packages("knitr")
```

or, within RStudio, click on the `Packages` tab in the Output Pane, choose `Install`, and enter the name in the resulting dialog box.

Because there are so many contributed packages, it is hard to know which one to use to solve your own problems. If you can't get help from someone with more experience, we suggest reading the CRAN *task views* at `https://cloud.r-project.org/web/views`. These are reviews of available packages written by experts in dozens of different subject areas.

2.6 | Getting help

The function q() and the other functions we have been discussing so far are examples of built-in functions. There are many functions in R which are designed to do all sorts of things, and we'll discuss some more of them in the next section. But first we want to tell you how to get help about features of R that you have heard about, and how to find out about features that solve new problems.

2.6.1 Built-in help pages

The online help facility can help you to see what a particular function is supposed to do. There are a number of ways of accessing the help facility.

If you know the name of the function that you need help with, the help() function is likely sufficient. It may be called with a string or function name as an argument, or you can simply put a question mark (?) in front of your query. For example, for help on the q() function, type

```
?q
```

or

```
help(q)
```

or just hit the F1 key while pointing at q in RStudio. Any of these will open a help page containing a description of the function for quitting R.

Another commonly used function in R is mean(). The first part of the help page for mean from within RStudio is shown in Figure 2.1. (There

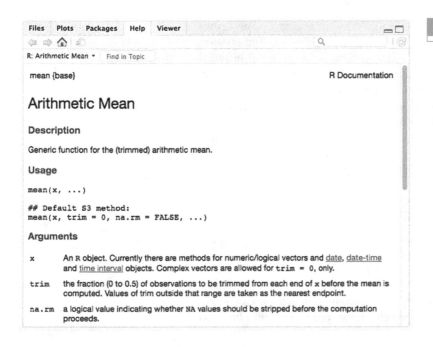

Fig. 2.1 Help page for ?mean.

may be small differences in the display on your system.) This tells us that mean() will compute the ordinary arithmetic average or it will do something called "trimming" if we ask for it.

To compute the mean of the values of the x vector created earlier, we simply type

```
mean(x)

## [1] 5
```

2.6.2 Built-in examples

A useful supplement to help() is the example() function, which runs examples from the end of the help page:

```
example(mean)

##
## mean> x <- c(0:10, 50)
##
## mean> xm <- mean(x)
##
## mean> c(xm, mean(x, trim = 0.10))
## [1] 8.75 5.50
```

These examples show simple use of the mean() function as well as how to use the trim argument. (When trim = 0.1, the highest 10% and lowest 10% of the data are deleted before the average is calculated.)

2.6.3 Finding help when you don't know the function name

One way to explore the help system is to use help.start(). This brings up an Internet browser, such as Google Chrome or Firefox. The browser will show you a menu of several options, including a listing of installed packages. (The base package contains many of the routinely used functions; other commonly used functions are in utils or stats.) You can get to this page within RStudio by using the Help | R Help menu item.

Another function that is often used is help.search(), abbreviated as a double question mark. For example, to see if there are any functions that do optimization (finding minima or maxima), type

```
??optimization
```

or

```
help.search("optimization")
```

The result of a such a search in the RStudio Help pane is shown in Figure 2.2.

Your results will likely be different, depending on which R packages are installed on your system. We can then check for specific help on a function like nlm() by typing

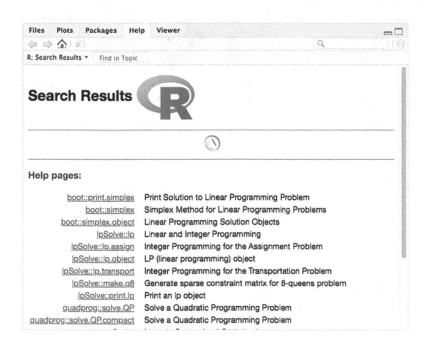

Fig. 2.2 Result of
??optimization.

```
?nlm
```

in the R console, or just clicking on the link in the displayed page.

Web search engines such as Google can also be useful for finding help on R. Including 'R' as a keyword in such a search will often bring up the relevant R help page. You may find pages describing functions that you do not have installed, because they are in user-contributed packages. The name of the R package that is needed is usually listed at the top of the help page. You can usually install them by typing

```
install.packages("packagename")
```

This will work as long as the package is available in the CRAN repository. Google may also find discussions of similar questions to yours on sites like https://stackoverflow.com/, where discussions about R are common.

Another function to note is RSiteSearch() which will do a search in the R-help mailing list and other web resources. For example, to bring up information on the treatment of missing values in R, we can type

```
RSiteSearch("missing")
```

The sos package gives help similar to RSiteSearch(), but organized differently, and triggered by a triple question mark. For example, try typing

```
library(sos)
???optimization
```

and compare the results to the ones returned by RSiteSearch().

2.7 | Useful R features

In this section we introduce some useful features of R and RStudio.

2.7.1 Some built-in graphics functions

Two basic plots are the histogram and the scatterplot. The codes below were used to produce the graphs that appear in Figures 2.3 and 2.4.

```
hist(islands)
```

```
x <- seq(1, 10)
y <- x^2 - 10 * x
plot(x, y)
```

Note that the x values are plotted along the horizontal axis.

Another useful plotting function is the `curve()` function for plotting the graph of a univariate mathematical function on an interval. The left and right endpoints of the interval are specified by `from` and `to` arguments, respectively.

A simple example involves plotting the sine function on the interval $[0, 6\pi]$:

```
curve(expr = sin, from = 0, to = 6 * pi)
```

The output is displayed in Figure 2.5. The `expr` parameter is either a function (whose output is a numeric vector when the input is a numeric

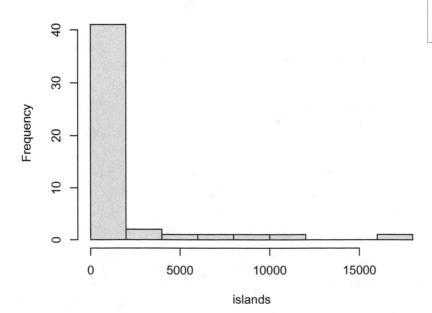

Histogram of islands

Fig. 2.3 A histogram of the areas of the world's 48 largest landmasses. See Section 3.1.3 for ways to improve this figure.

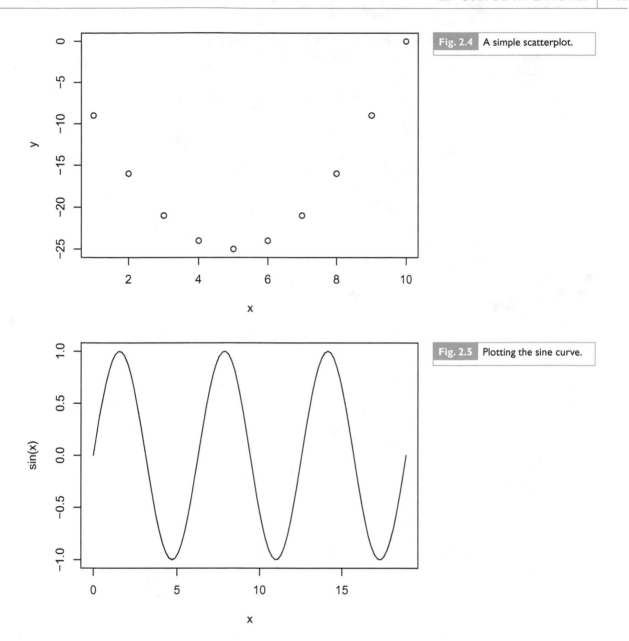

Fig. 2.4 A simple scatterplot.

Fig. 2.5 Plotting the sine curve.

vector) or an expression in terms of x. An example of the latter type of usage is:

```
curve(x^2 - 10 * x, from = 1, to = 10)
```

More information on graphics can be found in Chapter 3.

2.7.2 Some elementary built-in functions

The sample median

The sample median measures the middle value of a data set. If the data are $x[1] \leq x[2] \leq \cdots \leq x[n]$, then the median is $x[(n+1)/2]$ if n is odd, or $\{[x[n/2] + x[n/2 + 1]\}/2$ if n is even.

For example, the median of the values: 10, 10, 18, 30, 32 is 18, and the median of 40, 10, 10, 18, 30, 32 is the average of 18 and 30, i.e. 24.

This calculation is handled by R as follows:

```
median(x)   # computes the median or 50th percentile of the data in x
```

Other summary measures

Summary statistics can be calculated for data stored in vectors. In particular, try

```
var(x)       # computes the variance of the data in x
summary(x)   # computes several summary statistics on the data in x
length(x)    # number of elements in x
min(x)       # minimum value of x
max(x)       # maximum value of x
pmin(x, y)   # pairwise minima of corresponding elements of x and y
pmax(x, y)   # pairwise maxima of   x and y
range(x)     # difference between maximum and minimum of data in x
IQR(x)       # interquartile range:  difference between 1st and 3rd
             # quartiles of data in x
```

For an example of the calculation of pairwise minima of two vectors, consider

```
x <- 1:5
y <- 7:3
pmin(x,y)

## [1] 1 2 3 4 3
```

Exercises

1 The following are a sample of observations on incoming solar radiation at a greenhouse.

```
11.1 10.6 6.3  8.8  10.7 11.2 8.9 12.2
```

   (a) Assign the data to an object called solar.radiation.
   (b) Find the mean, median, range, and variance of the radiation observations.
   (c) Add 10 to each observation of solar.radiation, and assign the result to sr10. Find the mean, median, range, and variance of sr10. Which statistics change, and by how much?
   (d) Multiply each observation by -2, and assign the result to srm2. Find the mean, median, range, and variance of srm2. How do the statistics change now?
   (e) Plot a histogram of the solar.radiation, sr10, and srm2.

2 Calculate $\sum_{n=1}^{15} \min(2^n, n^3)$. (Hint: the min() function will give the wrong answer.)

3 Calculate $\sum_{n=1}^{15} \max(2^n, n^3)$.

2.7.3 Presenting results using R Markdown

We do some calculations and produce some graphics for ourselves, just to understand what is in our data, but often our work is intended for a wider audience. That usually means accompanying it with text explaining the background and interpretation in some sort of complete document.

There are many forms of document, such as web pages, printed reports or books, and so on. There are also many ways to produce documents: word processors like Microsoft Word, online systems for producing blogs, typesetting systems like LaTeX. In most of these, including graphics and results of computations is a chore: for example, you save a graph in R to a file, then import the file into your document. It is also error-prone: you may import the wrong file, change the calculation but forget to import the new graph, or change the text but forget to update the computation, among other errors.

R Markdown is one way to make this easier. It is a mixture of Markdown, a simple way to write a document in a plain text file, and "chunks" of code in R or another computer language. When you "render" the input into a document, R runs the code, automatically collects printed output and graphics and inserts them into the final document. This is well supported in RStudio. We recommend that students produce their assignments and projects in R Markdown and instructors produce presentation material that way as well.

The simplest way to start is to ask RStudio to produce an initial template; then you delete the sample material, add your own, and render it. Using the menus in RStudio, choose File|New File|R Markdown.... You will be offered a list of document types to produce. Pick one at this point, but don't worry too much about the choice: it will be easy to choose a different output format later. For example, if we choose an HTML document (a web page), a new file will open in the editor, showing content something like Figure 2.6. In this template, the first part (between the

Fig. 2.6 Sample R Markdown template.

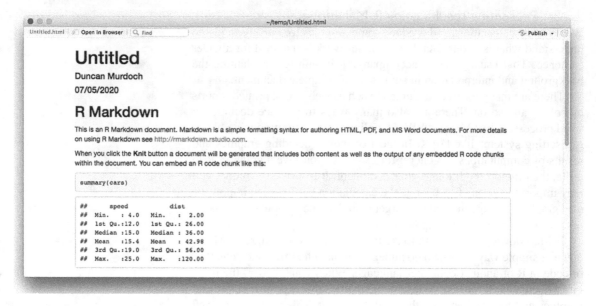

Fig. 2.7 Output from R Markdown template.

two `---` lines) is called the "YAML."[3] It contains information that will be used when rendering your document.

[3] YAML is actually an abbreviation for Yet Another Markup Language.

The actual document starts after the YAML. Headings are marked with an initial `##`, and text is written out in an essentially normal way. Instructions within the template tell you how to include code chunks that will display results, e.g.,

```
```{r cars}
summary(cars)
```
```

or produce a plot

```
```{r pressure, echo=FALSE}
plot(pressure)
```
```

Each of the above examples has a header line that tells R how to process the chunk. In the first example the defaults are used, so R will evaluate `summary(cars)` and insert the code and the results into the document. In the second example `echo=FALSE` is used, so R will evaluate `plot(pressure)` and insert the plot, but won't show the R code. To do the rendering, click on `Knit` in the top of the pane. This will ask to save the file if you haven't already done that, then render it and display the result on the screen (Figure 2.7).

If we decide we want printed output instead of a web page, we can click on the small downward pointing arrow beside `Knit`, and choose `Knit to PDF` or `Knit to Word`, and we'd get that format. It's very easy to use, and we recommend it. We have used a similar system to produce this book.

2.8 | Logical vectors and relational operators

We have used the `c()` function to put numeric vectors together as well as character vectors. R also supports logical vectors. These contain two different elements: TRUE and FALSE, as well as NA for missing.[4]

2.8.1 Boolean algebra

To understand how R handles TRUE and FALSE, we need to understand a little *Boolean algebra*. The idea of Boolean algebra is to formalize a mathematical approach to logic.

Logic deals with statements that are either true or false. We represent each statement by a letter or variable, e.g. *A* is the statement that the sky is clear, and *B* is the statement that it is raining. Depending on the weather where you are, those two statements may both be true (there is a "sunshower"), *A* may be true and *B* false (the usual clear day), *A* false and *B* true (the usual rainy day), or both may be false (a cloudy but dry day).

Boolean algebra tells us how to evaluate the truth of compound statements. For example, "*A* and *B*" is the statement that it is both clear and raining. This statement is only true during a sunshower. "*A* or *B*" says that it is clear or it is raining, or both: anything but the cloudy dry day. This is sometimes called an *inclusive or*, to distinguish it from the *exclusive or* "*A* xor *B*," which says that it is either clear or raining, but *not* both. There is also the "not *A*" statement, which says that it is not clear.

There is a very important relation between Boolean algebra and set theory. If we interpret *A* and *B* as sets, then we can think of "*A* and *B*" as the set of elements which are in *A* and are in *B*, i.e. the intersection $A \cap B$. Similarly "*A* or *B*" can be interpreted as the set of elements that are in *A* or are in *B*, i.e. the union $A \cup B$. Finally, "not *A*" is the complement of *A*, i.e. A^c.

Because there are only two possible values (true and false), we can record all Boolean operations in a table. On the first line of Table 2.1 we list the basic Boolean expressions, on the second line the equivalent way to code them in R, and in the body of the table the results of the operations.

2.8.2 Logical operations in R

One of the basic types of vector in R holds logical values. For example, a logical vector may be constructed as

```
a <- c(TRUE, FALSE, FALSE, TRUE)
```

[4] Some authors use T for TRUE and F for FALSE. We discourage this, because T and F are variables that the user can change, whereas TRUE and FALSE are constants that can't be changed. Imagine the confusion if you run `T <- FALSE`!

Table 2.1	*Truth table for Boolean operations*				
Boolean	A	B	not A	not B	A and B	A or B
R	A	B	!A	!B	A & B	A | B
	TRUE	TRUE	FALSE	FALSE	TRUE	TRUE
	TRUE	FALSE	FALSE	TRUE	FALSE	TRUE
	FALSE	TRUE	TRUE	FALSE	FALSE	TRUE
	FALSE	FALSE	TRUE	TRUE	FALSE	FALSE

The result is a vector of 4 logical values. Logical vectors may be used as indices:

```
b <- c(13, 7, 8, 2)
b[a]

## [1] 13  2
```

The elements of b corresponding to TRUE are selected.

If we attempt arithmetic on a logical vector, e.g.

```
sum(a)

## [1] 2
```

then the operations are performed after converting FALSE to 0 and TRUE to 1, so by summing we count how many occurrences of TRUE are in the vector.

There are two versions of the Boolean operators. The usual versions are &, | and !, as listed in the previous section. These are all vectorized, so we see for example

```
!a

## [1] FALSE  TRUE  TRUE FALSE
```

If we attempt logical operations on a numerical vector, 0 is taken to be FALSE, and any non-zero value is taken to be TRUE:

```
a & (b - 2)

## [1]  TRUE FALSE FALSE FALSE
```

The operators && and || are similar to & and |, but behave differently in two respects. First, they are *not* vectorized: only one calculation is done, and in newer versions of R, you'll get an error if you try to use them on longer vectors. Second, they are guaranteed to be evaluated from left to right, with the right-hand operand only evaluated if necessary. For example, if A is FALSE, then A && B will be FALSE regardless of the value of B, so B needn't be evaluated. This can save time if evaluating B would be very slow, and may make calculations easier, for example if evaluating B would cause an error when A was FALSE. This behavior is sometimes called *short-circuit evaluation*.

2.8.3 Relational operators

It is often necessary to test relations when programming. R allows for equality and inequality relations to be tested using the relational operators: <, >, ==, >=, <=, !=.[5] Some simple examples follow.

```
threeM <- c(3, 6, 9)
threeM > 4     # which elements are greater than 4

## [1] FALSE  TRUE  TRUE
```

[5] Be careful with tests of equality. Because R works with only a limited number of decimal places rounding error can accumulate, and you may find surprising results, such as 49 * (4 / 49) not being equal to 4.

```
threeM == 4    # which elements are exactly equal to 4
```

```
## [1] FALSE FALSE FALSE
```

```
threeM >= 4    # which elements are greater than or equal to 4
```

```
## [1] FALSE  TRUE   TRUE
```

```
threeM != 4    # which elements are not equal to 4
```

```
## [1] TRUE TRUE TRUE
```

```
threeM[threeM > 4] # elements of threeM which are greater than 4
```

```
## [1] 6 9
```

```
four68 <- c(4, 6, 8)
four68 > threeM # four68 elements exceed corresponding threeM elements
```

```
## [1]  TRUE FALSE FALSE
```

```
four68[threeM < four68] # print them
```

```
## [1] 4
```

Exercises

1 Use R to identify the elements of the sequence $\{2^1, 2^2, \ldots, 2^{15}\}$ that exceed the corresponding elements of the sequence $\{1^3, 2^3, \ldots, 15^3\}$.

2 More complicated expressions can be constructed from the basic Boolean operations. Write out the truth table for the *xor* operator, and show how to write it in terms of *and*, *or*, and *not*.

3 Venn diagrams can be used to illustrate set unions and intersections. Draw Venn diagrams that correspond to the *and*, *or*, *not*, and *xor* operations.

4 DeMorgan's laws in R notation are `!(A & B) == (!A) | (!B)` and `!(A | B) == (!A) & (!B)`. Write these out in English using the *A* and *B* statements above, and use truth tables to confirm each equality.

5 Evaluation of a square root is achieved using the `sqrt()` function, but a warning will be issued when the argument is negative. Consider the following code which is designed to test whether a given value is positive before checking whether the square root of the value is less than 5.

```
testValue <- 7
(testValue > 0) & (sqrt(testValue) < 5)
```

```
## [1] TRUE
```

```
testValue <- -7
(testValue > 0) & (sqrt(testValue) < 5)
```

```
## Warning in sqrt(testValue): NaNs produced
```

```
## [1] FALSE
```

Modify the code so that it continues to give the correct answer but without the warning.

6 Under what circumstances would B need to be evaluated in the expression A || B?

7 Using the values of a and b from this section, predict the output from each of these expressions, and then try them in R.

```
min(b)
min(a)
max(a)
length(a)
b * a
```

8 Logical vectors in R can contain NA as well as TRUE or FALSE, so truth tables like Table 2.1 really need 9 rows, not 4. Write out what you think the other 5 rows should be with NA interpreted as "unknown," and compare your table to results from R.

2.9 | Data frames, tibbles, and lists

Data sets frequently consist of more than one column of data, where each column represents measurements of a single variable. Each row usually represents a single observation. This format is referred to as *case-by-variable format*.

Most data sets are stored in R as data frames or tibbles. Tibbles (discussed in Chapter 5) are very similar to data frames. The discussion below mostly applies equally to data frames and tibbles, but for brevity we won't keep writing "and tibbles." Both are like matrices, but with the columns having their own names. Several data frames come with R. An example is women which contains the average heights (in inches) and weights (in pounds) of American women aged 30 to 39:

```
women

##    height weight
## 1      58    115
## 2      59    117
## 3      60    120
## 4      61    123
## 5      62    126
## 6      63    129
## 7      64    132
## 8      65    135
## 9      66    139
## 10     67    142
## 11     68    146
## 12     69    150
## 13     70    154
## 14     71    159
## 15     72    164
```

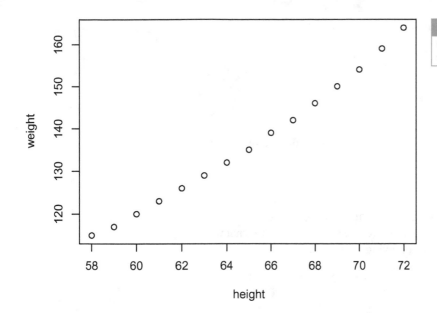

Fig. 2.8 A graphical summary of the two-variable data frame, women.

We have displayed the entire data frame, a practice not normally recommended, since data frames can be very large, and not much can be learned by scanning columns of numbers. (This is one difference between data frames and tibbles: the latter print in a more compact format.)

Other ways to view the data are through the use of the summary() function as shown below, or by constructing an appropriate graph such as in Figure 2.8, obtained by executing the command

```
plot(weight ~ height, data = women).
```

```
summary(women)
```

```
##      height         weight
##  Min.   :58.0   Min.   :115.0
##  1st Qu.:61.5   1st Qu.:124.5
##  Median :65.0   Median :135.0
##  Mean   :65.0   Mean   :136.7
##  3rd Qu.:68.5   3rd Qu.:148.0
##  Max.   :72.0   Max.   :164.0
```

For larger data frames, a quick way of counting the number of rows and columns is important. The functions nrow() and ncol() play this role:

```
nrow(women)
```

```
## [1] 15
```

```
ncol(women)
```

```
## [1] 2
```

We can get both at once using dim() (for *dimension*):

```
dim(women)
```

```
## [1] 15  2
```

and can get summary information using `str()` (for *structure*):

```
str(women)
## 'data.frame':       15 obs. of  2 variables:
##  $ height: num  58 59 60 61 62 63 64 65 66 67 ...
##  $ weight: num  115 117 120 123 126 129 132 135 139 142 ...
```

In fact, `str()` works with almost any R object, and is often a quick way to find what you are working with.

2.9.1 Extracting data frame elements and subsets

We can extract elements from data frames using similar syntax to what was used with matrices. Consider the following examples: [6]

[6] Extraction is different for tibbles: see Section 5.2.

```
women[7, 2]

## [1] 132

women[3, ]

##   height weight
## 3     60    120

women[4:7, 1]

## [1] 61 62 63 64
```

Data frame columns can also be addressed using their names using the `$` operator. For example, the weight column can be extracted as follows:

```
women$weight

##  [1] 115 117 120 123 126 129 132 135 139 142 146 150 154 159 164
```

Thus, we can extract all heights for which the weights exceed 140 using

```
women$height[women$weight > 140]

## [1] 67 68 69 70 71 72
```

The `with()` function allows us to access columns of a data frame directly without using the `$`. For example, we can divide the weights by the heights in the women data frame using

```
with(women, weight/height)

##  [1] 1.982759 1.983051 2.000000 2.016393 2.032258 2.047619 2.062500
##  [8] 2.076923 2.106061 2.119403 2.147059 2.173913 2.200000 2.239437
## [15] 2.277778
```

See `help(with)` for more information.

2.9.2 Taking random samples from populations

The `sample()` function can be used to take samples (with or without replacement) from larger finite populations. Suppose, for example, that we have a data frame called `fluSurvey` consisting of 15000 entries, and we would like to randomly select 8 entries (without replacement) for detailed study. If the entries have been enumerated (say, by the use of an ID index) from 1 through 15000, we could select the 8 numbers with

```
sampleID <- sample(1:15000, size = 8, replace = FALSE)
sampleID

## [1]  2459    14 10406  6900 14106  3413 13097 12060
```

The above numbers have been chosen randomly (or at least approximately so), and the random rows of `fluSurvey`, a supposedly existing data frame, can now be extracted with

```
fluSample <- fluSurvey[sampleID,]
```

The result is a new data frame consisting of 8 rows and the same number of columns as `fluSurvey`.

2.9.3 Constructing data frames

Use the `data.frame()` function to construct data frames from vectors that already exist in your workspace:

```
xy <- data.frame(x, y)
xy

##   x y
## 1 1 7
## 2 2 6
## 3 3 5
## 4 4 4
## 5 5 3
```

For another example, consider

```
xynew <- data.frame(x, y, new = 10:1)
```

2.9.4 Data frames can have non-numeric columns

Columns of data frames can be of different types. For example, the built-in data frame `chickwts` has a numeric column and a factor. Again, the `summary()` function provides a quick peek at this data set.

```
summary(chickwts)

##      weight          feed
## Min.   :108.0   casein   :12
## 1st Qu.:204.5   horsebean:10
## Median :258.0   linseed  :12
```

```
## Mean    :261.3    meatmeal :11
## 3rd Qu.:323.5    soybean  :14
## Max.    :423.0    sunflower:12
```

Here, displaying the entire data frame would have been a waste of space, as can be seen from:

```
nrow(chickwts)

## [1] 71
```

An important point to be aware of is that in older versions of R (before 4.0.0), the data.frame() function automatically converted character vectors to factors. As an example, consider the following data that might be used as a baseline in an obesity study:

```
gender <- c("M", "M", "F", "F", "F")
weight <- c(73, 68, 52, 69, 64)
obesityStudy <- data.frame(gender, weight)
```

The vector gender is clearly a character vector, and in R 4.0.0 or later it will be left that way in the data frame:

```
obesityStudy$gender

## [1] "M" "M" "F" "F" "F"
```

If you want the older behavior, use the stringsAsFactors = TRUE argument when you create the data frame:[7]

[7] In older versions of R, execute options(stringsAsFactors = FALSE) to get the new default.

```
obesityStudy <- data.frame(gender, weight, stringsAsFactors = TRUE)
obesityStudy$gender

## [1] M M F F F
## Levels: F M
```

Now, suppose we wish to globally change F to Female in the data frame. An incorrect approach is

```
wrongWay <- obesityStudy
whereF <- wrongWay$gender == "F"
wrongWay$gender[whereF] <- "Female"

## Warning in '[<-.factor'('*tmp*', whereF, value = structure(c(2L, 2L, NA, :
invalid factor level, NA generated

wrongWay$gender

## [1] M    M    <NA> <NA> <NA>
## Levels: F M
```

The correct approach is through the levels of the obesityStudy$gender factor:

```
levels(obesityStudy$gender)[1] <- "Female"  # F is the 1st level -- why?
obesityStudy$gender  # check that F was really replaced by Female

## [1] M       M      Female Female Female
## Levels: Female M
```

2.9.5 Lists

Data frames are actually a special kind of list, or structure. Lists in R can contain any other objects. You won't often construct these yourself, but many functions return complicated results as lists. You can see the names of the objects in a list using the names() function, and extract parts of it:

```
names(d)  # Print names of objects in list d
d$x       # Print the x component of d
```

The list() function is one way of organizing multiple pieces of output from functions. For example,

```
x <- c(3, 2, 3)
y <- c(7, 7)
z <- list(x = x, y = y)
z

## $x
## [1] 3 2 3
##
## $y
## [1] 7 7
```

There are several functions which make working with lists easy. Two of them are lapply() and vapply(). The lapply() function "applies" another function to every element of a list and returns the results in a new list; for example,

```
lapply(z, mean)

## $x
## [1] 2.666667
##
## $y
## [1] 7
```

In a case like this, it might be more convenient to have the results in a vector; the vapply() function does that. It takes a third argument to tell R what kind of result to expect from the function. In this case each result of mean should be a number, so we could use

```
vapply(z, mean, 1)

##        x        y
## 2.666667 7.000000
```

where the 1 just serves as an example of the type of output expected. If mean() had returned a different kind of result, vapply() would have given an error. If we expect more than a single value, the results will be organized into a matrix, e.g.

```
vapply(z, summary, numeric(6))
##            x y
## Min.    2.000000 7
## 1st Qu. 2.500000 7
## Median  3.000000 7
## Mean    2.666667 7
## 3rd Qu. 3.000000 7
## Max.    3.000000 7
```

Chapter 5 discusses other functions for transforming lists and data frames.

Exercises

1 Consider the built-in data frame Formaldehyde.
  (a) Extract the elements of the third row of this data frame.
  (b) Extract the elements of the carb (carbohydrate) column.
  (c) Use the plot() function to identify the relation between optden (optical density) and carb.
2 Consider the built-in USArrests data frame.
  (a) Determine the number of rows and columns for this data frame.
  (b) Calculate the median of each column of this data frame.
  (c) Find the average per capita murder rate (Murder) in regions where the percentage of the population living in urban areas (UrbanPop) exceeds 77%. Compare this with the average per capita murder rate where urban area population is less than 50%.
  (d) Construct a new data frame consisting of a random sample of 12 of the records of the USArrests data frame, where the records have been sampled without replacement.

2.10 | Data input and output

When in an R session, it is possible to read and write data to files outside of R, for example on your computer's hard drive. Before we can discuss some of the many ways of doing this, it is important to know where the data are coming from or going to.

2.10.1 Changing directories

In the RStudio Files Pane you can navigate to the directory where you want to work, and choose Set As Working Directory from the More menu item. Alternatively you can run the R function setwd(). For example, to work with data in the folder mydata on the C: drive, run

```
setwd("c:/mydata")        # or setwd("c:\\mydata")
```

After running this command, all data input and output will default to the mydata folder in the C: drive.[8]

[8] If you are accustomed to folder names in Windows, you might have expected this to be written as "c:\mydata". However, R treats the backslash character "\" as a special "escape" character, which modifies the interpretation of the next character. If you really want a backslash, you need to double it: the first backslash tells the second backslash not to be an escape. Because other systems use a forward slash "/" in their folder names, and because doubling the backslash is tedious in Windows, R accepts either form.

2.10.2 dump() and source()

Suppose you have constructed an R object called usefuldata. In order to save this object for a future session, type

```
dump("usefuldata", "useful.R")
```

This stores the command necessary to create the vector usefuldata into the file *useful.R* on your computer's hard drive. The choice of filename is up to you, as long as it conforms to the usual requirements for filenames on your computer.

To retrieve the vector in a future session, type

```
source("useful.R")
```

This reads and executes the command in *useful.R*, resulting in the creation of the usefuldata object in your global environment. If there was an object of the same name there before, it will be replaced.

To save all of the objects that you have created during a session, type

```
dump(list = objects(), "all.R")
```

This produces a file called *all.R* on your computer's hard drive. Using source("all.R") at a later time will allow you to retrieve all of these objects.

Example 2.4
To save existing objects humidity, temp and rain to a file called *weather.R* on your hard drive, type

```
dump(c("humidity", "temp", "rain"), "weather.R")
```

Exercises

1 Use a text editor to create a file consisting of the line

```
randomdata <- c(64, 38, 97, 88, 24, 14, 104, 83)
```

Save it to a file called randomdata.

2 Source the file randomdata into R and confirm the randomdata vector was created.

3 Create a vector called numbers which contains

```
3 5 8 10 12
```

Dump `numbers` to a file called *numbers.R* and delete `numbers` using the `rm()` function. Using `ls()`, confirm that `numbers` has been deleted. Now, use the source command to retrieve the vector `numbers`.

2.10.3 Redirecting R output

By default, R directs the output of most of its functions to the screen. Output can be directed to a file with the `sink()` function.

Example 2.5
Consider the greenhouse data in `solar.radiation`. The command `mean(solar.radiation)` prints the mean of the data to the screen. To print this output to a file called *solarmean.txt* instead, run

```
sink("solarmean.txt")      # Create a file solarmean.txt for output
mean(solar.radiation)      # Write mean value to solarmean.txt
```

All subsequent output will be printed to the file *solarmean.txt* until the command

```
sink()            # Close solarmean.txt; print new output to screen
```

is invoked. This returns subsequent output to the screen.

2.10.4 Saving and retrieving image files

The vectors and other objects created during an R session are stored in the workspace known as the global environment. When ending an R session, we have the option of saving the workspace in a file called a workspace image. If we choose to do so, a file called by default *.RData* is created in the current working directory (folder) which contains the information needed to reconstruct this workspace. In Windows, the workspace image will be automatically loaded if R is started by clicking on the icon representing the file *.RData*, or if the *.RData* file is saved in the directory from which R is started. If R is started in another directory, the `load()` function may be used to load the workspace image.

It is also possible to save workspace images without quitting. For example, we could save all current workspace image information to a file called *temp.RData* by typing

```
save.image("temp.RData")
```

Again, we can begin an R session with that workspace image, by clicking on the icon for *temp.RData*. Alternatively, we can type `load("temp.RData")` after entering an R session. Objects that were already in the current workspace image will remain, unless they have the same name as objects in the workspace image associated with *temp.RData*. In the latter case, the current objects will be overwritten and lost.

2.10.5 The `read.table` function

The following data set consists of 4 observations on the three variables x, y, and z:

x	y	z
61	13	4
175	21	18
111	24	14
124	23	18

If such a data set is stored in a file called *pretend.dat* in the directory *myfiles* on the *C:* drive, then it can be read into an R data frame. This can be accomplished by typing

```
pretend.df <- read.table("c:/myfiles/pretend.dat", header = TRUE)
```

The result is a data frame called `pretend.df` to which the usual data frame operations apply, such as `pretend.df$x` which would extract the first column of data.

Comma-separated values (CSV) files can be read in using the `sep = ","` argument in `read.table()`.

In practice, it is unusual for data files to be as *clean* as `pretend.df`. More often, data files are littered with blanks and other oddities. For example, suppose *file1.txt* has the following contents:

```
x, y, z
3,  ,  4
51, 48, 23
23, 33, 111
```

Reading in such a file with blank missing values is accomplished using

```
dataset1 <-
read.table("file1.txt", header = TRUE, sep = ",", na.string = " ")
```

In the above code, the `na.string` parameter replaces blank values with the NA missing value symbol. The contents of the data frame are

```
> dataset1
   x  y   z
1  3 NA   4
2 51 48  23
3 23 33 111
```

For another example, suppose the fields in *file2.txt* are separated by tabs and the contents, when viewed in a text editor, appear as follows:

```
x        y        z
33       223
32       88       2
3                 7
```

Reading in such a file with columns separated by tabs with blank missing values can be carried out using

```
dataset2 <-
read.table("file2.txt", header = TRUE, sep = "\t", na.string = " ")
```

The outcome of this is to produce a data frame with the following contents:

```
> dataset2
   x   y  z
1 33 223 NA
2 32  88  2
3  3  NA NA
```

Section 5.3 describes *tidyverse* functions for reading data from a file.

Exercises

1 Display the row 1, column 3 element of `pretend.df`.

2 Use two different commands to display the y column of `pretend.df`.

Chapter exercises

1 Calculate 11^2, 111^2 and 1111^2, and note the pattern in the sequence of results. Now, compute 11111111^2. In order to see all of the digits, try `options(digits = 18)` before carrying out the calculation. Finally, calculate 111111111^2. Did you obtain the correct answer? Why or why not?

2 How might you correct the following statement: "There are 10 kinds of people: those that understand binary and those that do not."

3 Consider the built-in data frame `chickwts`.

(a) Create a subset of the data frame called `chickwts300p` which contains all observations for which the weight exceeds 300.

(b) Create another subset called `chickwtsLinseed` which contains all observations for which the chicks were fed linseed.

(c) Calculate the average weight of the chicks who were fed linseed.

(d) Calculate the average weight of the chicks who were not fed linseed.

4 Consider the built-in data frame `cars`.

(a) Consult the help page to determine the number of observations in the data set as well as the number of variables. Also, what are the names of the variables?

(b) Find the mean stopping distance for all observations for which the speed was 20 miles per hour.

(c) Construct a scatterplot relating stopping distance to speed. What kind of relationship do you observe?

5 Assign the data set in *rnf6080.dat*[9] to a data frame called rain.df. Use the `header = FALSE` option.

(a) Display the row 2, column 4 element of `rain.df`.

(b) What are the names of the columns of `rain.df`.

(c) Display the contents of the 2nd row of the `rain.df` data set.

(d) Use the following command to re-label the columns of this data frame:

[9] This data set is available at www.statprogr.science/data/rnf6080.dat.

```
names(rain.df) <- c("year", "month", "day", seq(0, 23))
```

(e) Create a new column called `daily` which is the sum of the 24 hourly columns.

(f) Plot a histogram of the daily rainfall amounts.

6 Plot the graph of the function
$$f(x) = \begin{cases} 3x + 2, & x \le 3 \\ 2x - 0.5x^2, & x > 3 \end{cases}$$
on the interval $[0, 6]$.

7 The goal of this exercise is for you to use artificial data to see what the advantages of factors are over numeric and character vectors.

(a) Use the `sample()` function to construct a vector called `dieRolls` which simulates the results of 1000000 tosses of a 6-sided die.

(b) Convert `dieRolls` to a factor called `dieRollsFactor`. Change the levels of the factor using the code

```
levels(dieRollsFactor) <- c("One", "Two", "Three", "Four", "Five",
                            "Six")
```

(c) Create a character version of the vector using

```
dieRollsChar <- as.character(dieRollsFactor)
```

(d) Apply the `table()` function to each of `dieRolls`, `dieRollsFactor`, and `dieRollsChar`, and compare the results as well as how the information in each of the data sets is displayed.

(e) Run the code

```
system.time(table(dieRolls))
system.time(table(dieRollsFactor))
system.time(table(dieRollsChar))
```

to compare the length of time required to construct the 3 tables, using each data type. Which table was produced most quickly? Which was the slowest?

(f) Run the code

```
dump("dieRolls", "dieRolls.R")
dump("dieRollsFactor", "dieRollsFactor.R")
dump("dieRollsChar", "dieRollsChar.R")
```

Investigate the properties of the files *dieRolls.R*, *dieRollsFactor.R*, and *dieRollsChar.R*. Which one requires the smallest amount of memory? Which file takes the most memory?

8 What are the contents of the object `gender` after the following code is run?

```
gender <- c("M", "M", "F", "F", "F")
whereF <- (gender == "F")
gender[whereF] <- "Female"
```

9 Construct the data frame `charnum` in the following way:

```
char <- c("2", "1", "0")
num <- 0:2
charnum <- data.frame(char, num, stringsAsFactors = TRUE)
```

The `as.numeric()` function *coerces* character data to become numeric (when possible). Apply `as.numeric()` to `char` and to `charnum$char`. Can you explain why there is a difference in the results?

3

Programming statistical graphics

Users of statistical computing need to produce graphs of their data and the results of their computations. In this chapter we start with a general overview of how this is done in R, and learn how to draw some basic plots. We then discuss some of the issues involved in *choosing* a style of plot to draw: it is not always an easy choice, and there are plenty of bad examples in the world to lead us astray. We will talk briefly about customizing graphs, and then move on to alternate packages for producing graphics.

There are several different graphics systems in R. The oldest one is most directly comparable to the original S graphics, and is now known as base graphics. You can think of base graphics as analogous to drawing with ink on paper. You build up a picture by drawing fixed things on it, and once something is drawn, it is permanent, though you might be able to cover it with something else, or move to a clean sheet of paper. Since the very beginning, base graphics has been designed to allow easy production of good quality scientific plots.

The `grid` package provides the basis for a newer graphics system. It also has facilities to produce good quality graphics, but the programmer has access to the individual pieces of a graph, and can modify them: a graph is more like a physical model being built and displayed, rather than just drawn. The `ggplot2` and `lattice` packages provide functions for high level plots based on `grid` graphics.

Both base and `grid` graphics are designed to be "device independent." Directions are given where to draw and these drawing commands work on any device, such as a printer, laptop or even a mobile phone. The actual look of a graph will vary slightly from one device to another (e.g. on paper versus in a window on your screen), because of different capabilities.

In `ggplot2` the code to draw a plot is an abstract description of the intention of what to show in the plot, rather than how to draw it. The package translates that description into `grid` commands when you ask to draw it. We will discuss this in some detail in Section 3.4.

There are other more exotic graphics systems available in R as well, providing interactive graphics, 3D displays, etc. Some of these will be mentioned briefly in Section 3.5.

3.1 | Simple high level plots

In this section we will discuss several basic plots. The functions to draw these in R are called "high level" because you don't need to worry about the details of where the ink goes; you just describe the plot you want, and R does the drawing.

3.1.1 Bar charts and dot charts

The most basic type of graph is one that summarizes a single set of numbers. Bar charts and dot charts do this by displaying a bar or dot whose length or position corresponds to the number.

Example 3.1

Figure 3.1 displays a basic bar chart based on a built-in data set. The `WorldPhones` matrix holds counts of the numbers of telephones in the major regions of the world for a number of years. The first row of the matrix corresponds to the year 1951. In order to display these data graphically, we first extract that row.

```
WorldPhones51 <- WorldPhones[1, ]
WorldPhones51
```

```
##    N.Amer   Europe     Asia   S.Amer  Oceania   Africa Mid.Amer
##     45939    21574     2876     1815     1646       89      555
```

The default code to produce a bar chart of these data using the `barplot()` function is

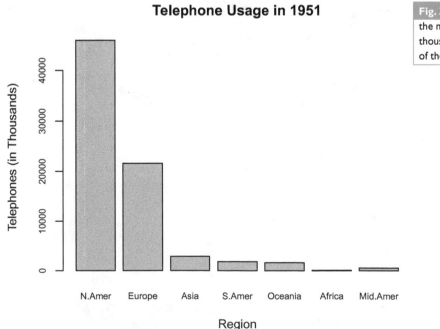

Telephone Usage in 1951

Fig. 3.1 A bar chart displaying the numbers of telephones (in thousands) in the various regions of the world in 1951.

```
barplot(WorldPhones51)
```

Some minor changes are required in order for the plot to be satisfactory: we'd like to display a title at the top, to include informative axis labels, and to reduce the size of the text associated with the axes. These changes can be carried out with the following code, yielding the result that appears in Figure 3.1.

```
barplot(WorldPhones51, main = "Telephone Usage in 1951", cex.names = 0.75,
        cex.axis = 0.75, ylab = "Telephones (in Thousands)", xlab="Region")
```

Understanding the code

The `cex.names = 0.75` argument reduced the size of the region names to 0.75 of their former size, and the `cex.axis = 0.75` argument reduced the labels on the vertical axis by the same amount. The `main` argument sets the main title for the plot, and the `ylab` and `xlab` arguments are used to include axis labels.

An alternative way to plot the same kind of data is in a dot chart (Figure 3.2):

```
dotchart(WorldPhones51, xlab = "Numbers of Phones ('000s)")
```

The values are shown by the horizontal positions of the dots.

Data sets having more complexity can also be displayed using these graphics functions. The `barplot()` function has a number of options which allow for side-by-side or stacked styles of displays, legends can be included using the `legend` argument, and so on.

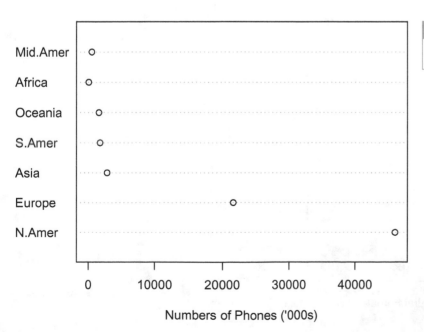

Fig. 3.2 World telephone counts in 1951 displayed as a dot chart.

Example 3.2

The VADeaths data set in R contains death rates (number of deaths per 1000 population per year) in various subpopulations within the state of Virginia in 1940.

```
VADeaths

##         Rural Male Rural Female Urban Male Urban Female
## 50-54        11.7          8.7       15.4          8.4
## 55-59        18.1         11.7       24.3         13.6
## 60-64        26.9         20.3       37.0         19.3
## 65-69        41.0         30.9       54.6         35.1
## 70-74        66.0         54.3       71.1         50.0
```

This data set may be displayed as a sequence of bar charts, one for each subgroup (Figure 3.3):

```
barplot(VADeaths, beside = TRUE, legend = TRUE, ylim = c(0, 90),
        ylab = "Deaths per 1000",
        main = "Death rates in Virginia")
```

Understanding the code

The bars correspond to each number in the matrix. The beside = TRUE argument causes the values in each column to be plotted side-by-side; legend = TRUE causes the legend in the top right to be added. The ylim = c(0, 90) argument modifies the vertical scale of the graph to make room for the legend. (We will describe other ways to place the legend in Section 3.3.) Finally, main = "Death rates in Virginia" sets the main title for the plot.

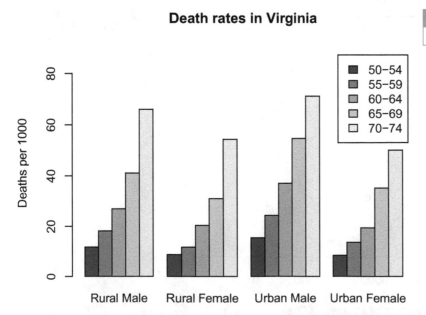

Death rates in Virginia

Fig. 3.3 An example of a complex bar chart.

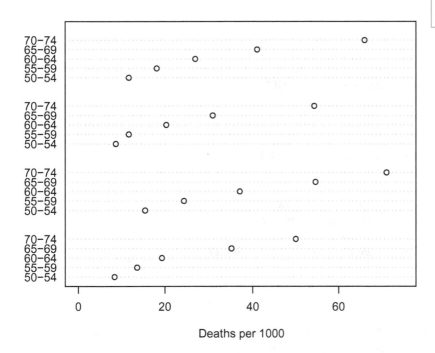

Death rates in Virginia

Deaths per 1000

Fig. 3.4 A dot chart interpretation of the Virginia Death Rate data set.

Again, the dot chart offers an alternative way of viewing the data (Figure 3.4). We will discuss criteria to use to choose between these alternatives in Section 3.2.

Example 3.3

```
dotchart(VADeaths, xlim = c(0, 75), xlab = "Deaths per 1000",
         main = "Death rates in Virginia", cex = 0.8)
```

Understanding the code

We set the x-axis limits to run from 0 to 75 so that zero is included, because it is natural to want to compare the total rates in the different groups. We have also set cex to 0.8. This shrinks the plotting character to 80% of its default size, but more importantly, shrinks the axis tick labels to 80% of their default size. For this example, the default setting would cause some overlapping of the tick labels, making them more difficult to read.

3.1.2 Pie charts

Pie charts display a vector of numbers by breaking up a circular disk into pieces whose angle (and hence area) is proportional to each number. For example, the letter grades assigned to a class might arise in the proportions, A: 18%, B: 30%, C: 32%, D: 10%, and F: 10%. These data are graphically displayed in Figure 3.5, which was drawn with the R code

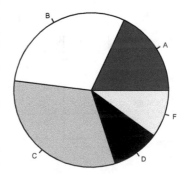

Fig. 3.5 A pie chart showing the distribution of grades in a class.

```
groupsizes <- c(18, 30, 32, 10, 10)
labels <- c("A", "B", "C", "D", "F")
pie(groupsizes, labels,
    col = c("grey40", "white", "grey", "black", "grey90"))
```

Pie charts are popular in non-technical publications, but they have fallen out of favor with statisticians. Some of the reasons why will be discussed in Section 3.2.

3.1.3 Histograms

A histogram is a special type of bar chart that is used to show the frequency distribution of a collection of numbers. Each bar represents the count of x values that fall in the range indicated by the base of the bar. Usually all bars have the same width; this is the default in R. In this case, the height of each bar is proportional to the number of observations in the corresponding interval. If bars have different widths, then the *area* of the bar should be proportional to the count; in this way the height represents the density (i.e. the frequency per unit of x).

In base graphics, hist(x, ...) is the main way to plot histograms. Here x is a vector consisting of numeric observations, and optional parameters in ... are used to control the details of the display.

An example of a histogram (of the areas of the world's largest landmasses) drawn with the default parameter settings was given in Section 2.7.1. The histogram bars decrease in height, roughly exponentially, in the direction of increasing land area (along the horizontal axis). It is often recommended that measurements from such *skewed* distributions be displayed on a logarithmic scale. This is demonstrated in Figure 3.6,

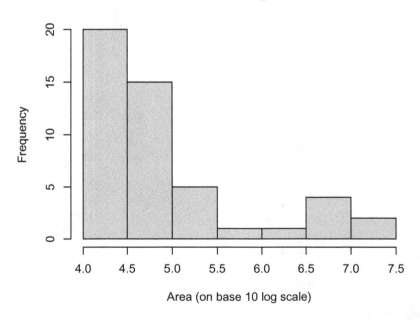

Areas of the World's Largest Landmasses

Area (on base 10 log scale)

Fig. 3.6 Histogram of landmass areas on the log scale, with better axis labeling and a title.

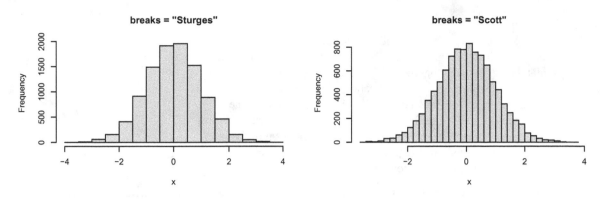

Fig. 3.7 Histograms of the values in a vector x of length 10000, using two different rules for setting the breaks.

together with better axis labeling and a title. Further improvements are illustrated in Appendix B.

```
hist(log(1000*islands, 10),  xlab = "Area (on base 10 log scale)",
    main = "Areas of the World's Largest Landmasses")
```

If you have n values of x, R, by default, divides the range into approximately $\log_2(n) + 1$ intervals, giving rise to that number of bars.

In the `islands` data set, there are

```
length(islands)
## [1] 48
```

measurements, so $n = 48$. Since

$$48 > 2^5 = 32$$

$$48 < 2^6 = 64$$

$$5 < \log_2(48) < 6$$

it can be seen that R should choose about 5 or 6 bars. In fact, it chose 8, because it also attempts to put the breaks at round numbers (multiples of 0.5 in this case).

The $\log_2(n) + 1$ rule (known as the "Sturges rule") is not always satisfactory for large values of n, giving too few bars. Current research suggests that the number of bars should increase proportionally to $n^{1/3}$ instead of $\log_2(n)$. The breaks = "Scott" and breaks = "Freedman-Diaconis" options provide variations on this choice. Figure 3.7 shows the results for a simulated 10000 point data set, generated from a symmetric distribution, using the "Sturges" and "Scott" rules.

3.1.4 Boxplots

A boxplot (or "box-and-whisker plot") is an alternative to a histogram to give a quick visual display of the main features of a set of data. A rectangular box is drawn, together with lines which protrude from two opposing sides. The box gives an indication of the location and spread of the central portion of the data, while the extent of the lines (the "whiskers") provides an idea of the range of the bulk of the data. In some implementations, outliers (observations that are very different from the rest of the data) are plotted as separate points.

The basic construction of the box part of the boxplot is as follows:

1. A horizontal line is drawn at the median.
2. Split the data into two halves, each containing the median.
3. Calculate the upper and lower quartiles as the medians of each half, and draw horizontal lines at each of these values. Then connect the lines to form a rectangular box.

The box thus drawn defines the *interquartile range* (IQR). This is the difference between the upper quartile and the lower quartile. We use the IQR to give a measure of the amount of variability in the central portion of the data set, since about 50% of the data will lie within the box.

The lower whisker is drawn from the lower end of the box to the smallest value that is no smaller than 1.5 IQR below the lower quartile. Similarly, the upper whisker is drawn from the middle of the upper end of the box to the largest value that is no larger than 1.5 IQR above the upper quartile. The rationale for these definitions is that when data are drawn from the normal distribution or other distributions with a similar shape, about 99% of the observations will fall between the whiskers.

An annotated example of a boxplot is displayed in Figure 3.8. Boxplots are convenient for comparing distributions of data in two or more categories, with a number (say 10 or more) of numerical observations per category. For example, the `iris` data set in R is a well-studied data set of measurements of 50 flowers from each of three species of iris. Figure 3.9, produced by the code

```
boxplot(Sepal.Length ~ Species, data = iris,
        ylab = "Sepal length (cm)", main = "Iris measurements",
        boxwex = 0.5)
```

compares the distributions of the sepal length measurements between the different species. Here we have used R's formula-based interface to the graphics function: the syntax `Sepal.Length ~ Species` is read as "Sepal.Length depending on Species," where both are columns of the data frame specified by `data = iris`. The `boxplot()` function draws separate side-by-side boxplots for each species. From these, we can see substantial differences between the mean lengths for the species, and that there is one unusually small specimen among the *virginica* samples.

Fig. 3.8 Construction of a boxplot.

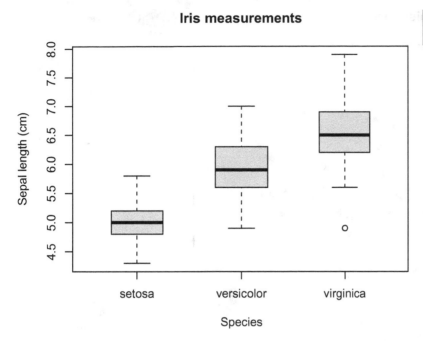

Iris measurements

Fig. 3.9 An example of side-by-side boxplots.

3.1.5 Scatterplots

When doing statistics and data science, most of the interesting problems have to do with the relationships between different variables. To study this, one of the most commonly used plots is the scatterplot, in which points (x_i, y_i), $i = 1, \ldots, n$ are drawn using dots or other symbols. These are drawn to show relationships between the x_i and y_i values. In R, scatterplots (and many other kinds of plots) are drawn using the `plot()` function. Its basic usage is `plot(x, y, ...)` where x and y are numeric vectors of the same length holding the data to be plotted. There are many additional optional arguments, and versions of `plot` designed for non-numerical data as well.

One important optional argument is `type`. The default is `type = "p"`, which draws a scatterplot. Line plots (in which line segments join the (x_i, y_i) points in order from first to last) are drawn using `type = "l"`. Many other types are available, including `type = "n"`, to draw *nothing*: this just sets up the frame around the plot, allowing other functions to be used to draw in it. Some of these other functions will be discussed in Section 3.3.

Many other types of graphs can be obtained with this function. We will show how to explore some of the options using some artificial data. Two vectors of numbers will be simulated, one from a standard normal distribution and the other from a Poisson distribution having mean 30.[1]

[1] See Chapter 5 for more information on the simulation of normal and Poisson random variables.

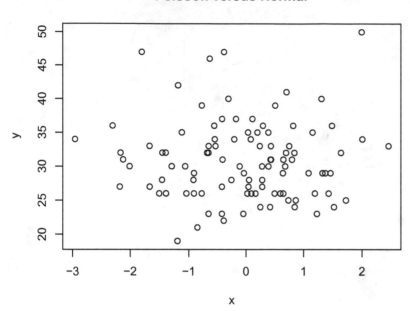

Poisson versus Normal

Fig. 3.10 An example of a scatterplot.

```
x <- rnorm(100)        # assigns 100 random normal observations to x
y <- rpois(100, 30)    # assigns 100 random Poisson observations
                       # to y; mean value is 30
mean(y)                # the resulting value should be near 30

## [1] 30.91
```

The `main` argument sets the main title for the plot. Figure 3.10 shows the result of

```
plot(x, y, main = "Poisson versus Normal")
```

Other possibilities you should try:

```
plot(x, y, pch = 16)       # changes the plot symbol to a solid dot
plot(x, y, type = 'l')     # plots a broken line (a dense tangle of line
                           # segments here)
plot(sort(x), sort(y), type = 'l')   # a plot of the sample "quantiles"
```

3.1.6 Plotting data from data frames

Example 3.4

The `Orange` data frame is in the `datasets` package installed with R. It consists of 35 observations on the age (in days since December 31, 1968) and the corresponding circumference of five different orange trees, with identifiers

```
unique(as.character(Orange$Tree))
```

```
## [1] "1" "2" "3" "4" "5"
```

(Since `Orange$Tree` is a factor, we use `as.character()` to get the displayed form, and `unique()` to select the unique values.)

To get a sense of how circumference relates to age, we might try the following:

```
plot(circumference ~ age, data = Orange)
```

Understanding the code

We have used the graphics formula and the `data` argument as in the earlier boxplot example. The plot function finds `circumference` and `age` in the `Orange` data frame, and plots the ordered pairs of (age, circumference) observations.

Figure 3.11 hides important information: the observations are not all from the same tree, and they are not all from different trees; they are from five different trees, but we cannot tell which observations are from which tree. One way to remedy this problem is to use a different plotting symbol for each tree. The `pch` parameter controls the plotting character. The default setting `pch = 1` yields the open circular dot. Other numerical values of this parameter will give different plotting characters. We can also ask for different characters to be plotted; for example, `pch = "A"` causes R to plot the character A.

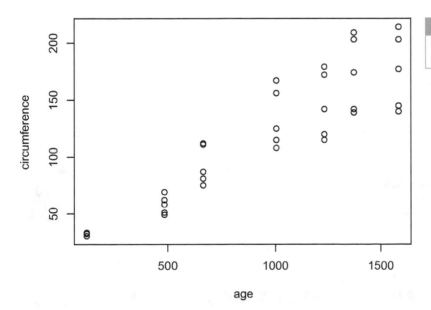

Fig. 3.11 A scatterplot of circumference versus age for five different orange trees.

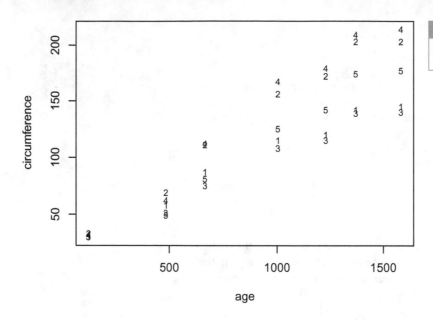

Fig. 3.12 A scatterplot of circumference versus age for five different orange trees.

Example 3.5

The following code can be used to identify the individual trees (Figure 3.12).

```
plot(circumference ~ age, data = Orange, pch = as.character(Tree),
     cex = 0.75)
```

Understanding the code

The `cex` parameter controls the size of the plotting character, and the `pch` parameter has been assigned the levels of the `Tree` column; because `Tree` is a factor, care must be taken in order that the level values are used, and not the factor codes, hence the use of `as.character()`.

There are many more optional arguments to the `plot()` function, described on the `?plot` and `?par` help pages.

3.1.7 QQ plots

Quantile-quantile plots (otherwise known as QQ plots) are a type of scatterplot used to compare the distributions of two groups or to compare a sample with a reference distribution.

In the case where there are two groups of equal size, the QQ plot is obtained by first sorting the observations in each group: $X[1] \leq \cdots \leq X[n]$ and $Y[1] \leq \cdots \leq Y[n]$. Next, draw a scatterplot of $(X[i], Y[i])$, for $i = 1, \ldots, n$.

When the groups are of different sizes, some scheme must be used to artificially match them. R reduces the size of the larger group to the size

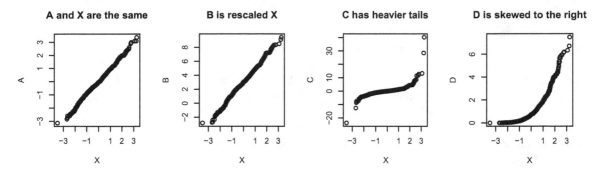

Fig. 3.13 Several examples of QQ plots.

of the smaller one by keeping the minimum and maximum values, and choosing equally spaced quantiles between. For example, if there were five X values but 20 Y values, then the X values would be plotted against the minimum, lower quartile, median, upper quartile and maximum of the Y values.

When plotting a single sample against a reference distribution, theoretical quantiles are used for one coordinate. R normally puts the theoretical quantiles on the x-axis and the data on the y-axis, but some authors make the opposite choice. To avoid biases, quantiles are chosen corresponding to probabilities $(i - 1/2)/n$: these are centered evenly between zero and one.

When the distributions of X and Y match, the points in the QQ plot will lie near the line $y = x$. We will see a different straight line if one distribution is a linear transformation of the other. On the other hand, if the two distributions are not the same, we will see systematic patterns in the QQ plot.

Example 3.6
The following code illustrates some common patterns (see Figure 3.13), using simulated data.

```
par(mfrow = c(1,4))
X <- rnorm(1000)
A <- rnorm(1000)
qqplot(X, A, main = "A and X are the same")

B <- rnorm(1000, mean = 3, sd = 2)
qqplot(X, B, main = "B is rescaled X")

C <- rt(1000, df = 2)
qqplot(X, C, main = "C has heavier tails")

D <- rexp(1000)
qqplot(X, D, main = "D is skewed to the right")
```

Understanding the code

The `mfrow` parameter of the `par()` function is giving a 1×4 layout (see Section B.3). The first plot is based on identical normal distributions, the second plot is based on normal distributions having different means and standard deviations, the third plot is based on a standard normal and a t distribution on 2 degrees of freedom, and the fourth plot is based on a standard normal compared with an exponential distribution. Since we used simulated random numbers here, you'll likely see slightly different results if you run the same code. More information about the functions `rnorm()`, `rt()` and `rexp()` is given in Chapter 5.

Exercises

1 Consider the `islands` vector discussed in this section.
   (a) Compare the histograms that result when using breaks based on Sturges' and Scott's rules. Make this comparison on the log-scale and on the original scale.
   (b) Construct a normal QQ plot, and compare the result with the plots in Figure 3.13; which one is most similar, and what does this tell you about this data set?
   (c) Construct a boxplot for these data on the log-scale as well as the original scale.
   (d) Construct a dot chart of the areas. Is a log transformation needed here?
   (e) Which form of graphic do you think is most appropriate for displaying these data?

2 The `stackloss` data frame contains 21 observations on four variables taken at a factory where ammonia is converted to nitric acid. The first three variables are `Air.Flow`, `Water.Temp`, and `Acid.Conc..` The fourth variable is `stack.loss`, which measures the amount of ammonia which escapes before being absorbed. (Read the help file for more information about this data frame.)
   (a) Use scatterplots to explore possible relationships between acid concentration, water temperature, and air flow and the amount of ammonia which escapes. Do these relationships appear to be linear or nonlinear?
   (b) Use the `pairs()` function to obtain all pairwise scatterplots among the four variables. Identify pairs of variables where there might be linear or nonlinear relationships.

3 Consider the `pressure` data frame. There are two columns— `temperature` and `pressure`.
   (a) Construct a scatterplot with `pressure` on the vertical axis and `temperature` on the horizontal axis. Are the variables related linearly or nonlinearly?
   (b) The graph of the following function passes through the plotted points reasonably well:

$$y = (0.168 + 0.007x)^{20/3}.$$

The differences between the pressure values predicted by the curve and the observed pressure values are called *residuals*. Here is a way to calculate them:

```
residuals <- with(pressure, pressure -
                          (0.168 + 0.007*temperature)^(20/3))
```

Construct a normal QQ plot of these residuals and decide whether they are normally distributed or whether they follow a skewed distribution.

(c) Now, apply the power transformation $y^{3/20}$ to the pressure data values. Plot these transformed values against temperature. Is a linear or nonlinear relationship evident now?

(d) Calculate residuals for the difference between transformed pressure values and those predicted by the straight line. Obtain a normal QQ plot, and decide whether the residuals follow a normal distribution or not.

4 What does a skewed distribution look like? How does a skewed distribution differ from a symmetric distribution, and how does a left-skewed distribution differ from a right-skewed distribution?

3.2 | Choosing a high level graphic

We have described bar, dot, and pie charts, histograms, boxplots, scatterplots, and QQ plots. There are many other styles of statistical graphics that we haven't discussed. How should a user choose which one to use?

The first consideration is the type of data. As discussed in the previous section, bar, dot, and pie charts display individual values, histograms, boxplots, and QQ plots display distributions, and scatterplots display pairs of values.

Another consideration is the audience. If the plot is for yourself or for a statistically educated audience, then you can assume a more sophisticated understanding. For example, a boxplot or QQ plot would require more explanation than a histogram, and might not be appropriate for the general public.

It is also important to have some understanding of how human visual perception works in order to make a good choice. There has been a huge amount of research on this and we can only touch on it here.

When looking at a graph, you extract quantitative information when your visual system *decodes* the graph. This process can be described in terms of unconscious measurements of lengths, positions, slopes, angles, areas, volumes, and various aspects of color. It has been found that people are particularly good at recognizing lengths and positions, not as good at slopes and angles, and their perception of areas and volumes can be quite inaccurate, depending on the shape. Most of us are quite good at recognizing differences in colors. However, up to 10% of men and a much smaller proportion of women are partially color-blind, and almost nobody is very good at making quantitative measurements from colors.

We can take these facts about perception into account when we construct graphs. We should try to convey the important information in ways that are easy to perceive, and we should try not to have conflicting messages in a graph.

For example, the bars in bar charts are easy to recognize, because the position of the ends of the bars and the length of the bars are easy to see. The area of the bars also reinforces our perception.

However, the fact that we see length and area when we look at a bar constrains us. We should normally base bar charts at zero, so that the position, length and area all convey the same information. If we are displaying numbers where zero is not relevant, then a dot chart is a better choice: in a dot chart it is mainly the position of the dot that is perceived.

Thinking in terms of visual tasks tells us that pie charts can be poor choices for displaying data. In order to see the sizes of slices of the pie, we need to make angle and area measurements, and we are not very good at those.

Finally, color can be very useful in graphs to distinguish groups from each other. The `RColorBrewer` package in R contains a number of *palettes*, or selections of colors. Some palettes indicate sequential groups from low to high, others show groups that diverge from a neutral value, and others are purely qualitative. These are chosen so that most people (even if color-blind) can easily see the differences.

3.3 | Low level graphics functions

Functions like `barplot()`, `dotchart()`, and `plot()` do their work by using low level graphics functions to draw lines and points, to establish where they will be placed on a page, and so on.

In this section we will describe a few of these low level functions, which are also available to users to customize their plots. More detail is given in Appendix B.

3.3.1 Adding to plots

Several functions exist to add components to existing graphs:

```
points(x, y, ...)              # adds points
lines(x, y, ...)               # adds line segments
text(x, y, labels, ...)        # adds text into the graph
abline(a, b, ...)              # adds the line $y = a + bx$
abline(h = y, ...)             # adds a horizontal line
abline(v = x, ...)             # adds a vertical line
polygon(x, y, ...)             # adds a closed and possibly filled polygon
segments(x0, y0, x1, y1, ...)  # draws line segments
arrows(x0, y0, x1, y1, ...)    # draws arrows
symbols(x, y, ...)             # draws circles, squares, thermometers, etc.
legend(x, y, legend, ...)      # draws a legend
```

The optional arguments to these functions specify the color, size, and other characteristics of the items being added.

Example 3.7

Consider the `Orange` data frame again. In addition to using different plotting characters for the different trees, we will pass lines of best fit (i.e. least-squares regression lines) through the points corresponding to each tree.

The basic scatterplot is obtained from

```
plot(circumference ~ age, pch = as.numeric(as.character(Tree)),
    data = Orange)
```

The best-fit lines for the five trees can be obtained using the `lm()` function which relates circumference to age for each tree. A legend has been added to identify which data points come from the different trees.

```
abline(lm(circumference ~ age, data = Orange, subset = Tree == "1"),
    lty = 1)
abline(lm(circumference ~ age, data = Orange, subset = Tree == "2"),
    lty = 2)
abline(lm(circumference ~ age, data = Orange, subset = Tree == "3"),
    lty = 3, lwd = 2)
abline(lm(circumference ~ age, data = Orange, subset = Tree == "4"),
    lty = 4)
abline(lm(circumference ~ age, data = Orange, subset = Tree == "5"),
    lty = 5)
legend("topleft", legend = paste("Tree", 1:5), lty = 1:5, pch = 1:5,
    lwd = c(1, 1, 2, 1, 1))
```

In these plots `lty` gives the line type, and `lwd` gives the line width. The left panel of Figure 3.14 shows the resulting lines. The right panel shows an alternative way of displaying the data, using the `lines()` function and

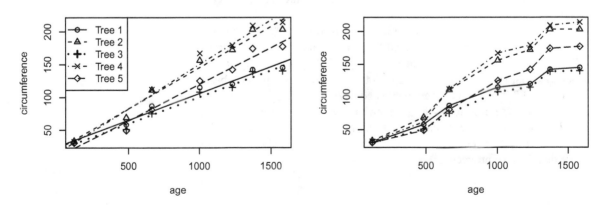

Fig. 3.14 A scatterplot of circumference versus age for five orange trees, with overlaid trend lines, using different line types for each tree. Left panel: best-fit straight lines have been obtained using least-squares; right panel: broken lines are used to interpolate the data.

without obtaining the least-squares regression lines. The details are left as an exercise for the reader.

Exercises

1 The breakdown of music preferences for a class of university students is: 40% prefer rock, 10% prefer country, 15% prefer hip-hop and the rest prefer alternative. Construct an appropriate plot to display these data.

2 Write code that produces the figure in the right panel of Figure 3.14. Add an appropriate legend to the bottom right corner of the plot.

3 Obtain an analogous set of plots to those displayed in Figure B.4, but with enough room for the respective titles: "Histogram-Sturges," "Histogram-FD," "Density Estimate," "Boxplot," "QQ Plot," "Trace Plot."

4 Re-do the plots of Figure B.4, but this time, apply the six graphics functions to a variable X which is defined by $X = Z^2$, where Z is a simulated standard normal random variable as in the example. Comment on the changes that you see in the plots. (The variable X is an example of a chi-squared random variable on 1 degree of freedom.)

5 Refer to the previous question. Construct another set of six plots as in Figure B.4, but this time apply the data in `EuStockMarkets` (i.e. apply the code of B.4 to `z` where `z <- EuStockMarkets`). Comment on the results, and use the `summary()` function to gain further insight. Which of the six plots are useful descriptors of this data set, and which may be limited in their usefulness?

3.4 | Graphics as a language: `ggplot2`

The `ggplot2` package by Hadley Wickham is based on a "grammar of graphics": the idea that statistical graphics is a language that conveys meaning; the words of this language are charts and components of the charts. Rather than describing the ink that goes on the page, the code describes the message you want to send.

The ideas behind `ggplot2` were first described in a 1999 book called *The Grammar of Graphics* by Leland Wilkinson, and a second expanded edition was published in 2005. They were expanded again and popularized when Wickham published `ggplot2` in 2007. Our own description is based on version 3.3.2 of that package, published in 2020.

The `ggplot2` package gives a somewhat abstract but very rich way to describe graphics. We will start our discussion with an example showing how to re-draw the bar chart of the world telephones of Example 3.1, adding more detail as we proceed.

Example 3.8
To plot the world phone data that we saw at the start of this chapter, we would write

```
library(ggplot2)
region <- names(WorldPhones51)
phones51 <- data.frame(Region = factor(region, levels = region),
                       Telephones = WorldPhones51)
ggplot(data = phones51, aes(x = Region, y = Telephones)) + geom_col()
```

Understanding the code

The first lines of this snippet are needed to load the plotting package and to prepare a data frame consisting of the telephone counts that correspond to the various world regions. The new feature is in the ggplot invocation where aes says that we want the Region names on the x-axis in their original order, and the telephone counts on the y-axis. We want to display the data using bars, hence the use of the geom_col function. The statistic to display is the identity, i.e. just the value itself. The result is shown in Figure 3.15.

The general idea in ggplot2 is that plots are described by a sum of objects produced by function calls. As with any addition in R, we use +, but you should think of the whole expression as a way to describe the plot as a combination of different components. The main components of a plot are shown in Table 3.1.

Most ggplot2 plot expressions start with a call to the ggplot() function. Its first argument is data, and that's where we specify the data component of the plot, which is always a data frame or tibble.[2] In

[2] ggplot2 fits into the *tidyverse*, described in Chapter 5.

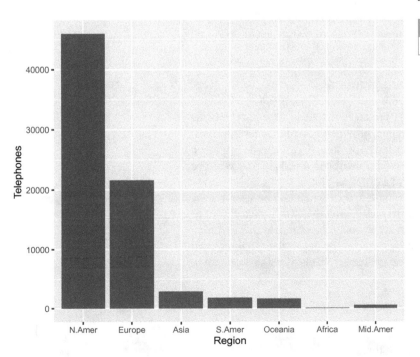

Fig. 3.15 Re-doing Figure 3.1 using ggplot2.

Table 3.1	*The main components of a ggplot2 plot.*
ggplot2 name	Description
data	your data frame
aes()	"aesthetics": things like position, color, size, and shape that control how your data is encoded in the display
geom_*()	a geometric object or layer of the graph that represents the data

Example 3.8 we specified the argument name data explicitly, but since it is the first argument and every plot contains data, usually we will skip the argument name in the call to ggplot().

The second component of every plot is called the "aesthetic mapping" of the plot, or "aesthetics" for short. This doesn't refer to the appreciation of beauty; it refers to the ways that quantities in our data are expressed in the plot. We use the aes() function to specify the aesthetics. In Example 3.8 Region is shown on the x-axis, and Telephones is shown on the y-axis. The two aesthetics x and y are so common in plots that x is the first argument to aes() and y is the second, and here again we usually we omit the argument names.

The aesthetics don't tell us *how* Region is displayed on the x-axis, just that it is. To specify how it is displayed, we give one or more layers, using geom_*() function calls. In Example 3.8 we requested a bar plot by using the geom_col() function. Because Region is a factor, geom_col() displays one bar per level. Because we had aes(x = Region, y = Telephones) the bars are vertical. We could get horizontal bars by using aes(y = Region, x = Telephones). Try it!

In the remainder of this section we will describe graphics in ggplot2 in more detail.

3.4.1 Details of the ggplot2 grammar

As we've seen, ggplot2 plots are usually created as a sum of function calls. Each of those function calls produces a special object, which the ggplot2 code knows how to combine, provided you follow certain rules.

First, you need to start with a "ggplot" object. This can be produced by a call to ggplot() or to some other function that calls it, and it can be saved in a variable and used later in a different plot.

The "ggplot" object sets certain defaults which can be used by the layers of the plot. Normally the first argument specifies a data frame or tibble, and that data can be used in all layers of the plot. It's also common to specify aesthetics as the second argument, and again, these will be used everywhere unless overridden by other settings. Thus a first component to a ggplot2 plot could be produced as

```
g1 <- ggplot(phones51, aes(Region, Telephones))
```

Because we assigned the result to g1, it is not printed, and no graph is displayed. To display it, we can print that object:

Table 3.2 | *Less commonly used components of a ggplot2 plot.*

ggplot2 name	Description
scale_*()	scales: how the data maps to the plot
trans	transformations to the data within the scale
coord_*()	coordinate systems
theme_*()	themes: overall choice of color and other parts of the appearance
facet_*()	facets: subsetting the plot. See Section 3.4.5.

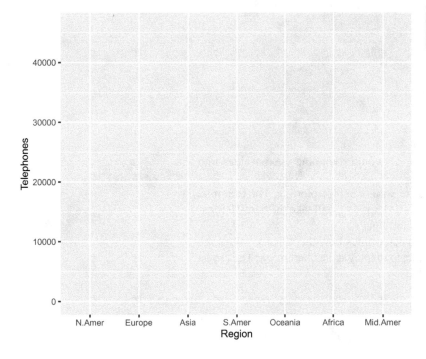

Fig. 3.16 A call to ggplot() with no layers added.

g1

and see the result in Figure 3.16. The ggplot() call is enough to establish the scale for the plot, but without layers, we don't see any data.

After our call to ggplot(), we will add other objects to change the display. The most common objects are the layers produced by the geom_*() functions; we will discuss them in the next section. Other less common components are shown in Table 3.2. The differences between scales, transformations, and coordinate systems need explaining. Scales are more qualitative than the others. We have seen two scales so far in Example 3.8. Because Region is a factor, it is automatically displayed using a discrete scale, and because Telephones is a number, it is displayed on a continuous scale. These automatic choices could be changed by adding in a call to a different scale_*() function. For example, using

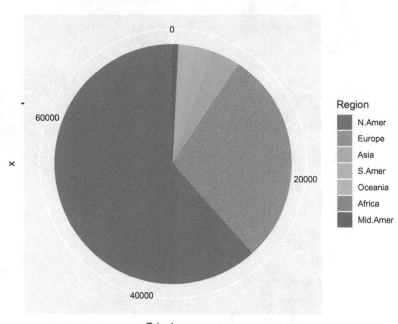

Fig. 3.17 Pie chart drawn by ggplot2.

scale_y_binned(n.breaks = 4) would round the y-axis values into five bins before plotting.

Transformations are changes to values before plotting. For example, scale_y_continuous(trans = "log10") will take the base 10 logarithm of the y-axis values before plotting.

Finally, the coordinate system determines how the x and y values are displayed on the plot. For example, to display a pie chart in ggplot2, you display a bar plot in polar coordinates:

```
ggplot(phones51, aes(x = "", y = Telephones, fill = Region)) +
    coord_polar(theta = "y") +
    geom_col()
```

The result is shown in Figure 3.17. We have changed the aesthetics, because now Region should be displayed by color, not by position in the plot. We want Telephones to control the angle theta, and the radius should be constant. ggplot2 automatically chooses colors and adds a legend to help us to decode the plot. The points we made in Section 3.2 still apply: Figure 3.15 is still a better display of these data.

The theme of a plot controls the general appearance. All of our plots have used the default theme_gray(), but others are available. There are ten complete themes shown on the ?theme_gray help page, and the theme() function can be used for near-infinite customization.

3.4.2 Layers in ggplot2

There are many ways to display data, and ggplot2 puts "ways to display data" into the geom_*() layer functions. Version 3.3.2 of ggplot2

Table 3.3 | *Some common ggplot2 layers.*

Function	Description
geom_col()	bar plots
geom_bar()	bar plots of counts
geom_histogram()	histograms
geom_point()	scatterplots
geom_jitter()	scatterplots with jittering
geom_line()	line plots
geom_contour()	contour plots
geom_contour_filled()	filled contour plots
geom_density_2d()	contour plots of density estimates
geom_boxplot()	boxplots
geom_violin()	violin plots

contains 52 of these functions, and others are available in other contributed packages. Table 3.3 lists a few of the commonly used ones.

Each kind of layer works with a different set of aesthetics. We have already seen x and y aesthetics; others that are commonly supported are

- alpha: transparency
- color (or colour)
- group: group, (described in Section 3.4.6)

Where appropriate, some others are supported:

- linetype
- size
- fill: the fill color
- weight: the statistical weight to give to each observation
- shape: the shape of point to plot
- stroke: the thickness of parts of points being plotted

Example 3.9
We produced the bar plot in Figure 3.15 using the layer function geom_col(). If we had used geom_point() or geom_line() instead, we would see points or lines respectively. In fact, Figure 3.18 shows how we can use all three:

```
ggplot(phones51, aes(Region, Telephones)) +
  geom_col() +
  geom_line(col = "blue", aes(x = as.numeric(Region))) +
  geom_point(col = "red")
```

Understanding the code
The ggplot() call sets up the scales and coordinate system, and sets the default theme. The geom_col() call draws the bars in the plot

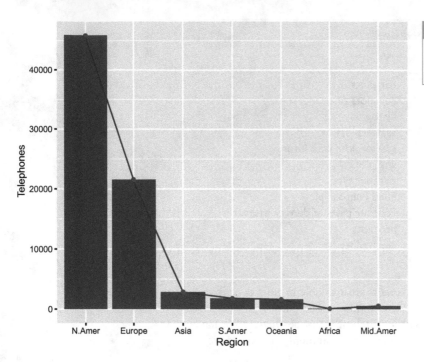

Fig. 3.18 Plot of world phone usage using `geom_col()`, `geom_point()`, and `geom_line()`.

as before, and `geom_point(col = "red")` draws points in red. The middle layer `geom_line(col = "blue", aes(x = as.numeric (Region)))` draws the blue line. The x aesthetic was replaced by a numeric version, because `Region` is a factor, and by default `ggplot2` won't join lines across its levels (see Section 3.4.6 for an explanation). The layers are drawn in the order specified, so we can see the lines on top of the bars, and the points on top of the lines. To gain a clearer view of the lines and points, we might increase the transparency of the bars, by replacing the line of code

```
geom_col() +
```

with

```
geom_col(alpha = 0.4)
```

Larger values of `alpha` increase the opaqueness of the bars.

Example 3.10

In Figure 3.8 we showed boxplots of the `iris` data using base graphics. A similar plot could be produced in `ggplot2` with this code:

```
ggplot(iris, aes(x = Species, y = Sepal.Length)) + geom_boxplot()
```

Another view of the same data (Figure 3.19) using violin plots is produced by the similar code:

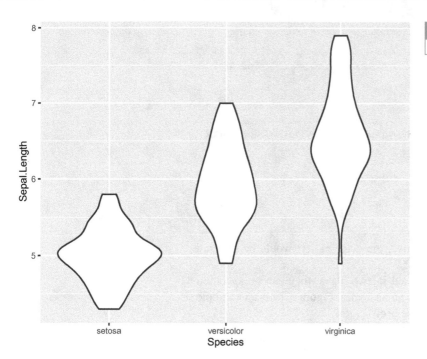

Fig. 3.19 Violin plot of the iris data.

```
ggplot(iris, aes(x = Species, y = Sepal.Length)) + geom_violin()
```

In a violin plot, a rough estimate of the PDF is used to obtain the width of the plot. This gives somewhat more information about the distribution than we saw in the boxplot: for example, we can see that setosa appears to have a high concentration of sepal lengths very close to 5 cm.

3.4.3 Setting colors

There are several different ways to identify colors in R. They can be specified by name; the function `colors()` lists hundreds of names recognized by R:

```
str(colors())
```

```
##  chr [1:657] "white" "aliceblue" "antiquewhite" "antiquewhite1" ...
```

They can also be constructed using hexadecimal (base 16) codes for the levels of red, green, and blue. For example, red would be specified as `"#FF0000"`, where `FF`, the base 16 representation of 255, is the maximum level of red, and both green and blue have zero contribution.

R also maintains a palette of a small number of colors that can be referenced by number. Since version 4.0.0, there have been several choices of palettes, choosable by name:

```
palette.pals()
```

```
##  [1] "R3"          "R4"          "ggplot2"
##  [4] "Okabe-Ito"   "Accent"      "Dark 2"
```

```
##  [7]  "Paired"           "Pastel 1"         "Pastel 2"
##  [10] "Set 1"            "Set 2"            "Set 3"
##  [13] "Tableau 10"       "Classic Tableau"  "Polychrome 36"
##  [16] "Alphabet"
```

```
palette("R3")
```

With this choice of colors (the same as in previous versions of R), we see

```
palette()
##  [1]  "black"   "red"     "green3"  "blue"    "cyan"    "magenta"
##  [7]  "yellow"  "gray"
```

For example, with this palette active, the color `"red"` would be selected by specifying color number 2.

In `ggplot2`, colors can be used in two ways: they can be specified explicitly, or color can be used as an aesthetic. Figure 3.18 is an example of specifying a color explicitly. We used

```
geom_point(col = "red")
```

to choose red points. Any of the standard R specifications for red would have worked equally well: `"red"`, `"#FF0000"`, or, assuming we are using the `"R3"` palette, the number 2.[3] For the bars in a `geom_col()` layer, `col` controls the outline color, and argument `fill` controls the fill color.

The second way to specify color in `ggplot2` is to use the `col` or `fill` aesthetic. In this case, determining the final result is more complicated, as it depends on the type of variable mapped to the aesthetic. For a discrete variable like `phones51$Region`, `ggplot2` will construct a palette of values and map each level of the variable to a different color. By default, the palette is a set of colors evenly spaced around the color wheel. If you don't want to use that palette (perhaps because it isn't a good choice for color-blind viewers), you can choose another. For example, to use one of the palettes discussed in Section 3.2, use `scale_fill_brewer()`:

[3] We used the argument name `col` as an abbreviation for `color`. Base graphics requires the abbreviated name, while `ggplot2` would accept `color` or `colour` as well.

```
ggplot(phones51, aes(Region, Telephones, fill = Region)) +
  geom_col() +
  scale_fill_brewer(palette = "Set2")
```

The result is shown in Figure 3.20.

When the mapped variable is continuous, `ggplot2` will default to a gradient scale from light blue to dark blue, produced by the `scale_fill_gradient()` function. For example,

```
ggplot(phones51, aes(Region, Telephones, fill = Telephones)) +
  geom_col()
```

The result is shown in Figure 3.21.

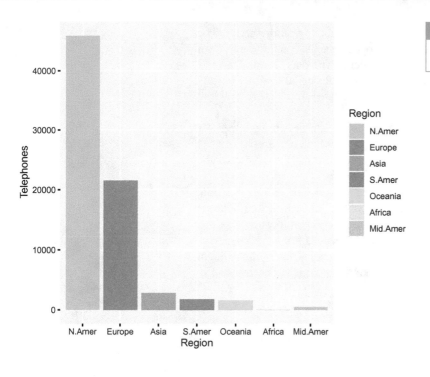

Fig. 3.20 Plot of world phone usage using the RColorBrewer Set2 palette for Region.

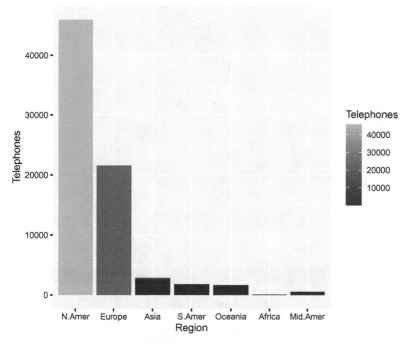

Fig. 3.21 Plot of world phone usage using the gradient palette for Telephones.

3.4.4 Customizing the look of a graph

Besides colors, there are a lot of other customizations one might want to make to a graph. We mentioned 11 different aesthetic mappings in Section 3.4.2 and gave details about setting colors in the previous section.

There are several functions to change the labeling on the graph. The ggtitle() function sets a title at the top, and xlab() and ylab() set titles on the axes. These are all just convenient "wrappers" for the labs() function, which can set labels in all of these places, as well as on any legends shown in the graph if you assign the label to the corresponding aesthetic name.

The theme() and theme_*() functions mentioned in Section 3.4.1 can be used to change many details of the overall look of a graph.

The scale_*() functions described in Sections 3.4.1 and 3.4.3 can be used to customize the mapping for each aesthetic.

The annotate() function is interesting. It works like a layer function, but with fixed vectors of aesthetics, not values taken from the data set for the plot. For example, to add some text to a plot at location x = 1, y = 2, one could use annotate("text", x = 1, y = 2, text = "Label"). The first argument ("text" in this case) is part of the name of the "geom" to use. Geoms have names like GeomText and correspond to a subset of the geom_*() functions.[4]

[4] Other functions share geoms. For example geom_histogram() uses the same geom as geom_bar().

Example 3.11

The data set windWin80 from the MPV package contains pairs of observations of wind speed at the Winnipeg International Airport. The columns give the wind speed in km per hour at midnight (h0) and noon (h12).

A proposed model for the joint probability density function of these two measurements is

$$f_{X_1, X_2}(x_1, x_2) = \frac{\alpha_1 \alpha_2 x_1^{\alpha_1 - 1} x_2^{\alpha_2 - 1} e^{-x_1^{\alpha_1}/\beta_2 - x_2^{\alpha_2}/(\beta_0 + \beta_1 x_1)}}{\beta_2(\beta_0 + \beta_1 x_1)}, \quad \text{for } x_1 \geq 0, x_2 \geq 0.$$

The parameters $\alpha_1, \alpha_2, \beta_0, \beta_1$, and β_2 must be nonnegative. The values $\alpha_1 = 3/2, \alpha_2 = 5/3, \beta_0 = 108, \beta_1 = 5.3$, and $\beta_2 = 65$ were estimated from the data; we would like to plot the data and the contours of this density on the same plot.

A first attempt at this plot can be obtained using the following code.

```
# Compute values from the proposed density function
a1 <- 3/2; a2 <- 5/3; b0 <- 108; b1 <- 5.3; b2 <- 65
grid <- with(MPV::windWin80,
             expand.grid(x1 = seq(0, max(h0), len=101),
                         x2 = seq(0, max(h12), len=101)))
grid$z <- with(grid, a1*a2*exp(-x1^a1/b2 - x2^a2/
                   (b0+b1*x1))*x1^(a1-1)*x2^(a2-1)/(b2*(b0+b1*x1)) )
# Plot the data on top of the density function
ggplot(MPV::windWin80, aes(x = h0, y = h12)) +
  geom_contour(data = grid, aes(x = x1, y = x2, z = z) ) +
  geom_point()
```

Understanding the code

The first thing we did was to define R variables corresponding to the parameters in the formula for the model. We used `a1`, `a2`, `b0`, `b1` and `b2` for $\alpha_1, \alpha_2, \beta_0, \beta_1,$ and β_2 respectively. We then used the `expand.grid()` function to create a grid of values in `x1` and `x2`; these were stored in a data frame. We added a third column to the data frame using the formula for the joint PDF.

Our plot includes a regular scatterplot in `h0` and `h12`, but before plotting the points, we plotted contours using the grid values.

Improving the plot

After your first attempt at drawing a plot, you should look for ways to improve it. In the case of Figure 3.22, we can see these issues:

- The points appear to fall on a regular grid of values, because the original data were rounded to the nearest integer. This might hide some points if they exactly overlap. A way to deal with overlapping points is *jittering*: move each point slightly by a random amount. If two points were overlapping in the original, they probably won't be overlapping after each is randomly moved. The `geom_jitter()` layer function does this for us in `ggplot2`.
- The labels `h0` and `h12` on the plot mean should be made more informative using `xlab()` and `ylab()`.
- There appear to be too many points outside the widest contour line, and too few inside the smallest ones where the peak of the PDF occurs. This could be a subtle problem with the model, so it is worth pointing it out

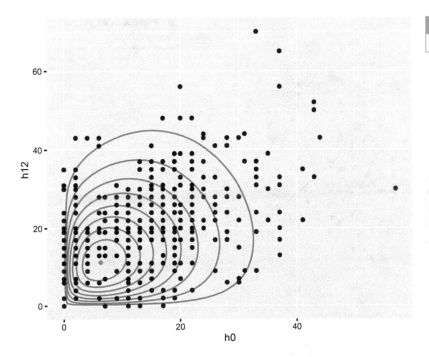

Fig. 3.22 First attempt at plot described in Example 3.11.

to the viewer. To do this, we could add an estimated PDF function to the plot using `geom_density2d()`: this will estimate the PDF from the points. We could then compare the two densities to see if they agree approximately.

- Adding two sets of contours to the same plot would be confusing. We'll need to draw them in different colors. We'll use white in `geom_density2d()`, since we are only adding it for reference: it's not the main point of the plot.
- The grid lines are going to make the plot too busy, so we can remove them using a call to `theme()`.
- Finally, we'll add some annotations to point out our areas of concern.

```r
ggplot(MPV::windWin80, aes(x = h0, y = h12)) +
    geom_density2d(col = "white") +
    geom_contour(data = grid, aes(x = x1, y = x2, z = z) ) +
    geom_jitter() +
    xlab("Wind speed at midnight (km/h)") +
    ylab("Wind speed at noon (km/h)") +
    theme(panel.grid = element_blank()) +
    annotate("text", x = 46, y = 20, hjust = 0, label = "Too many points") +
    annotate("segment", x = 46, y = 20, xend = 35, yend = 34) +
    annotate("text", x = 5, y = 50, vjust = -1, label = "Too few points") +
    annotate("segment", x = 5, y = 50, xend = 6, yend = 11)
```

The result is shown in Figure 3.23.

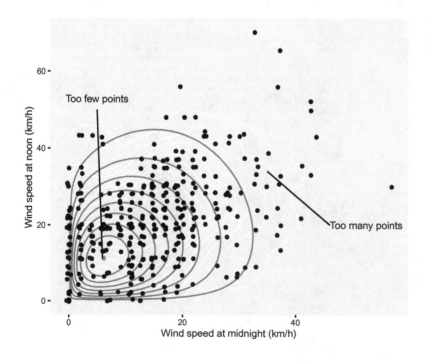

Fig. 3.23 Annotated, jittered, and improved plot described in Example 3.11.

Understanding the code

To remove the grid, we set it to the special value `element_blank()`. We drew our text annotations outside the cloud of points to make them more visible, then added line segments to point to the region we were actually talking about. The `hjust = 0` argument in the first one puts the text to the right of the reference point; `vjust = -1` puts the second text one line above its reference point.

3.4.5 Faceting

A strategy for displaying relations among three or more variables is to divide the data into subsets using the values of some of the variables, and then draw multiple plots of the values of the other variables in each of those subsets.

In `ggplot2` this is called "faceting," and the `facet_wrap()` and `facet_grid()` functions are used to implement it. The `facet_wrap()` function draws these plots side-by-side, wrapping the display to the next line once there are more than a few. Its first argument describes the variables to use for subsetting. This can be expressed by listing them in the `vars()` function, or giving a formula using ~.

Example 3.12

To study the trends over time in the `WorldPhones` data, we first need to convert it to a data frame.

```
phones <- data.frame(Year = as.numeric(rep(rownames(WorldPhones), 7)),
                     Region = rep(colnames(WorldPhones), each = 7),
                     Telephones = as.numeric(WorldPhones))
```

If we are particularly interested in the changes in the distribution between regions over time, we might plot similar bar charts for each year by specifying `facet_wrap(vars(Year))` or `facet_wrap(~ Year)`.

```
ggplot(phones, aes(x = Region, y = Telephones, fill = Region)) +
  geom_col() +
  facet_wrap(vars(Year)) +
  theme(axis.text.x = element_blank(), axis.ticks.x = element_blank()) +
  xlab(element_blank())
```

The results are shown in Figure 3.24. In this plot, we suppressed the x-axis labels and tick marks, as the legend seemed sufficient to identify the regions.

The `facet_grid()` function arranges the plots in a rectangle whose rows define one set of variables for subsetting, and whose columns represent another. These can be specified using `vars()` in the `rows` and `cols` arguments, or using a formula for `rows` and skipping `cols`. It also has an

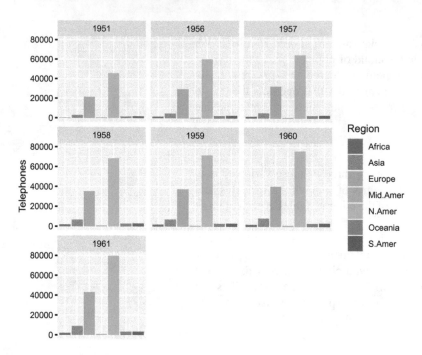

Fig. 3.24 Trends in phone usage.

argument `margins`, which adds a row ignoring the `cols` variables, and a column ignoring the `rows` variables.[5]

[5] As of version 3.3.2 of `ggplot2`, there's a bug that stops `margins` from being used when an expression is used for one of the row or column variables.

Example 3.13

The `mpg` data frame in `ggplot2` contains fuel economy data for 38 models of cars from 1999 to 2008. The `cty` and `hwy` columns measure miles per gallon in city and highway, respectively. Engine displacement in litres is given in the `displ` column, and `cyl` holds the number of cylinders.

One would expect that fuel economy is worse in larger engines and with more cylinders, but it's not obvious how these would affect the relation between city and highway efficiency. To study this, we could subset the data according to values of `displ` and `cyl` and draw scatterplots of `cyl` versus `hwy` for each. However, `displ` is a continuous variable, and even though it is rounded to one decimal place, there are still 35 different values, so the subsets would be too small.

A way to address this is to break `displ` into a smaller number of subsets based on ranges of values. The `cut_*()` functions in `ggplot2` do this in a few different ways: `cut_number()` gives equal numbers of cases per subset, `cut_interval()` gives equal ranges of values per subset, and `cut_width()` gives ranges with a specified width. We'll use `cut_number()`.

```
ggplot(mpg, aes(hwy, cty)) +
  geom_point() +
  facet_grid(cut_number(displ, 3) ~ cyl)
```

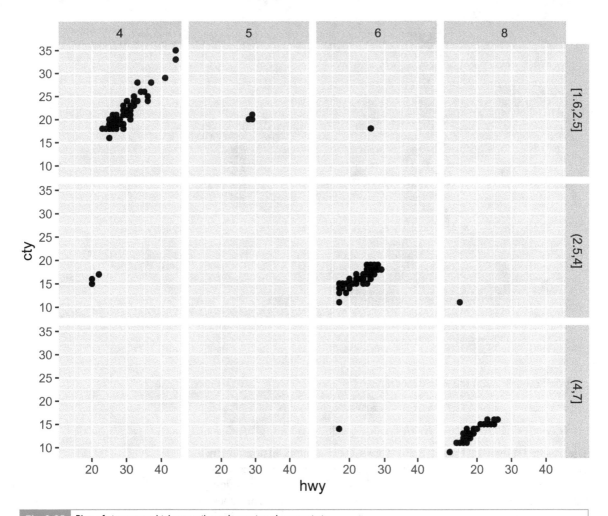

Fig. 3.25 Plot of city versus highway mileage by engine characteristic.

The result is shown in Figure 3.25. We can see in the plot that there is a change in the relation of `cty` and `hwy` with size of engine (smaller engines perform better in the city), but since `displ` and `cyl` are quite closely related, we can't determine whether this effect is more closely related to one of them than the other.

3.4.6 Groups in `ggplot2`

Some layer functions (e.g. `geom_point()`) draw one thing for each observation, while others (e.g. `geom_histogram()`) look at groups of points and compute what to draw once per group. There are two ways that `ggplot2` uses to determine groups. The usual way is to look at all of the discrete variables mentioned in the plot, and creating a group out of every unique combination of levels. Groups can also be set explicitly, by specifying the `group` aesthetic.

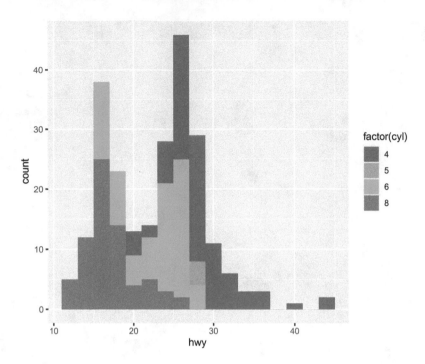

Fig. 3.26 Plotting histograms separately by group.

For example, with the `mpg` data set,

```
ggplot(mpg, aes(hwy, fill = factor(cyl))) +
    geom_histogram(binwidth = 2)
```

The result (shown in Figure 3.26) draws each group's histogram in a different color, and stacks them in the plot. The `geom_histogram()` parameter `binwidth` sets the size of each bin. To draw the bars side-by-side, you could use the parameter `position = "dodge"`. That doesn't look very good in this data set (try it!), but can be a good strategy with just two or three groups. If we had used `aes(hwy, group = cyl)` we would get the same grouping (the variable used with `group` doesn't need to be a factor), but it would be invisible, since all groups would be drawn in the default color.

Exercises

1 Re-draw the histogram of the `islands` data (Figure 3.6) using `ggplot2` functions. To do this, you will first need to store the data in a data frame as in

```
landmasses <- data.frame(area = log(1000*islands, 10))
```

Which of the following replicates the original histogram exactly?

```
ggplot(landmasses, aes(area)) +
geom_histogram(binwidth=.5)
```

or

```
ggplot(landmasses, aes(area)) +
geom_histogram(binwidth=.5, boundary=TRUE)
```

2 Construct violin plots of the egg lengths for each host species using data from the cuckoos data frame (*DAAG* package). Compare with the corresponding side-by-side boxplots for the same data.

3 Construct a scatterplot of the egg breadths versus the egg lengths for the data in cuckoos. Is there evidence of a linear relationship between length and breadth? Now, re-draw the scatterplot for the subset of the cuckoos data where robin is the host species. Note the vaguely linear relationship between length and breadth, and then construct a similar plot for the meadow.pipit subset. Is the relationship linear or nonlinear?

3.5 | Other graphics systems

Besides base graphics and ggplot2, there are many other graphics systems supported within R. These are each very rich systems and we won't discuss them in detail, but we will give the flavor of a few of them.

3.5.1 The lattice package

The lattice package is a high level graphics system for R that pre-dated ggplot2. Ideas similar to faceting (Section 3.4.5) are central to it: conditioning scatterplots reduce the effort required to repeat similar plots for multiple subsets of data.

Example 3.14

To show the trends over time in the WorldPhones data as in Figure 3.27, we could use

```
library(lattice)
xyplot(Telephones ~ Year | Region, data = phones)
```

Understanding the code

We first convert the matrix to a data frame. The formula Telephones ~ Year | Region says to plot Telephones against Year conditional on the Region; Figure 3.27 shows the result.

We refer readers to *Lattice: Multivariate Data Visualization with R*, by Sarkar, for a full discussion of lattice.

3.5.2 The grid package

Both ggplot2 and lattice are implemented using the grid package. This package uses a different mental model of graphics than the base

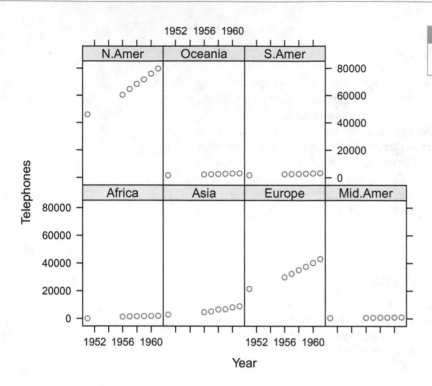

Fig. 3.27 Trends in telephone usage plotted using the `lattice` package.

graphics we discussed earlier. A chart is thought of as a hierarchy of graphical objects (which `grid` calls "grobs") within rectangular regions with associated coordinate systems ("viewports"). This mental model makes transformations and modifications of the display possible, something that can't really be done in base graphics.

Example 3.15
The following code illustrates the basic use of viewports. The result is shown in Figure 3.28.

```
library(grid)
grid.rect()         # draw black rectangle containing original viewport
vp <- viewport(h = 0.4, w = 0.6, angle = 60)
pushViewport(vp)    # create viewport rotated 60 degrees (counter clockwise)
                    # with height 40% and width 60% of original box
grid.rect(gp = gpar(col = "red")) # draw red rectangle around new viewport
pushViewport(vp)    # create new viewport nested in previous viewport,
                    # rotated 60 degrees and with height 40%
                    # and width 60% of previous viewport.
grid.rect(gp = gpar(col = "blue")) # draw blue rectangle around viewport
```

Understanding the code
First, a rectangle is drawn, containing the original viewport (a 1 × 1 square). A viewport having height 0.4 and width 0.6, and rotated at an angle

of 60°, is then pushed. A red rectangle is drawn showing the outline of the viewport. Finally, the same operation is repeated, creating a viewport, rotated by a further 60° and which has a height and width which are 40% and 60% of the size of the previously drawn viewport. The small blue rectangle shows the outline of the new viewport.

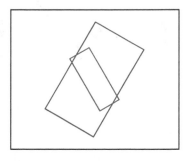

Fig. 3.28 Simple demonstration of the effect of rotating viewports using the `grid` package.

See Example 4.5 for a further indication of the power of the `grid` approach to graphics. We recommend *R Graphics* by Murrell for readers interested in learning about `grid`.

3.5.3 Interactive graphics

The graphics systems that we have discussed so far are designed for static graphics, typically printed on a page. Packages within R also support many kinds of interactive graphics.

The `rgl` package is designed for three-dimensional, rotatable displays. It includes functions modeled on the base graphics functions to set up plots, and also ways to display them on screen or on a web page. We give examples of its use in the Chapter Exercises and in Example 4.2 in the next chapter.

The `plotly` package is designed for interactive graphics on web pages using the open source `plotly.js` Javascript library. Especially helpful is the function `ggplotly()` that can convert most `ggplot2` graphs into interactive form.

The `leaflet` package provides an interface to the Leaflet library that is written in Javascript for web browsers. It is particularly well integrated with RStudio.

Example 3.16
Executing this code:

```
library(leaflet)
leaflet() %>%
  addTiles() %>%
  addMarkers(lng = 174.768, lat = -36.852, popup = "The birthplace of R")
```

in RStudio will result in the display of an interactive map with a marker in Auckland, New Zealand. Figure 3.29 shows the initial display.

Understanding the code
The `%>%` symbols are described in Section 4.2.5. You should read this code as instructions to create a `leaflet()` display, add map tiles to it, then add markers at the location of Auckland.

Besides `rgl`, `plotly` and `leaflet`, there are many other packages that provide interactive graphics of various sorts. Explore!

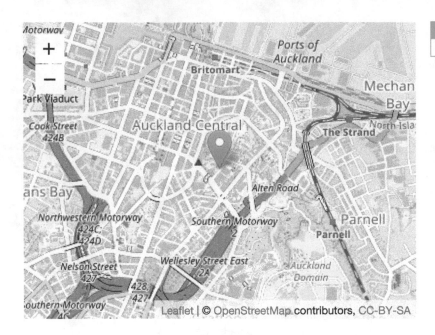

Fig. 3.29 A map showing the birthplace of R.

Leaflet | © OpenStreetMap contributors, CC-BY-SA

Chapter exercises

1 Consider the `islands` data set again. In particular, try out the following code.

```
hist(log(islands,10), breaks = "Scott", axes = FALSE, xlab = "area",
                    main = "Histogram of Landmass Areas")
axis(1, at = 1:5, labels = 10^(1:5))
axis(2)
box()
```

(a) Explain what is happening at each step of the above code.
(b) Add a subtitle to the plot such as "Base-10 Log-Scale."
(c) Modify the code to incorporate the use of the Sturges rule in place of the Scott rule. In this case, you will need to use the `round()` function to ensure that excessive numbers of digits are not used in the axis labels.

2 Consider the `pressure` data frame again.

(a) Plot `pressure` against `temperature`, and use the following command to pass a curve through these data:

```
curve((0.168 + 0.007*x)^(20/3), from = 0, to = 400, add = TRUE)
```

(b) Now, apply the power transformation $y^{3/20}$ to the pressure data values. Plot these transformed values against temperature. Is a linear or nonlinear relationship evident now? Use the `abline()` function to pass a straight line through the points. (You need an intercept and slope for this—see the previous part of this question to obtain appropriate values.)
(c) Add a suitable title to the graph.

(d) Re-do the above plots, but use the `mfrow()` function to display them in a 2×1 layout on the graphics page. Repeat once again using a 1×2 layout.

3 Use the `xyplot()` function to display the orange tree data (in `Orange`) in a sequence of five panels, one panel for each tree.

4 Code to produce an interactive perspective plot of the bivariate density discussed in Example 3.11 is as follows:

```
wind2D <- function(x,y) a1*a2*exp(-x^a1/b2 -
    y^a2/(b0+b1*x))*x^(a1-1)*y^(a2-1)/(b2*(b0+b1*x))
library(rgl)
a1 <- 3/2; a2 <- 5/3; b0 <- 108; b1 <- 5.3; b2 <- 65
persp3d(wind2D, xlim = c(0,50), ylim = c(0, 60), polygon_offset = 1)
```

(a) Experiment with additional arguments, such as `front = "lines"` or `col = "lightgreen"`, or change the transparency of the figure using the `alpha` parameter.

(b) Experiment with different values of the model parameters. How does the shape change for different values of `a1` and `a2`?

5 **Data Visualization Project.** This exercise gives the reader additional exposure to functions in the *lattice* package.

The `anorexia` data frame in the *MASS* package contains weight measurements for young female anorexia patients before and after a study comparing two types of treatments and a control. The three columns of the data frame are:

- `Treat`, a factor containing levels
  - `Cont` (Control—no therapy)
  - `CBT` (Cognitive Behavioral Therapy)
  - `FT` (Family Therapy)

- `Prewt`: Weight of patient before study period, in pounds
- `Postwt`: Weight of patient after study period, in pounds

(a) We usually want to compare the change in weight between the treatment groups. For this purpose, we construct a new column which subtracts the pre-study weights from the post-study weights:

```
library(MASS) # contains anorexia data set
anorexia$change <- with(anorexia, Postwt - Prewt)
```

In this context, a negative change is bad. The therapies should increase the weight if they are effective.

(b) The factor of interest is `Treat`. We want to know if the measured changes in weight are different for the different therapies. If there is no difference from the control group (where nothing was done), we would conclude that the therapies are not useful.

(c) Side-by-side dot plots[6] allow us to see differences between the different treatment groups:

[6] Boxplots could also be used—try `bwplot` in place of `dotplot`.

```
dotplot(Treat ~ change, data = anorexia, xlab = "weight change",
    ylab="treatment")
```

Observe that the treatments (Family Therapy and CBT) sometimes lead to better increases in weight than the control group, but there is a lot of overlap among the measurement distributions. This is not very strong evidence in favor of the therapies.

(d) Another way to visualize pre/post data is to use a scatterplot relating the post-study data to the pre-study data, with an overlaid smoothing curve. Here we do that for each treatment group.

```
xyplot(Postwt ~ Prewt|Treat, data = anorexia,
    type=c("p", "smooth"), span=.75)
```

(The span argument controls the amount of smoothing in the curve.) You should now see a clear difference between the control group and the treatment groups. For pre-study weights above 82 pounds, the control is not having a good effect, but the other therapies are. For pre-study weights below about 80–82 pounds, it does not seem to make a difference.

(e) We can reconstruct the dot plots now to take this new information into account. Create a factor which separates the very low pre-weight subject from the others as follows:

```
anorexia$lowPrewt <- factor(anorexia$Prewt < 82)
levels(anorexia$lowPrewt) <- c("Higher Preweight",
    "Very Low Preweight")
```

(f) Now construct new dot plots, conditional on whether the pre-study weight was very low or not:

```
dotplot(Treat ~ change|lowPrewt, data = anorexia,
    xlab = "weight change",   ylab="treatment")
```

Observe that for subjects with a very low pre-study weight, there are no differences, but for subjects with a high enough pre-study weight, the therapies really appear to help, especially the Family Therapy.

(g) Re-draw all of the above plots using ggplot2 functions.

4

Programming with R

Programming involves writing relatively complex systems of instructions. There are two broad styles of programming: the imperative style (used in R, for example) involves stringing together instructions telling the computer what to do. The declarative style (used in HTML in web pages, for example, and to some extent in `ggplot2`, as described in Section 3.4) involves writing a description of the end result, without giving the details about how to get there. Within each of these broad styles, there are many subdivisions, and a given program may involve aspects of several of them. For example, R programs may be procedural (describing what steps to take to achieve a task), modular (broken up into self-contained packages), object-oriented (organized to describe operations on complex objects), and/or functional (organized as a collection of functions which do specific calculations without having external side-effects), among other possibilities. In this book we will concentrate on the procedural aspects of programming.

As described in Chapter 1, R statements mainly consist of expressions to be evaluated. Most programs are very repetitive, but the amount of repetition depends on the input. In this chapter we start by describing several *flow control* statements that control how many times statements are repeated. The remainder of the chapter gives advice on how to design and debug programs.

4.1 Flow control

4.1.1 The `for()` loop
One of the goals of this book is to introduce stochastic simulation. Simulations are often very repetitive: we want to see patterns of behavior, not just a single instance.

The `for()` statement allows one to specify that a certain operation should be repeated a fixed number of times.

Syntax

```
for (name in vector)  { commands }
```

This sets a variable called name equal to each of the elements of vector, in sequence. For each value, whatever commands are listed within the curly braces will be performed. The curly braces serve to group the commands so that they are treated by R as a single command. If there is only one command to execute, the braces are not needed.

Example 4.1

The factorial $n!$ counts how many ways n different objects could be ordered. It is defined as

$$n! = 1 \cdot 2 \cdot 3 \cdots (n-1) \cdot n.$$

One way to calculate it would be to use a `for()` statement. For example, we could find the value of 100! using the code

```
n <- 100
result <- 1
for (i in 1:n)
    result <- result * i
result

## [1] 9.332622e+157
```

Understanding the code

The first line sets a variable named n to 100, and the second line initializes result to 1, i.e. a product with no terms. The third line starts the `for()` statement: the variable i will be set to the values 1, 2, ..., n in succession. Line 4 multiplies result by i in each of those steps, and the final line prints it.

There is also a `factorial()` function built in to R; it is much faster than the `for()` loop. But in many cases, you will want to write your own loops.

Example 4.2

In the 1960s, IBM sold a large computer called the System/360. (We do mean large: each computer filled a room.) Some programs needed unpredictable numbers, so they used the following scheme (called RANDU):

- Start with an odd integer x between 1 and $2^{31} - 1$ inclusive.
- Multiply it by 65539, and take the remainder when dividing by 2^{31}. (These numbers have particularly simple binary representations, so these operations are very fast.) This gives a new value for x.
- Repeat to generate a somewhat unpredictable sequence of numbers. Divide them by 2^{31} to put them on the scale from 0 to 1.

We can implement RANDU in a for loop. Suppose we want 1000 unpredictable numbers.

```
results <- numeric(1000)
x <- 123
for (i in 1:1000) {
  x <- (65539*x) %% (2^31)
  results[i] <- x / (2^31)
}
```

Understanding the code

In the first line, we set up a vector to hold the results. The second line sets a "seed" value. The `for()` loop in lines 3–6 first updates x, then divides it by 2^{31} and stores the result in the result vector. This is done for entries 1 to 1000.

We can plot these numbers, and it appears that RANDU works well (Figure 4.1):

```
plot(1:1000, results)
```

If you change the value of the seed, you will see a different pattern, and the pattern is hard to predict if you don't know that RANDU was used. However, RANDU has a terrible flaw that was not found for several years, but is obvious with modern computer graphics: all successive triplets fall into a small subset of the 1 by 1 by 1 cube, so if you know two successive values, you can make a good prediction of the next. We can use the `rgl` package mentioned in Section 3.5.3 to explore it.

```
library(rgl)
plot3d(results[1:998], results[2:999], results[3:1000])
```

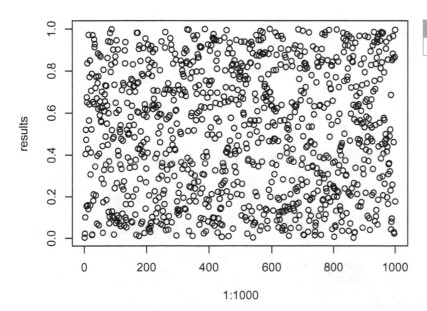

Fig. 4.1 One thousand values from the RANDU algorithm.

Here we are plotting successive triplets of points in three dimensions. If you do this yourself, you'll be able to rotate the display; certain orientations show the pattern very strikingly. Try it!

Example 4.3

The Fibonacci sequence is a famous sequence in mathematics. The first two elements are defined as [1, 1]. Subsequent elements are defined as the sum of the preceding two elements. For example, the third element is 2 ($= 1+1$), the fourth element is 3 ($= 1+2$), the fifth element is 5 ($= 2+3$), and so on.

To obtain the first 12 Fibonacci numbers in R, we can use

```
Fibonacci <- numeric(12)
Fibonacci[1] <- Fibonacci[2] <- 1
for (i in 3:12)
  Fibonacci[i] <- Fibonacci[i - 2] + Fibonacci[i - 1]
```

Understanding the code

The first line sets up a numeric vector of length 12 with the name `Fibonacci`. This vector consists of 12 zeros.

The second line updates the first two elements of `Fibonacci` to the value 1.

The next lines update the third element, fourth element, and so on according to the rule defining the Fibonacci sequence. In particular, `Fibonacci[3]` is assigned the value of `Fibonacci[1]` + `Fibonacci[2]`, i.e. 2. `Fibonacci[4]` is then assigned the latest value of `Fibonacci[2]` + `Fibonacci[3]`, giving it the value 3. The `for()` loop updates the third through 12th element of the sequence in this way.

To see all 12 values, type in

```
Fibonacci
##  [1]   1   1   2   3   5   8  13  21  34  55  89 144
```

Example 4.4

Suppose a car dealer promotes two options for the purchase of a new $20,000 car. The first option is for the customer to pay up front and receive a $1000 rebate. The second option is "0%-interest financing" where the customer makes 20 monthly payments of $1000 beginning in one month's time.

Because of option 1, the effective price of the car is really $19,000, so the dealer really is charging some interest rate i for option 2. We can calculate this value using the formula for the present value of an annuity:

$$19000 = 1000 \left(\frac{1 - (1 + i)^{-20}}{i} \right).$$

By multiplying both sides of this equation by i and dividing by 19,000, we get the form of a *fixed-point* problem:[1]

$$i = (1 - (1 + i)^{-20})/19.$$

By taking an initial guess for i and plugging it into the right side of this equation, we can get an "updated" value for i on the left. For example, if we start with $i = 0.006$, then our update is

$$i = (1 - (1 + 0.006)^{-20})/19 = 0.00593.$$

By plugging this updated value into the right-hand side of the equation again, we get a new update:

$$i = (1 - (1 + 0.00593)^{-20})/19 = 0.00586.$$

This kind of fixed-point iteration usually requires many iterations before we can be confident that we have the solution to the fixed-point equation. Here is R code to work out the solution after 1000 iterations:

```
i <- 0.006
for (j in 1:1000) {
    i <- (1 - (1 + i)^(-20)) / 19
}
i

## [1] 0.004935593
```

[1] A fixed-point problem arises when we want to solve an equation of the form $x = f(x)$, for some function $f(x)$. Note that the unknown value is on both sides of the equation.

Example 4.5
The `for()` loop can be used in the programming of graphics. Figure 4.2 illustrates its use in the repeated pushing of viewports, in the context of *grid* graphics. In this case, 100 viewports are pushed, each has height and width which are 90% of the height and width of the previous viewport, and each is positioned slightly off-center, at the point (0.46, 0.5) relative to the previously pushed viewport. Also, each viewport has been rotated by a growing number of degrees, starting at 1, and increasing by 1, at each iteration. Circles having diameter equal to the height of the current viewport are drawn at each iteration. The resulting pattern indicates the kind of complex results that can be obtained from the `grid` approach to graphics, using only a few lines of code.

Fig. 4.2 Demonstration of rotation of viewports using a for loop.

```
library(grid)
for (i in 1:100) {
    vp <- viewport(x = .46, h = .9, w = .9, angle = i)
    pushViewport(vp)
    grid.circle()
}
```

Exercises

1 Modify the code to generate the Fibonacci sequence in the following ways:

(a) Change the first two elements to 2 and 2.

(b) Change the first two elements to 3 and 2.

(c) Change the update rule from summing successive elements to taking differences of successive elements. For example, the third element is defined as the second element minus the first element, and so on.

(d) Change the update rule so that each element is defined as the sum of three preceding elements. Set the third element as 1 in order to start the process.

2 Let f_n denote the nth Fibonacci number.

(a) Construct a sequence of ratios of the form $f_n/f_{n-1}, n = 1, 2, \ldots, 30$. Does the sequence appear to be converging?

(b) Compute the golden ratio $(1 + \sqrt{5})/2$. Is the sequence converging to this ratio? Can you prove this?

3 In each of the following, determine the final value of `answer`. Check your result by running the code in R.

(a)
```
answer <- 0
for (j in 1:5) answer <- answer + j
```

(b)
```
answer <- NULL
for (j in 1:5) answer <- c(answer, j)
```

(c)
```
answer <- 0
for (j in 1:5) answer <- c(answer, j)
```

(d)
```
answer <- 1
for (j in 1:5) answer <- answer * j
```

(e)
```
answer <- 3
for (j in 1:15) answer <- c(answer, (7 * answer[j]) %% 31)
```

Inspect this last sequence of numbers. If you did not know the rule used to determine this sequence, would you be able to predict successive elements?

4 Refer to the car dealer promotion example in this section. Calculate the first 20 updates of the interest rate i, starting with $i = 0.006$. Repeat with a starting value of $i = 0.005$, and with a starting value of $i = 0.004$. Based on these observations, what is the true value of i (up to 5-digit accuracy)?

5 Use a fixed-point iteration to determine the solution (in $[0, 1]$) of the equation $x = \cos(x)$. Use a starting value of 0.5. How many iterations does it take before you have an answer which is accurate in the first 2 digits? ...in the first 3 digits? ...in the first 4 digits? What happens if you change the starting value to 0.7? ...to 0.0?

6 Repeat the previous question, but using the equation $x = 1.5\cos(x)$. (The solution is near $x = 0.9148565$.)

   (a) Does the fixed-point iteration converge? If not, modify the equation so that $x = \cos(x)/30 + 44x/45$. Does the iteration converge now?

   (b) Can you show that the solutions to these two equations are the same?

   (c) Compute the absolute value of the derivative of $1.5\cos(x)$ and of $\cos(x)/30 + 44x/45$. There is a theorem in numerical analysis which says that if this quantity is less than 1, then the fixed-point iteration will converge if the starting guess is close enough to the solution. Does this explain the behavior that you observed in part (a)?

7 Refer to the *grid* graphics example. Modify the code so that rectangles are created instead of circles. Center the rectangles at (.5, .5) instead of (.46, .5), and set the angle of rotation to `0` instead of `i`. Comment on the result.

4.1.2 The `if()` statement

Earlier, we learned about logical vectors and relational operators. The subscripting device is a powerful way to perform different operations on different parts of vectors. The `if()` statement allows us to control which statements are executed, and sometimes this is more convenient.

Syntax

```
if (condition) {commands when TRUE}
if (condition) {commands when TRUE} else {commands when FALSE}
```

This statement causes a set of commands to be invoked if `condition` evaluates to `TRUE`. The `else` part is optional, and provides an alternative set of commands which are to be invoked in case the logical variable is `FALSE`. Be careful how you type this. If you put the `else` part on a new line, you may see something like this:

```
if (condition) {
    # do TRUE
}

else {
  ^

## Error: unexpected 'else' in "else"
```

R executed the first three lines before you entered the `else`. This meant it wasn't expecting an `else`, and it signalled an error.[2] To avoid this problem, a common convention for typing `if ... else` is to put the `else` on the same line as the previous closing brace:

```
if (condition) {
    # do TRUE
} else {
    # do FALSE
}
```

[2] If these lines had appeared within a block of commands in curly braces, they wouldn't have triggered an error, because R would collect all the lines before it starts to act on any of them: but it is still a good idea to avoid this ambiguity.

This way it is very clear that the statement is incomplete until the very end.

R also allows numerical values to be used as the value of `condition`. These are converted to logical values using the rule that zero becomes `FALSE`, and any other value becomes `TRUE`.

Missing values are not allowed for the condition, and will trigger an error.

Example 4.6
A simple example:

```
x <- 3
if (x > 2) y <- 2 * x else y <- 3 * x
```

Since `x > 2` is `TRUE`, `y` is assigned `2 * 3 = 6`. If it hadn't been true, `y` would have been assigned the value of `3 * x`.

The `if()` statement is often used inside user-defined functions. The following is a typical example.

Example 4.7
The correlation between two vectors of numbers is often calculated using the `cor()` function. It is supposed to give a measure of linear association. We can add a scatterplot of the data as follows.

```
corplot <- function(x, y, plotit) {
    if (plotit == TRUE) plot(x, y)
    cor(x, y)
}
```

We can apply this function to two vectors without plotting by typing

```
corplot(c(2, 5, 7), c(5, 6, 8), FALSE)
## [1] 0.953821
```

Example 4.8
The function that follows is based on the sieve of Eratosthenes, the oldest known systematic method for listing prime numbers up to a given value *n*. The idea is as follows: begin with a vector of numbers from 2 to *n*. Beginning with 2, eliminate all multiples of 2 which are larger than 2. Then move to the next number remaining in the vector, in this case, 3. Now, remove all multiples of 3 which are larger than 3. Proceed through all remaining entries of the vector in this way. The entry for 4 would have been removed in the first round, leaving 5 as the next entry to work with after 3; all multiples of 5 would be removed at the next step, and so on.

```
Eratosthenes <- function(n) {
# Return all prime numbers up to n (based on the sieve of Eratosthenes)
    if (n >= 2) {
        sieve <- seq(2, n)
        primes <- c()
        for (i in seq(2, n)) {
            if (any(sieve == i)) {
                primes <- c(primes, i)
                sieve <- c(sieve[(sieve %% i) != 0], i)
            }
        }
        return(primes)
    } else {
        stop("Input value of n should be at least 2.")
    }
}
```

Here are some examples of the use of this function:

```
Eratosthenes(50)

##  [1]  2  3  5  7 11 13 17 19 23 29 31 37 41 43 47
```

```
Eratosthenes(-50)

## Error in Eratosthenes(-50): Input value of n should be at least 2.
```

Understanding the code

The purpose of the function is to provide all prime numbers up to the given value n. The basic idea of the program is contained in the lines:

```
sieve <- seq(2, n)
primes <- c()
for (i in seq(2, n)) {
    if (any(sieve == i)) {
        primes <- c(primes, i)
        sieve <- sieve[(sieve %% i) != 0]
    }
}
```

The sieve object holds all the candidates for testing. Initially, all integers from 2 through n are stored in this vector. The primes object is set up initially empty, eventually to contain all of the primes that are less than or equal to n. The composite numbers in sieve are removed, and the primes are copied to primes.

Each integer i from 2 through n is checked in sequence to see whether it is still in the vector. The any() function returns a TRUE if at least one of the logical vector elements in its argument is TRUE. In the case that i is still in the `sieve` vector, it must be a prime, since it is the smallest number that has not been eliminated yet. All multiples of `i` are eliminated, since they are necessarily composite, and `i` is appended to `primes`. The expression `(sieve %% i) == 0` would give `TRUE` for all elements of `sieve` which are multiples of `i`; since we want to eliminate these elements and save all other elements, we can negate this using `!(sieve %% i == 0)` or `sieve %% i != 0`. Then we can eliminate all multiples of `i` from the `sieve` vector using

```
sieve <- sieve[(sieve %% i) != 0]
```

Note that this eliminates `i` as well, but we have already saved it in `primes`.

If the supplied argument `n` is less than 2, then the function output would be meaningless. To avoid this, we cause an error to be triggered if a value smaller than 2 is supplied by the user.

Exercises

1 Does the `Eratosthenes()` function work properly if `n` is not an integer? Is an error message required in this case?

2 Use the idea of the `Eratosthenes()` function to prove that there are infinitely many primes. Hint: Suppose all primes were less than m, and construct a larger value n that would not be eliminated by the sieve.

3 A twin prime is a pair of primes (x, y), such that $y = x + 2$. Construct a list of all twin primes less than 1000.[3]

4 A bank offers a guaranteed investment certificate (GIC) which pays an annual interest rate of 4% (compounded annually) if the term is 3 years or less, or 5% if the term is more than 3 years. Write a function which takes the initial investment amount, P, and the number of interest periods (i.e. years) as arguments and which returns the amount of interest earned over the term of the GIC. That is, return I, where $I = P((1 + i)^n - 1)$.

5 Mortgage interest rates can sometimes depend on whether the mortgage term is *open* or *closed*. Use the formula

$$R = \frac{Pi}{1 - (1 + i)^{-n}}$$

to create a function to calculate a monthly mortgage payment R where i is an interest rate (compounded monthly), P is the original principal, and n is the length of the term (in months). The function should take `n`, `P`, and `open` as arguments. If `open==TRUE`, then take $i = 0.005$; otherwise, take $i = 0.004$.

[3] It has been known since ancient times that there are infinitely many primes. It remains a conjecture as to whether there is an infinite set of twin primes.

4.1.3 The `while()` loop

Sometimes we want to repeat statements, but the pattern of repetition isn't known in advance. We need to do some calculations and keep going as long as a condition holds. The `while()` statement accomplishes this.

Syntax

```
while (condition) {statements}
```

The condition is evaluated, and if it evaluates to FALSE, nothing more is done. If it evaluates to TRUE the statements are executed, condition is evaluated again, and the process is repeated.

Example 4.9

Suppose we want to list all Fibonacci numbers less than 300. We don't know beforehand how long this list is, so we wouldn't know how to stop the for() loop at the right time, but a while() loop is perfect:

```
Fib1 <- 1
Fib2 <- 1
Fibonacci <- c(Fib1, Fib2)
while (Fib2 < 300) {
    Fibonacci <- c(Fibonacci, Fib2)
    oldFib2 <- Fib2
    Fib2 <- Fib1 + Fib2
    Fib1 <- oldFib2
}
```

Understanding the code

The central idea is contained in the lines

```
while (Fib2 < 300) {
    Fibonacci <- c(Fibonacci, Fib2)
```

That is, as long as the latest Fibonacci number created (in Fib2) is less than 300, it is appended to the growing vector Fibonacci.

Thus, we must ensure that Fib2 actually contains the updated Fibonacci number. By keeping track of the two most recently added numbers (Fib1 and Fib2), we can do the update

```
Fib2 <- Fib1 + Fib2
```

Now Fib1 should be updated to the old value of Fib2, but that has been overwritten by the new value. So before executing the above line, we make a copy of Fib2 in oldFib2. After updating Fib2, we can assign the value in oldFib2 to Fib1.

In order to start things off, Fib1, Fib2, and Fibonacci need to be initialized. That is, within the loop, these objects will be used, so they need to be assigned sensible starting values.

To see the final result of the computation, type

```
Fibonacci
## [1]   1   1   1   2   3   5   8  13  21  34  55  89 144 233
```

Caution

Increasing the length of a vector element by element as in Fibonacci <- c(Fibonacci, Fib2) in a for() or while() loop should be avoided if the number of such operations is likely to be large. R will have to keep allocating new vectors, each one element longer than the last one, and this will slow the process down substantially.

Exercises

1 The variable `oldFib2` isn't strictly necessary. Rewrite the Fibonacci `while()` loop with the update of `Fib1` based just on the current values of `Fib1` and `Fib2`.
2 In fact, `Fib1` and `Fib2` aren't necessary either. Rewrite the Fibonacci `while()` loop without using *any* variables except `Fibonacci`.
3 Determine the number of Fibonacci numbers less than 1000000.
4 Recall the car dealer interest rate example in Example 4.4. Use a `while()` loop to iteratively calculate the interest rate i which satisfies the fixed-point equation

$$i = (1 - (1 + i)^{-20})/19.$$

Use a starting guess of $i = 0.006$. Stop the calculation when two successive values of the interest rate are less than 0.000001 apart.

What happens when you try other starting guesses?
5 Referring to the previous exercise, modify your code so that it also computes the number of iterations required to get two successive values of the interest rate that are less than 0.000001 apart.

4.1.4 Newton's method for root finding

Newton's method is a popular numerical method to find a root of an algebraic equation:[4]

$$f(x) = 0.$$

[4] Alternatively, we say that it is finding a zero of the function $f(x)$.

If $f(x)$ has derivative $f'(x)$, then the following iteration should converge to a root of the above equation if started close enough to the root.

$$x_0 = \text{initial guess}$$

$$x_n = x_{n-1} - \frac{f(x_{n-1})}{f'(x_{n-1})}.$$

The idea is based on the Taylor approximation

$$f(x_n) \approx f(x_{n-1}) + (x_n - x_{n-1})f'(x_{n-1}). \tag{4.1}$$

Newton's method is equivalent to setting $f(x_n) = 0$ and solving for x_n in (4.1). Even though (4.1) is only an approximation, we hope that the solution x_n should give a close approximation to the root. Be careful: there are many examples where x_n will fail to converge to a root unless x_{n-1} is already sufficiently close, and some where it will fail regardless of the starting value.

Example 4.10
Suppose $f(x) = x^3 + 2x^2 - 7$. Then, if x_0 is close enough to one of the three roots of this equation,

$$x_n = x_{n-1} - \frac{x_{n-1}^3 + 2x_{n-1}^2 - 7}{3x^2 + 4x}$$

will converge to a root.

An R version of this could be implemented as follows:

```
x <- x0
f <- x^3 + 2 * x^2 - 7
tolerance <- 0.000001
while (abs(f) > tolerance) {
    f.prime <- 3 * x^2 + 4 * x
    x <- x - f / f.prime
    f <- x^3 + 2 * x^2 - 7
}
x
```

Understanding the code

We start with x equal to x_0, and evaluate $f(x_0)$. Then, as long as $|f(x_i)|$ is more than 0.000001, we update x using Newton's method. Notice that we don't need a variable `i`. Because Newton's method is a recursive formula where the new value can be calculated from the old one, there is no need to know which iteration we are on when doing the updates.

Exercises

1 The equation

$$x^7 + 10000x^6 + 1.06x^5 + 10600x^4 + 0.0605x^3 + 605x^2 + 0.0005x + 5$$

has exactly one real root. How many iterations of Newton's method are required to find this root if the initial guess is $x = 0$?

2 Use Newton's method to find a zero of

$$f(x) = x^4 + 3x^3 - 2x^2 - 7$$

using an initial guess of $x = 1$.

3 Modify the above function so that it finds one of the zeros of

$$f(x) = \cos(x) + e^x$$

using an initial guess of $x = -1.5$.

4 Find a minimizer of the function

$$f(x) = (x - 3)^4 + 7(x - 2)^2 + x.$$

5 How many zeros does the function

$$f(x) = \frac{5x - 3}{x - 1}$$

have? What are they? Describe the behavior of Newton's method applied to this function if the initial guess is

(a) 0.5

(b) 0.75

(c) 0.2

(d) 1.25

6 How many zeros does the function

$$f(x) = (x^2 - 6x + 9)e^{-x}$$

have? What are they? Describe the behavior of Newton's method applied to this function if the initial guess is

(a) 3

(b) 3.2

(c) 2.99

(d) 3.01

7 Refer to the car dealer interest rate example in Example 4.4. Use Newton's method to calculate the interest rate i which satisfies

$$i = (1 - (1 + i)^{-20})/19.$$

Use $i = 0.006$ as your starting guess. How many iterations are required for two successive values of i to be within 0.000001 of each other?

4.1.5 The `repeat` loop, and the `break` and `next` statements

Sometimes we don't want a fixed number of repetitions of a loop, and we don't want to put the test at the top of the loop the way it is in a `while()` loop. In this situation we can use a `repeat` loop. This loop repeats until we execute a `break` statement.

Syntax
```
repeat { statements }
```

This causes the statements to be repeated endlessly. The statements should normally include a `break` statement, typically in the form

```
if (condition) break
```

but this is not a requirement of the syntax.

The `break` statement causes the loop to terminate immediately. `break` statements can also be used in `for()` and `while()` loops. The `next` statement causes control to return immediately to the top of the loop; it can also be used in any loop.

The `repeat` loop and the `break` and `next` statements are used relatively infrequently. It is usually easier to understand code when the test is clearly displayed at the top, and when that is the only exit from the loop (as in the `for` and `while` loops). However, sometimes these statements help to make programs clearer.

Example 4.11

We can repeat the Newton's algorithm example from the previous section using a `repeat` loop:

```
x <- x0
tolerance <- 0.000001
repeat {
    f <- x^3 + 2 * x^2 - 7
    if (abs(f) < tolerance) break
    f.prime <- 3 * x^2 + 4 * x
    x <- x - f / f.prime
}
x
```

This version removes the need to duplicate the line that calculates f.

Exercises

1 Another algorithm for finding a zero of a function is called the *bisection algorithm*. This algorithm starts with two values x_1 and x_2 for which $f(x_1)$ and $f(x_2)$ have opposite signs. If $f(x)$ is a continuous function, then we know a root must lie somewhere between these two values. We find it by evaluating $f(x)$ at the midpoint, and selecting whichever half of the interval still brackets the root. We then start over, and repeat the calculation until the interval is short enough to give us our answer to the required precision.

   (a) Use a `repeat` loop to write a bisection algorithm to find a root to 6 decimal place accuracy of $f(x) = x^3 + 2x^2 - 7$, given that the root is known to lie between 0 and 2.

   (b) Prove that your bisection algorithm is guaranteed to converge for any continuous function which takes opposite signed values at 0 and 2, and calculate how many loops it will take.

2 We could implement the Sieve of Eratosthenes using a `while()` loop:

```
Eratosthenes <- function(n) {
    # Print prime numbers up to n (based on the sieve of Eratosthenes)
    if (n >= 2) {
        sieve <- seq(2, n)
        primes <- c()
        while (length(sieve) > 0) {
            p <- sieve[1]
            primes <- c(primes, p)
            sieve <- sieve[(sieve %% p) != 0]
        }
        return(primes)
    } else {
        stop("Input value of n should be at least 2.")
    }
}
```

   (a) Trace through this function until you understand why it works.

   (b) Show that once `p >= sqrt(n)` all remaining entries in `sieve` are prime.

(c) Modify this function using `break` to take advantage of the above result.

4.2 | Managing complexity through functions

Most real computer programs are much longer than the examples we give in this book. Most people can't keep the details in their heads all at once, so it is extremely important to find ways to reduce the complexity. There have been any number of different strategies of program design developed over the years. In this section we give a short outline of some of the strategies that have worked for us.

4.2.1 What are functions?

Functions are self-contained units of R code with a well-defined purpose. In general, functions take inputs, do calculations (possibly printing intermediate results, drawing graphs, calling other functions, etc.), and produce outputs. If the inputs and outputs are well defined, the programmer can be reasonably sure whether the function works or not: and once it works, can move on to the next problem.

Example 4.12

Suppose payments of R dollars are deposited annually into a bank account which earns constant interest i per year. What is the accumulated value of the account at the end of n years, supposing deposits are made at the end of each year?

The total amount at the end of n years is

$$R(1 + i)^{n-1} + \ldots + R(1 + i) + R$$

$$= R \frac{(1 + i)^n - 1}{i}$$

An R function to calculate the amount of an annuity is

```
annuityAmt <- function(n, R, i) {
    R*((1 + i)^n - 1) / i
}
```

If \$400 is deposited annually for 10 years into an account bearing 5% annual interest, we can calculate the accumulated amount using

```
annuityAmt(10, 400, 0.05)
## [1] 5031.157
```

R is somewhat unusual among computer languages in that functions are objects that can be manipulated like other more common objects such as vectors, matrices, and lists.

The definition of a function normally has the following structure:

1. the word `function`
2. a pair of round parentheses `()` which enclose the argument list. The list may be empty.
3. a single statement, or a sequence of statements enclosed in curly braces `{}`.

Like other R objects, functions are usually named. You should choose the names of your functions to succinctly describe the action of the function. For example, `var()` computes variances, and `median()` computes medians. The name is important: if you choose a name that you can't remember, you will waste time looking it up later. If you choose a name that is misleading about the action of the function (e.g. if we had named our `annuityAmt` function `annuityRate`), you will find your programs extremely hard to understand.

When R executes a function definition, it produces an object with three parts: the header, the body, and a reference to the environment in which the definition was executed.

The first two items in the function definition are used to create the header. The header to an R function describes the inputs, or "arguments." For example, the header of our `Eratosthenes` function above is `function(n)`. This tells us that the function takes one argument named `n`, which specifies the upper limit for the sieve. The header on `annuityAmt` is `function(n, R, i)`, telling us that it takes three arguments named `n`, `R`, and `i`. Functions may take any number of arguments. Again, choose their names to indicate their function.

To reduce the burden on the user of a function, we may give default values to some arguments: if the user doesn't specify the value, the default will be used. For example, we could have used the header

```
annuityAmt <- function(n, R = 1, i = 0.01)
```

to indicate that if a user called `annuityAmt(24)` without specifying `R` and `i`, then we should act as though `R = 1` and `i = 0.01`.

The second part of a function is the body. This is a single statement, or sequence of statements in curly braces. They specify what computations are to be carried out by the function. In the original `Eratosthenes` example, the body was

```
{
    if (n >= 2) {
        sieve <- seq(2, n)
        primes <- c()
        for (i in seq(2, n)) {
            if (any(sieve == i)) {
                primes <- c(primes, i)
                sieve <- c(sieve[(sieve %% i) != 0], i)
            }
        }
        return(primes)
```

```
    } else {
        stop("Input value of n should be at least 2.")
    }
}
```

At some point in the body of the function there is normally a statement like `return(primes)` which specifies the output value of the function. (In R all functions produce a single output. In some other languages functions may produce no output, or multiple outputs.) If there is no `return()` statement, then the value of the last statement executed is returned. This is how `annuityAmt` returns its value.

The third part of a function is the hardest part to understand, because it is the least concrete: the environment of the function. We won't give a complete description here, but will limit ourselves to the following circular definition: the environment is a reference to the environment in which the function was defined.

What we mean by this is the following. In our `Eratosthenes` function, we made use of two quite different sorts of objects: n, `sieve`, `primes` and i were all defined locally within the function. There is no ambiguity about what they mean. But `seq`, c, `any`, `return`, and `stop` are not defined there: they were part of the R environment where `Eratosthenes` was defined. (They are all functions, and the local variables were not: this is commonly the case, but it is by no means necessary.)

The really interesting thing is the following. Within the `Eratosthenes` function, we could have defined a new function. *Its* environment would include n, `sieve`, `primes`, and i. For example, we might want to make the removal of multiples of the prime values clearer by putting that operation into a small function called `noMultiples`:

```
Eratosthenes <- function(n) {
    # Print all prime numbers up to n (based on the sieve of Eratosthenes)
    if (n >= 2) {

        noMultiples <- function(j) sieve[(sieve %% j) != 0]

        sieve <- seq(2, n)
        primes <- c()
        for (i in seq(2, n)) {
            if (any(sieve == i)) {
                primes <- c(primes, i)
                sieve <- c(noMultiples(i), i)
            }
        }
        return(primes)
    } else {
        stop("Input value of n should be at least 2.")
    }
}
```

The `noMultiples` function defines j in its header, so j is a local variable, and it finds `sieve` in its environment.

Exercises

1 Verify that the objects `var`, `cos`, `median`, `read.table`, and `dump` are all functions.[5]

2 Suppose Mr. Ng deposits a certain amount (say, *P*) of money in a bank where the interest rate is `i.r`, and interest is compounded. If he leaves the money in the bank for *n* interest conversion periods, it will accumulate to

$$P(1 + i.r)^n.$$

(a) Write an R function called `compound.interest()` which computes this amount. Your function should have three arguments.

(b) Often, one interest conversion period is equal to 1 month. In this case, how much will Mr. Ng have in the bank at the end of 30 months, if he deposits $1000, and the interest rate is 1% per month?

3 Write a function which uses the bisection algorithm to calculate the zero of a user-supplied function.

[5] It is conventional to refer to functions with parentheses after the name, i.e. as `var()`, `cos()`, etc. We didn't do that here in order to avoid the ambiguity: do we mean the `var` object, or the result returned by a call to `var()`?

4.2.2 Scope of variables

The "scope" of a variable tells us where the variable would be recognized. For example, variables defined within functions have local scope, so they are only recognized within the function. A variable could be created with the same name in a different function but there is no risk of a clash.

Example 4.13

In this example we create two functions `f` and `g`, both with local variables named `x`. `g` is called by `f` and modifies its instance of `x` without affecting the `x` in `f`.

```
f <- function() {
    x <- 1
    g()        # g will have no effect on our local x
    return(x)
}
g <- function() {
    x <- 2     # this changes g's local x, not the one in f
}
f()

## [1] 1
```

In R, scope is controlled by the environment of functions. Variables defined at the console have global scope, meaning they are visible in any user-defined function. Variables defined in a function are visible in the function, and in functions defined within it.

Using local variables rather than globals helps tremendously in programming, because while you are writing the function, you don't need to worry about some other part of the program changing the values of your variables. You can predict their values from the code you write, and be sure that once you get it correct, you can trust it.

We have mentioned that function arguments can have default values. In fact, the default values can refer to any local variables in the function. This works because the arguments aren't evaluated until they are first used; at that point, you need to make sure the default value exists. If the argument is never used, the default will never be evaluated.

Packages have their own scope (known as their "namespace"), but the details of namespaces are beyond the scope of this text.

4.2.3 Returning multiple objects

We said in Section 4.2.1 that R functions always return a single object. But sometimes you want to return more than one thing! The trick here is to return them in a list() or vector.

Example 4.14

For example, our annuityAmt() function simply calculated the amount of the annuity at the end of n years. But we might also want to know the present value, which is $(1 + i)^{-n}$ times the amount. We return both in this function:

```
annuityValues <- function(n, R, i) {
    amount <- R*((1 + i)^n - 1) / i
    PV <- amount * (1 + i)^(-n)
    list(amount = amount, PV = PV)
}
annuityValues(10, 400, 0.05)

## $amount
## [1] 5031.157
##
## $PV
## [1] 3088.694
```

4.2.4 Using S3 classes to control printing

In the annuityValues() example, the display of the results wasn't very pleasing. To produce a nicer looking display, we could use a number of calls to the cat() or print() functions instead of returning the list of values. But then the function would be less useful in other calculations: other functions might want to do further calculations on the results, without printing them.

A general solution to this problem is to declare the type of the return value, and to tell R how to print things like that. This is a kind of *object oriented* programming. In fact, there are several ways to do this, and a full discussion is beyond the scope of this text, but in this section we will show one of the simplest ways: using *S3 methods*.

Besides having values, objects in R may have named *attributes*. The S3 class is (in the simplest case) a character string named `class` containing the class of the object.

Example 4.15

We can assign the class to our annuity values with code like this:

```
values <- annuityValues(10, 400, 0.05)
class(values) <- "annuity"
```

To make use of it, we need to define one or more methods. We'll define a print-method:

```
print.annuity <- function(x, ...) {
  cat("An annuity object with present value", x$PV, "and final value",
      x$amount, "\n")
  invisible(x)
}
values

## An annuity object with present value 3088.694 and final value 5031.157

values$PV

## [1] 3088.694
```

Understanding the code

In the S3 system, there are "generic functions" like `print()` and methods like `print.annuity()`. By convention, the method is named with the name of the generic function, a dot, then the name of the class. When R prints the value, it sees that the `values` object is of class `"annuity"`, and calls the method for that class, `print.annuity()`. When we extract the `PV` component from the list, we no longer have an `"annuity"` object and it prints as a number.

The arguments to a `print` method need to be compatible with the generic function; `print.classname(x, ...)` is generally a good choice.

By convention `print` methods should return the value being printed, but they need to do it in a way so that it doesn't print again, or you'd get an infinite loop. The `invisible()` function marks a result so that it won't print.

4.2.5 The `magrittr` pipe operator

The `magrittr` package defines the "pipe operator" `%>%`, and many other packages also make these available. The idea behind `%>%` is fairly simple: rather than typing a function call as `f(x, y)`, it is typed as `x %>% f(y)`.

We can read this as "start with x, and use `f(y)` to modify it." This sometimes (as in Example 3.16 using `leaflet`) leads to more readable code than the equivalent standard notation. In that example we wrote

```
leaflet() %>%
  addTiles() %>%
  addMarkers(lng = 174.768, lat = -36.852,
             popup = "The birthplace of R")
```

instead of the equivalent

```
addMarkers(addTiles(leaflet()),
           lng = 174.768, lat = -36.852,
           popup = "The birthplace of R")
```

Using the pipe makes the successive calculations more obvious.

The pipe operator is particularly helpful when used with functions whose main purpose is to modify their first argument, and the *tidyverse* packages described in Chapter 5 were designed with this in mind. However, any function can be used with `%>%`: if the object that is being "piped in" isn't the first argument of the function, the special placeholder `.` can be used to mark where it should appear.[6] For example, the base graphics code to draw the boxplot in Figure 3.9 was

```
boxplot(Sepal.Length ~ Species, data = iris,
        ylab = "Sepal length (cm)",
        main = "Iris measurements",
        boxwex = 0.5)
```

but if `library(magrittr)` had been used to make the pipe operator available, it could have been written as

```
iris %>% boxplot(Sepal.Length ~ Species, data = .,
        ylab = "Sepal length (cm)",
        main = "Iris measurements",
        boxwex = 0.5)
```

[6] There is a proposal to include a new pipe operator `|>` in R version 4.1.0, to be released around the time this book prints. The proposed usage is similar to `%>%`, but not identical. In particular, piping a result into a later argument is likely to be handled differently.

4.3 | The `replicate()` function

Section 4.1 was about flow control. The `for()`, `while()`, and `repeat` loops allow increasing flexibility in looping. In this section we describe a step in the opposite direction: the `replicate()` function.

The `replicate()` function is something like a `for()` loop, with a few differences. For one thing, the syntax looks like a function call:

```
replicate(n, { statements })
```

This says to evaluate the statements *n* times. Another difference is that it returns the result of each evaluation, whereas the `for()` loop does not return the values. If the value in each step is a vector, it returns a matrix:

```
replicate(5, 1:3)
```

```
##      [,1] [,2] [,3] [,4] [,5]
## [1,]    1    1    1    1    1
## [2,]    2    2    2    2    2
## [3,]    3    3    3    3    3
```

Finally, there's a difference in scoping. Changes made within a for() loop have global scope, but the replicate() function evaluates the statements in a local scope, much as a function evaluates its body. Thus the following implementation of the RANDU algorithm gives repetitive output:

```
x <- 123
replicate(10, {
  x <- (65539*x) %% (2^31)
  x / (2^31)
})
```

```
##  [1]  0.003753834 0.003753834 0.003753834 0.003753834 0.003753834
##  [6]  0.003753834 0.003753834 0.003753834 0.003753834 0.003753834
```

We'll see examples in Chapter 6 where these properties are very convenient in simulations of random processes.

4.4 | Miscellaneous programming tips

4.4.1 Always edit code in the editor, not in the console

Sometimes we make errors when we write code. It is easy in the R console to use the up-arrow to retrieve a previous command, change it, and then run it again. However, we strongly discourage this style of programming.

A much better style is to write your commands in the editor, and run them from there. If you get it wrong, fix it in the editor and try again. This way you work towards having a script that does a long calculation correctly, rather than ending up with a console history containing all of your errors. It is also easier to start from the beginning and re-run many lines, if they are all in the editor.

4.4.2 Documentation using

The # symbol is a simple way of inserting comments such as titles and descriptions into R functions and scripts. R ignores all text from the # character to the end of the line.

It is good practice to add a title and short description to any function that you create, so that you and other users can be reminded later of the purpose of the function. It is surprising how easy it is to forget the purpose of a function created only a few weeks or months ago.

It is also sometimes useful to describe what a particular line of code does. This is especially useful when an obscure command has been used.

When working in RStudio, the "Code" menu offers several entries to make this very easy. You can use "Code | Comment/Uncomment lines" to add (or remove) comment markers from a range of lines. If your comments take up too much space on a line (or too little), you can "Code | Reflow Comment" to get more evenly spaced lines.

4.4.3 Neatness counts!

When first programming, it is tempting to think that the only goal is to get a program that works. When it gives the expected result in a few tests, you're done. In Section 4.6.1 we'll talk about ways to improve your testing. But more importantly, you want to write code that "obviously" works, and that means writing clearly, and formatting your code neatly. In this section we'll give some tips for formatting.

1. Use spacing and line breaks to make long expressions easier to read. It's generally a good idea to put spaces around most operators in expressions, and to break long expressions into multiple lines. For example, in R the expressions

```
x1<-a+b+c
y12< -a+b+c
```

are confusingly similar, but very different: the first one assigns the value of a + b + c to x1, while the second compares y12 to -a + b + c. If we add some spaces around the assignment, comparison, and addition operators (but not the negative sign), they'll be easier to read:

```
x1  <- a + b + c
y12 < -a + b + c
```

We added two spaces after x1 so that the very similar expressions on the right would line up, making it easier to spot the differences. With this formatting the differences stand out, and if they were not intentional they would be easy to fix.

2. Indent according to the logical organization of your program. In Sections 4.1 and 4.2 we described flow control and functions, both ways to logically organize your program. These techniques help make your program more understandable, but if the reader doesn't see them the way R does, they can be a source of a huge amount of confusion. We thus make the following recommendation regarding indentation:

Put opening braces "{" at the end of a line, and closing ones "}" at the start of a line, indented equally to the line that started the block. Indent lines within the block consistently, e.g. by 2 or 4 spaces. For example, on page 110 we defined the complex function Eratosthenes containing if statements and for loops in its body. We used four spaces of indentation to indicate each additional level of nesting, and so it is clear where the body starts and ends, and the scope of each flow control statement. Putting the closing brace at the end of the line has the additional beneficial effect in R of preventing a syntax error when the if statement is complete before the else statement is seen.

3. Use informative and consistently formatted variable names. Once you are writing a long program, it becomes hard to remember what the variables do. Mathematical style is to use single letters for variables

(perhaps with different typefaces, or accents, superscripts or subscripts), but this doesn't work in programming: you are generally restricted to a single typeface without any modifications. This makes it important to use longer names for things, for example `wheelRadius` instead of r_1. It is also important to adopt a consistent style for names containing two or more words. We like *camel case* as in `wheelRadius`, but others advocate separators such as `wheel_radius`. Unfortunately the names of R functions are inconsistent in this so we can't give a single recommendation, but you should aim to be consistent within your own programs.

Exercises

1 Compute 10!, 50!, 100!, and 1000!.

2 (a) Using `factorial()`, create a function which computes the binomial coefficient
$$\binom{n}{m}.$$

(b) Compute $\binom{4}{2}$, $\binom{50}{20}$, and $\binom{5000}{2000}$.

(c) The `sum()` function can be used to sum up all elements of its argument, while the `log()` and `exp()` functions take the natural logarithm and exponential of all elements in their argument. Use these functions to create an improved function to compute binomial coefficients.

(d) Compute $\binom{4}{2}$, $\binom{50}{20}$, and $\binom{5000}{2000}$ using the improved version.

3 Refer to Exercise 2 of Section 4.2.1 in which you created a function called `compound.interest()`. Often, the interest rate is quoted as a nominal annual rate, compounded monthly. To obtain the monthly rate, the nominal annual rate is simply divided by 12. More generally, if there are m interest conversion periods in a year, the nominal annual rate is divided by m to obtain the effective interest rate for the appropriate conversion period. (e.g. If the compounding is daily, the nominal annual rate is divided by 365.)

Fix `compound.interest()` so that a nominal annual interest rate j and m, the number of conversion periods per year are part of the argument. The effective rate $i.r$ is assigned j/m in the body of the function. (You may delete $i.r$ from the argument list.)

4 Use the new `compound.interest()` function to compute the amount accumulated from $1000 at an annual rate of 12%, compounded daily. Compare this with the amount accumulated if the compounding is monthly or yearly.

5 Suppose Ms. Wu wishes to take out a mortgage on a house. She wants to know what her periodic payments will be. If P is the initial amount mortgaged, $i.r$ is the effective interest rate, and n is the length of the mortgage, then the periodic payment R is given by
$$R = \frac{Pi.r}{1 - (1 + i.r)^{-n}}.$$

(a) Construct a function called `mortgage.payment()` which employs this formula.

(b) Calculate Ms. Wu's monthly payments, if the initial amount is $100,000, the interest rate is 1%, and the number of interest conversion periods is 300.

6 Use the `annuityAmt()` function to compute accumulated amounts after 10 years, with periodic payments of $400, but with a vector of interest rates ranging from 0.01 through 0.20, by increments of 0.01.

4.5 | Some general programming guidelines

Writing a computer program to solve a problem can usually be reduced to following this sequence of steps:

1. Understand the problem.
2. Work out a general idea for how to solve it.
3. Translate your general idea into a detailed implementation.
4. Check: does it work?
   Is it good enough?
   If yes, you are done!
   If no, go back to step 2.

Example 4.16

We wish to write a program which will sort a vector of integers into increasing order.

1. *Understand the problem.* A good way to understand your programming problem is to try a specific case. You will often need to consider a simple case, but take care not to make it too trivial. For the sorting problem, we might consider sorting the vector consisting of the elements $3, 5, 24, 6, 2, 4, 13, 1$.

   We will write a function to be called `sort()` for which we could do the following:

   ```
   x <- c(3, 5, 24, ..., 1)
   sort(x)
   ```

   The output should be the numbers in increasing order: $1, 2, 3, 4, 5, 6, 13, 24$.

2. *Work out a general idea.* A first idea might be to find where the smallest value is, and put it aside. Then repeat, with the remaining values, setting aside the smallest value each time.

   An alternative idea: compare successive pairs of values, starting at the beginning of the vector, and running through to the end. Swap pairs if they are out of order.

   After checking, you will find that the alternative idea doesn't work. Try using this idea on $2, 1, 4, 3, 0$, for example. After running through it, you should end up with $1, 2, 3, 0, 4$.

   In your check of this alternate idea, you may notice that the largest value always lands at the end of the new vector. (Can you prove to yourself that this should always happen?) This means that we can sort the vector by starting at the beginning of the vector, going through all adjacent pairs, then repeating this procedure for all but the last value, and so on.

3. *Detailed implementation.* At the implementation stage, we need to address specific coding questions. In this sorting problem, one question to be addressed is: how do we swap x[i] and x[i+1]?

   Here is a way to swap the value of x[3] with that of x[4]:

```
save <- x[3]
x[3] <- x[4]
x[4] <- save
```

Note that you should not over-write the value of x[3] with the value of x[4] before its old value has been saved in another place; otherwise, you will not be able to assign that value to x[4].

   We are now ready to write the code:

```
sort <- function(x) {
    # x is initially the input vector and will be modified to form
    # the output
    # first is compared with last
    for(last in length(x):2) {
        for(first in 1:(last-1)) {
            if(x[first] > x[first + 1]) {      # swap the pair
                save <- x[first]
                x[first] <- x[first + 1]
                x[first + 1] <- save
            }
        }
    }
    return (x)
}
```

4. *Check.*

   Always begin testing your code on simple examples to identify obvious bugs.

```
sort(c(2, 1))
```

```
## [1] 1 2
```

```
sort(c(2, 24, 3, 4, 5, 13, 6, 1))
```

```
## [1]  1  2  3  4  5  6 13 24
```

Try the code on several other numeric vectors. What is the output when the input vector has length 1?

```
sort(1)
```

```
## Error in if (x[first] > x[first + 1]) {: missing value where TRUE/FALSE
needed
```

The problem here is that when `length(x) == 1`, the value of `last` will take on the values `1:2`, rather than no values at all. This doesn't require a redesign of the function, we can fix it by handling this as a special case at the beginning of our function:

```r
sort <- function(x) {
    # x is initially the input vector and will be modified to form
    # the output

    if (length(x) < 2) return (x)

    # last is the last element to compare with

    for(last in length(x):2) {
        for(first in 1:(last - 1)) {
            if(x[first] > x[first + 1]) {     # swap the pair
                save <- x[first]
                x[first] <- x[first + 1]
                x[first + 1] <- save
            }
        }
    }
    return (x)
}
```

Test the new version:

```r
sort(1)
```

```
## [1] 1
```

Success! (Or at least we hope so. Have we missed anything?)

4.5.1 Top-down design

Working out the detailed implementation of a program can appear to be a daunting task. The key to making it manageable is to break it down into smaller pieces which you know how to solve. One strategy for doing that is known as "top-down design." Top-down design is similar to outlining an essay before filling in the details:

1. Write out the whole program in a small number (1–5) of steps.
2. Expand each step into a small number of steps.
3. Keep going until you have a program.

Example 4.17
The sort algorithm described in Example 4.16 is known as a "bubble sort." The bubble sort is easy to program and is efficient when the vector x is short, but when x is longer, more efficient methods are available. One of these is known as a "merge sort."

The general idea of a merge sort is to split the vector into two halves, sort each half, and then merge the two halves. During the merge, we only need to compare the first elements of each sorted half to decide which is the smallest value overall. Remove that value from its half; then the second value becomes the smallest remaining value in this half, and we can proceed to put the two parts together into one sorted vector.

So how do we do the initial sorting of each half? We could use a bubble sort, but a more elegant procedure is to use a merge sort on each of them. This is an idea called *recursion*. The `mergesort()` function which we will write below can make calls to itself. Because of variable scoping, new copies of all of the local variables will be created each time it is called, and the different calls will not interfere with each other.

Understanding the idea

It is often worthwhile to consider small numerical examples in order to ensure that we understand the basic idea of the algorithm, before we proceed to designing it in detail. For example, suppose x is $[8, 6, 7, 4]$, and we want to construct a sorted result r. Then our merge sort would proceed as follows:

1. Split x into two parts: $y \leftarrow [8, 6]$, $z \leftarrow [7, 4]$
2. Sort y and z: $y \leftarrow [6, 8]$, $z \leftarrow [4, 7]$
3. Merge y and z:

   (a) Compare $y_1 = 6$ and $z_1 = 4$: $r_1 \leftarrow 4$; Remove z_1; z is now $[7]$.
   (b) Compare $y_1 = 6$ and $z_1 = 7$: $r_2 \leftarrow 6$; Remove y_1; y is now $[8]$.
   (c) Compare $y_1 = 8$ and $z_1 = 7$: $r_3 \leftarrow 7$; Remove z_1; z is now empty.
   (d) Append remaining values of y onto r: $r_4 \leftarrow 8$

4. Return $r = [4, 6, 7, 8]$

Translating into code

It is helpful to think of the translation process as a stepwise process of refining a program until it works.

We begin with a general statement, and gradually expand each part. We will use a double comment marker ## to mark descriptive lines that still need expansion. We will number these comments so that we can refer to them in the text; in practice, you would probably not find this necessary. After expanding, we will change to the usual comment marker to leave our description in place.

We start with just one aim, which we can use as our first descriptive line:

```
## 1.  Use a merge sort to sort a vector
```

We will slowly expand upon previous steps, adding in detail as we go. A simple expansion of step 1 follows from recognizing that we need an input vector x which will be processed by a function that we are naming `mergesort`. Somehow, we will sort this vector. In the end, we want the output to be returned:

```
# 1.   Use a merge sort to sort a vector
mergesort <- function (x) {
    ## 2:     sort x into result
    return (result)
}
```

We now expand step 2, noting how the merge sort algorithm proceeds:

```
# 1.   Use a merge sort to sort a vector
mergesort <- function (x) {
    # 2:     sort x into result
    ## 2.1: split x in half
    ## 2.2: sort each half
    ## 2.3: merge the 2 sorted parts into a sorted result
    return (result)
}
```

Each substep of the above needs to be expanded. First, we expand step 2.1.

```
# 2.1: split x in half
len <- length(x)
x1 <- x[1:(len %/% 2)]
x2 <- x[(len %/% 2 + 1):len]
```

Be careful with "edge" cases; usually, we expect to sort a vector containing more than one element, but our sort function should be able to handle the simple problem of sorting a single element. The code above does not handle len < 2 properly.

We must try again, fixing step 2.1. The solution is simple: if the length of x is 0 or 1, our function should simply return x. Otherwise, we proceed to split x and sort as above. This affects code outside of step 2.1, so we need to correct our outline. Here is the new outline, including the new step 2.1:

```
# 1.   Use a merge sort to sort a vector
mergesort <- function (x) {
    # Check for a vector that doesn't need sorting
    len <- length(x)
    if (len < 2) result  <- x
    else {
        # 2: sort x into result
        # 2.1: split x in half
        y <- x[1:(len %/% 2)]
        z <- x[(len %/% 2 + 1):len]
        ## 2.2: sort y and z
        ## 2.3: merge y and z into a sorted result
    }
    return(result)
}
```

Step 2.2 is very easy to expand, because we can make use of our `mergesort()` function, even though we haven't written it yet! The key idea is to remember that we are not executing the code at this point, we are designing it. We should assume our design will eventually be successful, and we will be able to make use of the fruits of our labor. So step 2.2 becomes

```
# 2.2: sort y and z
y <- mergesort(y)
z <- mergesort(z)
```

Step 2.3 is more complicated, so let's take it slowly. We know that we will need a `result` vector, but let's describe the rest of the process before we code it. We repeat the whole function here, including this expansion and the expansion of step 2.2:

```
# 1.  Use a merge sort to sort a vector
mergesort <- function (x) {
    # Check for a vector that doesn't need sorting
    len <- length(x)
    if (len < 2) result  <- x
    else {
        # 2: sort x into result
        # 2.1: split x in half
        y <- x[1:(len %/% 2)]
        z <- x[(len %/% 2 + 1):len]
        # 2.2: sort y and z
        y <- mergesort(y)
        z <- mergesort(z)
        # 2.3: merge y and z into a sorted result
        result <- c()
        ## 2.3.1:   while (some are left in both piles)
        ## 2.3.2:       put the smallest first element on the end
        ## 2.3.3:       remove it from y or z
        ## 2.3.4:   put the leftovers onto the end of result
    }
    return(result)
}
```

The final steps are now easy to expand. Steps 2.3.2 and 2.3.3 end up intertwined, because they both depend on the test of which of $y[1]$ and $z[1]$ is smallest.

```
# 1.  Use a merge sort to sort a vector
mergesort <- function (x) {
    # Check for a vector that doesn't need sorting
    len <- length(x)
    if (len < 2) result  <- x
    else {
        # 2: sort x into result
```

```
    # 2.1: split x in half
    y <- x[1:(len %/% 2)]
    z <- x[(len %/% 2 + 1):len]
    # 2.2: sort y and z
    y <- mergesort(y)
    z <- mergesort(z)
    # 2.3: merge y and z into a sorted result
    result <- c()
    # 2.3.1:   while (some are left in both piles)
    while (min(length(y), length(z)) > 0) {
        # 2.3.2:       put the smallest first element on the end
        # 2.3.3:       remove it from y or z
        if (y[1] < z[1]) {
            result <- c(result, y[1])
            y <- y[-1]
        } else {
            result <- c(result, z[1])
            z <- z[-1]
        }
    }
    # 2.3.4:   put the leftovers onto the end of result
    if (length(y) > 0)
        result <- c(result, y)
    else
        result <- c(result, z)
    }
    return(result)
}
```

Exercises

1 Modify the `mergesort` function described in this section so that it takes a logical argument (called `decreasing`) which causes sorting in decreasing order when set to TRUE.

2 The system of equations

$$f(x, y) = 0$$
$$g(x, y) = 0$$

can be solved numerically using a form of Newton's method. Assign initial guesses to each of x_0 and y_0. Then perform the following iteration, for $n = 1, 2, \ldots$:

$$x_n = x_{n-1} - (g_{y,n-1}f_{n-1} - f_{y,n-1}g_{n-1})/d_{n-1},$$

$$y_n = y_{n-1} - (f_{x,n-1}g_{n-1} - g_{x,n-1}f_{n-1})/d_{n-1},$$

where

$$f_{x,n-1} = \frac{\partial f}{\partial x}(x_{n-1}, y_{n-1})$$

$$f_{y,n-1} = \frac{\partial f}{\partial y}(x_{n-1}, y_{n-1})$$

$$g_{x,n-1} = \frac{\partial g}{\partial x}(x_{n-1}, y_{n-1})$$

$$g_{y,n-1} = \frac{\partial g}{\partial y}(x_{n-1}, y_{n-1})$$

$$f_{n-1} = f(x_{n-1}, y_{n-1})$$

$$g_{n-1} = g(x_{n-1}, y_{n-1})$$

and

$$d_{n-1} = f_{x,n-1}g_{y,n-1} - f_{y,n-1}g_{x,n-1}.$$

The iteration is terminated when the function values are close enough to 0.

(a) Write a function which will perform this iteration.

(b) Apply the function to the system

$$x + y = 0$$
$$x^2 + 2y^2 - 2 = 0.$$

Find the two solutions to this system analytically as a check on your numerical result.

4.6 Debugging and maintenance

Computer errors are called *bugs*. Removing these errors from a program is called *debugging*. Debugging is difficult, and one of our goals is to write programs that don't have bugs in them: but sometimes we make mistakes.

We have found that the following five steps help us to find and fix bugs in our own programs:

1. Recognize that a bug exists.
2. Make the bug reproducible.
3. Identify the cause of the bug.
4. Fix the error and test.
5. Look for similar errors.

We will consider each of these in turn.

4.6.1 Recognizing that a bug exists

Sometimes this is easy; if the program doesn't work, there is a bug. However, in other cases the program seems to work, but the output is incorrect, or the program works for some inputs, but not for others. A bug causing this kind of error is much more difficult to recognize.

There are several strategies to make it easier. First, follow the advice in previous sections of this text, and break up your program into simple, self-contained functions. Document their inputs and outputs. Within the function, test that the inputs obey your assumptions about them, and think of test inputs where you can see at a glance whether the outputs match your expectations.

In some situations, it may be worthwhile writing *two* versions of a function: one that may be too slow to use in practice, but which you are sure is right, and another that is faster but harder to be sure about. Test that both versions produce the same output in all situations.

When errors only occur for certain inputs, our experience shows that those are often what are called *edge cases*: situations which are right on the boundary between legal and illegal inputs. Test those! For example, test what happens when you try a vector of length zero, test very large or very small values, etc.

4.6.2 Make the bug reproducible

Before you can fix a bug, you need to know where things are going wrong. This is *much* easier if you know how to trigger the bug. Bugs that only appear unpredictably are extremely difficult to fix. The good news is that for the most part computers are predictable: if you give them the same inputs, they give you the same outputs. The difficulty is in working out what the necessary inputs are.

For example, a common mistake in programming is to misspell the name of a variable. Normally this results in an immediate error message, but sometimes you accidentally choose a variable that actually does exist. Then you'll probably get the wrong answer, and the answer you get may appear to be random, because it depends on the value in some unrelated variable.

The key to tracking down this sort of problem is to work hard to make the error reproducible. Simplify things as much as possible: start a new empty R session, and see if you can reproduce it. Once you can reproduce the error, you will eventually be able to track it down.

Some programs do random simulations. For those, you can make the simulations reproducible by setting the value of the random number seed (see Section 6.2) at the start.

4.6.3 Identify the cause of the bug

When you have confirmed that a bug exists, the next step is to identify its cause. If your program has stopped with an error, read the error messages. Try to understand them as well as you can. There are several thousand different error messages in R and we don't have space to list them all, but some common ones are shown in Figure 4.3. If your error is not there, try to guess what it means, or search online for the exact words in the message— or ask someone for help.

In R, you can obtain extra information about an error message using the `traceback()` function. When an error occurs, R saves information about the current stack of active functions, and `traceback()` prints this list.

```
sqrt(var)

## Error in sqrt(var): non-numeric argument to mathematical function
```

`var` is a function, not a vector of numbers that `sqrt` can handle.

```
mean("x")

## Warning in mean.default("x"): argument is not numeric or logical: returning
NA

## [1] NA
```

This is a warning that you can't take the mean of a character variable. You probably should have written `mean(x)`.

```
mean(X)

## Error in mean(X): object 'X' not found
```

You have no variable named `X`. Did you spell the name wrong? Remember that `x` and `X` are different names.

```
library(mass)

## Error in library(mass): there is no package called 'mass'
```

This could be a spelling error (there's a package named `MASS`), or perhaps you have forgotten to install the package.

```
if (x == NA) print("NA")

## Error in if (x == NA) print("NA"): missing value where TRUE/FALSE needed
```

`x == NA` gives `NA`, but the `if` statement needs `TRUE` or `FALSE`. Use `is.na(x)` to test for `NA`.

```
if (1:10 > 5) print("bigger")

## Warning in if (1:10 > 5) print("bigger"): the condition has length > 1 and
only the first element will be used
```

This is a warning that the `if` statement wants just a single test value, but `1:10 > 5` gives 10 values.

Fig. 4.3 Some common errors and warnings and their causes.

Example 4.18

In this function we calculate the coefficient of variation as the standard deviation of a variable, after dividing by its mean. However, our test case gives an error:

```
cv <- function(x) {
    sd(x / mean(x))
}

x1 <- rnorm(10)
cv(x1)
```

```
## Error in is.data.frame(x): object 'x1' not found
```

The error message talks about the function is.data.frame(), which we didn't use. To find out where it was called from, we use traceback():

```
traceback()
## 4: cv(x1)
## 3: sd(x/mean(x))
## 2: var(if (is.vector(x) || is.factor(x)) x else as.double(x), na.rm = na.rm)
## 1: is.data.frame(x)
```

This shows that our cv() function called the standard function sd(), and it called var(), and it ended up calling is.data.frame(). But notice that the only place x1 is mentioned is in our original call, so we need to look at it more closely. When we do, we discover that our original variable was named x1 (with an "ell," not a "one"), and that's the cause of the error.

The traceback() function shows *where* an error is happening, but it doesn't show *why*. Furthermore, many bugs don't trigger any error message, you just see that your program is giving the wrong answer.

How do you work out what is going wrong?

With proper planning beforehand, this step can be made somewhat easier. The advice above in Section 4.6.1 also helps here. If you have chosen meaningful names for variables, you will recognize when their content doesn't make sense. You can check what they contain by printing their values. For example,

```
cat("In myfunction, x=", x, "\n")
```

This will print the value of x, identifying where the message is coming from. The "\n" at the end tells R to go to a new line after printing. You may want to use print() rather than cat() to take advantage of its formatting, but remember that it can only print one thing at a time, so you would likely use it as

```
cat("In myfunction, x=\n")
print(x)
```

A more flexible way to examine the values in functions is to use the RStudio debugging facilities discussed in Section 4.6.6.

Another great way to understand what is going wrong in a small function is to simulate it by hand. Act as you think R would act, and write down the values of all variables as the function progresses. In combination with the techniques described above, this can also identify misconceptions about R. If your simulation would print different results than the real R prints, then you've identified a possible cause of your bug: R is not behaving as you expect. Most likely this is because you don't know R well enough yet, but it is possible that you have actually discovered a bug in R!

4.6.4 Fixing errors and testing

Once you have identified the bug in your program, you need to fix it. Try to fix it in such a way that you don't cause a different problem. Then test what you've done! You should put together tests that include the way you know that would reproduce the error, as well as edge cases, and anything else you can think of.

4.6.5 Look for similar errors elsewhere

Often when you have found and fixed a bug, you can recognize the kind of mistake you made. It is worthwhile looking through the rest of your program for similar errors, because if you made the mistake once, you may have made it twice.

4.6.6 Debugging in RStudio

The RStudio environment provides some very helpful support for understanding the cause of errors when debugging. For example, if we had entered Example 4.18 in the RStudio editor and executed it, we would have been offered the opportunity to produce a traceback in a single mouse click (Figure 4.4). While the ordering and numbering of the traceback entries is different, the information is the same, and that might be enough to spot the error. If not, you could look at the "Environment" pane at the top right of the display. It shows that x1 really does exist.

Fig. 4.4 Traceback of Example 4.18 in RStudio.

Fig. 4.5 Breaking at line 4 of Example 4.18 in RStudio.

If that's still not enough of a hint as to what went wrong, you can set a *breakpoint* within the `cv()` function, and examine the state of variables there. Do this by clicking just to the left of the line number "4" in the code editor. A small red "stop sign" will appear. To activate the breakpoint, click on "Source" in the top right of the code editor. This will run the whole file again, but with the breakpoint set, and execution will stop on line 4. The Environment pane will show the values of local variables in the function. In this case it tells you that `x` has value `x1` (Figure 4.5). Hopefully you will notice the typo at this point.

In more complicated debugging situations, you might make use of the controls that now appear at the top of the Console pane. You can click on Next to execute one line of code, or use the other controls to "step into" a function, finish the current function, resume normal execution, or stop debugging. Experiment!

4.6.7 The `browser()`, `debug()`, and `debugonce()` functions

If you are not using RStudio, the debugging facilities are still available, they are just a little less convenient. Instead of setting a breakpoint in the code editor, R allows you to call the function `browser()`. This will pause execution of your function, and allow you to examine (or change!) local variables, or execute any other R command, inside the evaluation environment of the function.

You can also execute a debugger command.

- `n` - "next"; execute the next line of code, single-stepping through the function
- `s` - "step into" function calls
- `f` - "finish" the current function

- c - "continue"; let the function continue running
- Q - quit the debugger

Another way to enter the browser is to use the debug() function. You mark function f for debugging using debug(f), and then the browser will be called when you enter the function. Turn off debugging using undebug(f). Alternatively, use debugonce() to mark the function, and debugging will be turned off after the first call.

Exercises

1 Consider the mergesort() function constructed in Example 4.17. Using either the debug() function or the debugging facilities in RStudio, run mergesort(c(3, 5, 4, 2)) and check the value of the x argument before any other calculation is completed, and then the values of y and z just before sorting them.

2 Consider the cv() function constructed in Example 4.18. Using either the debug() function or the debugging facilities in RStudio, run cv(c(-3, 10, -7)) and explain why it returns NaN. Suggest a more reasonable return value and modify the function to produce it.

4.6.8 Debugging magrittr pipes

The pipe operator discussed in Section 4.2.5 presents some challenges when debugging. Pipelines can be quite long and involve several function calls (sometimes multiple calls to the same function), but as far as R is concerned, each pipeline is a single statement, so it's hard to look at intermediate results.

There are two basic strategies for handling this: break up the pipeline into multiple statements, or insert the magrittr::debug_pipe() function. We illustrate both methods on a simple example.

Example 4.19
The magrittr package defines several small functions: add, subtract, and so on, to do arithmetic on R objects. We can use those to simulate a children's trick:

> Pick a number between 1 and 10, and keep it secret. Multiply your number by 3. Add 3. Multiply by 3 again. The digits of your current number add up to 9!

It's probably obvious to you how this works, but let's simulate it using R and pipes.

```
library(magrittr)
x <- sample(1:10, 1)
x %>% multiply_by(3) %>% add(5) %>% multiply_by(3)

## [1] 78
```

Oh no! The digits don't add up to 9! To debug this, we can rewrite the sequence, saving intermediate results:

```
r1 <- x %>% multiply_by(3); r1
## [1] 21
r2 <- r1 %>% add(5); r2
## [1] 26
r3 <- r2 %>% multiply_by(3); r3
## [1] 78
```

Now it's obvious that we didn't add 3 in the second step, we added 5.

The other way to debug this is to insert the `magrittr` function `debug_pipe()` into the pipe, e.g.

```
x %>% multiply_by(3) %>% debug_pipe() %>% add(5) %>%
    debug_pipe() %>% multiply_by(3)
```

This calls `browser()` between each step with the current value stored in x. It then passes x on to the next step with no changes. We can print x and recognize when it's not the right value. Try it!

We can check that our fix is correct by doing the calculation for every possible starting choice:

```
1:10 %>% multiply_by(3) %>% add(3) %>% multiply_by(3)
##  [1] 18 27 36 45 54 63 72 81 90 99
```

and now we see another bug: if 10 had been chosen, the sum of digits would be 18, so we should reword the magic trick to keep adding the digits until they get to a single digit.

4.7 | Efficient programming

When producing computer code, you may find that it runs slower than you want it to, even on today's fast computers. But take heart: there are always ways to speed up a program. The process is called *optimization*. In this section we will give a few examples of *hand optimization* in R: ways to rewrite your code so that it runs faster. Other possibilities are automatic optimization (not available in R, but some other programming platforms can do this), or hardware optimization, where you change your computer to run your programs faster, e.g. by buying a new one.

Optimization always requires some sort of trade-off. Hand optimization can be time consuming, and since optimized code can be harder to understand, errors can slip by undetected. You should always ensure that your code is correct before you try to optimize it because it will probably be harder to debug later. You should use judgment about whether optimization will be worthwhile.

4.7.1 Learn your tools

In order to write efficient code, you need to understand the platform you are working with. For example, R is designed to work with vectors. Operations on whole vectors are usually much faster than working one element at a time.

For example, summing two vectors could be done as follows:

```
X <- rnorm(100000)      # Xi ~ N(0, 1) i=1, ..., 100,000
Y <- rnorm(100000)      # Yi ~ N(0, 1) i=1, ..., 100,000
Z <- c()
for (i in 1:100000) {
    Z <- c(Z, X[i] + Y[i])  # this takes about 25 seconds
}
```

However, this is extremely inefficient in R. First, it reallocates the vector Z 100,000 times, increasing its length by one each time. Since we know the length of z in advance, we could allocate it once, and modify its entries:

```
Z <- rep(NA, 100000)
for (i in 1:100000) {
    Z[i] <- X[i] + Y[i]      # this takes about 0.15 seconds
}
```

Simply by avoiding the reallocations, we have got a speedup by a factor of approximately 170 times.

A more natural way to do this calculation in R is by vectorizing completely, i.e.

```
Z <- X + Y                 #    0.001 seconds (approx)
```

The fully vectorized calculation is another 150 times faster, i.e. 25,000 times faster than the original loop. If the original code had taken a year to run, the optimized code would be done in about 20 minutes, making the difference between an infeasible solution and a feasible one.

However, the original code in our example took 25 seconds to run, and the optimized version 1 millisecond: an impressive ratio, but still only a savings of 25 seconds. In this case the revised code is clearer and more obvious than the original so we think the effort was worthwhile. But if we had been forced to spend a lot of time on the optimization, and had ended up with obscure code that we wouldn't understand the next time we looked at it, we would judge the effort not to have been worth it.

4.7.2 Use efficient algorithms

Example 4.20

Think about the problem of recording grades in a spreadsheet. You have a pile of tests from a class. There are n tests, each with a name and grade. You also have a class list in a spreadsheet, and want to record the grades there.

A really slow algorithm

1. Read the name of the first student in the mark spreadsheet.
2. Randomly select one of the n tests.
3. If the names match, record the grade, and go on to the next student.
4. If not, put the test back, and randomly select another.
5. Continue until all grades have been recorded.

How bad is this algorithm? One answer to this question is to determine the expected time until we get our first matching grade.

Since there are n tests, the probability of a correct match is $1/n$. The number of draws until the first match is a geometric random variable with parameter $1/n$. The expected value for that random variable is known to be n. When we get to the second student, the expected value will be $n - 1$, because there is one less test to search. Overall, the expected time to completely record all of the grades is $\sum_{i=1}^{n} i = n(n - 1)/2$ times the amount of time to do one selection and check.

A slightly faster algorithm

1. Take the first test.
2. Scan through all the names in the spreadsheet until you find the matching name, and record the grade.
3. Repeat for each student.

For each test, this algorithm requires scanning an average of half the names in the list, so the total time is $n^2/2$ times the time to scan one name, plus n times the time to select a test from the pile. Even though this is a total of $n^2/2 + n = n(n + 2)/2$ steps, each step is faster than the steps above, so this algorithm is probably faster.

A much faster algorithm

1. First, sort the names in the spreadsheet into alphabetical order.
2. Take the first test.
3. Search for the name in the spreadsheet, using the alphabetical sorting to help.
4. Repeat for each student.

This is much faster, because searching through a sorted list can be quicker, using a bisection technique: check the middle name, then the middle name of whichever half the current test falls in, and so on. Each test takes about $\log_2 n$ comparisons before you'll find it, so the whole operation takes $n \log_2 n$ operations. For a medium to large class this is much better than the $n^2/2$ lookup time of the previous algorithm. For a class of 100, it's the difference between 5000 operations and fewer than 700.

We could go further, and sort the tests before recording them: since the tests and the class list will be in the same order, the recording would take just n steps. However, the sorting of the tests is probably much slower than sorting the names in the spreadsheet, since it requires physical sorting rather than just asking the computer to sort the names, and this will likely be slower than the algorithm above. On the other hand, it leaves the tests in sorted order so other future operations on them (e.g. looking up the test of a particular student) would be faster. It will require a judgment whether the additional investment now will pay off in saved time later.

4.7.3 Measure the time your program takes

Optimization is hard work, so you don't want to do it when it's not necessary. In many cases, it will take more time to optimize a program than you could ever hope to save from the optimization. Before starting to optimize, you should measure the amount of time your program is taking, as an upper bound on the amount of time you could possibly save.

In R, the system.time() function measures the execution time of evaluating expressions. For example,

```
X <- rnorm(100000)
Y <- rnorm(100000)
Z <- c()
system.time({
    for (i in 1:100000) {
        Z <- c(Z, X[i] + Y[i])
    }
})

##    user  system elapsed
##  19.442  12.651  32.209

Z <- rep(NA, 100000)
system.time({
    for (i in 1:100000) {
        Z[i] <- X[i] + Y[i]
    }
})

##    user  system elapsed
##   0.011   0.000   0.011

system.time(Z <- X + Y)

##    user  system elapsed
##       0       0       0
```

shows how we obtained the timing reported above.[7] The "user" time is the time dedicated to this particular task, the "system" time is how much time your system spent doing other tasks, and the "elapsed" time is the time we would have seen on a clock. The microbenchmark() function in the microbenchmark package automatically repeats operations a number of times to allow for measurement of very short durations, e.g.

```
library(microbenchmark)
microbenchmark(Z <- X + Y)

## Unit: microseconds
##        expr     min       lq     mean   median       uq      max neval
##  Z <- X + Y 132.245 365.6865  583.899  378.157  394.165 15927.88   100
```

[7] The times here are not exactly the same as before; this is typical, because other activities on the computer affect the results.

You may also be able to measure which particular parts of your program are the best targets for optimization. A famous rule of thumb in computing is the 90/10 rule: 90% of the execution time of your program comes from 10% of the code. We call code in the slow 10% the *bottlenecks*. The corollary is that if you can identify and optimize the bottlenecks, you can obtain a substantial speedup without even looking at 90% of the program.

Many software platforms offer *profilers* to help find the bottlenecks in your program. There are various kinds of profilers, but in general they monitor the program while it is running and report on where the execution time was spent. In R the profiler is controlled by the Rprof() function, and RStudio has a graphical display of its results, but a discussion of the details is beyond the scope of this text.

4.7.4 Be willing to use different tools

Much as we love it, we admit that R is not the only computing platform available, and it is not the best tool for all tasks. For raw speed, you are much better off using a compiled language like C, C++, or Fortran. R itself is written in C and Fortran, which is why the operations on vectors go so quickly: most of the work is done in compiled code.

A style of programming that we recommend is to do most of your work in R. In cases where you don't get acceptable speed, identify the bottlenecks, and consider translating those into a compiled language. R has extensive support for linking to code in other languages. Unfortunately this requires a level of technical detail that is again beyond the scope of this book.

4.7.5 Optimize with care

The famous computer scientist Donald Knuth once said, "Premature optimization is the root of all evil (or at least most of it) in programming." We have emphasized above that optimization is difficult and that it is not always advisable. We finish the chapter with this advice for writing efficient code:

1. Get it right.
2. Get it fast enough.
3. Make sure it's still right.

Chapter exercises

1 As mentioned in Example 4.2, the RANDU algorithm produces triplets of values that are very predictable. To see this, try the following. First, generate 3,000,000 values using RANDU. Round the values to three decimal places, and put them into a matrix with three columns, with the first value in column 1, the second in column 2, and the third in column 3, repeated through the whole vector of values. Then set x to 0.1 and find the subset of rows of the matrix where the first column equals x. Plot the second column versus the third column. Repeat this

for $x = 0.1, 0.2, \ldots, 0.9$ in an array of 9 plots. The pattern should be striking.

2 Write a function which will evaluate polynomials of the form

$$P(x) = c_n x^{n-1} + c_{n-1} x^{n-2} + \cdots + c_2 x + c_1.$$

Your function should take x and the vector of polynomial coefficients as arguments and it should return the value of the evaluated polynomial. Call this function `directpoly()`.

3 Refer to the previous question. For moderate to large values of n, evaluation of a polynomial at x can be done more efficiently using *Horner's Rule*:

(a) Set $a_n \leftarrow c_n$.
(b) For $i = n - 1, \ldots, 1$,

$$\text{set } a_i = a_{i+1} x + c_i.$$

(c) Return a_1. (This is the computed value of $P(x)$.)

Write an R function which takes arguments x and a vector of polynomial coefficients and which returns the value of the polynomial evaluated at x. Call the resulting function `hornerpoly()`. Ensure that your function returns an appropriate vector of values when x is a vector.

4 Do some timings to compare the algorithms used in the previous two questions.

(a) In particular, try the following code:

```
library(microbenchmark)
microbenchmark(directpoly(x = seq(-10, 10, length = 5000000),
                          c(1, -2, 2, 3, 4, 6, 7)),
              hornerpoly(x = seq(-10, 10, length = 5000000),
                          c(1, -2, 2, 3, 4, 6, 7)))
```

(b) What happens to the comparison when the number of polynomial coefficients is smaller? Try

$$P(x) = 2x^2 + 17x - 3.$$

5 Using a starting value of 2.9, find the time required for Newton's method to find the zero (to within 7-digit accuracy) of

(a) $(x - 3)e^{-x}$
(b) $(x^2 - 6x + 9)e^{-x}$

6 Repeat the previous question, using the bisection algorithm and the initial interval $[2.1, 3.1]$.

7 Do a timing comparison of the bubble sort (see Example 4.16) and the merge sort (see Example 4.17). Do the comparison for vectors of length 10, 1000, 10000, and 100000. (You may use the function `rnorm()` to generate vectors for this purpose.)

8 This exercise gives a taste of the graphical editing capability of *grid* (touched on briefly in Chapter 3). To create a graphical object (grob) with the information required to draw a triangle, execute the following:

```
b1 <- sqrt(1/cos(36*pi/180)^2-1)/2
b2 <- sin(72*pi/180)/(2*(1+cos(72*pi/180))) - (1-sin(72*pi/180))/2
triangle <- polygonGrob(c(0,.5,1), c(b2,b2+b1,b2),
      name = "triangle", gp = gpar(fill = "yellow", col = 0))
grid.draw(triangle)  # nothing appears until this line is executed
```

Next draw three rotated copies of the triangles, creating the impression of a star shape.

```
for (i in 0:2){
pushViewport(vp=viewport(angle=72*i))
grid.draw(triangle)
upViewport()
}
```

5

Complex programming in the *tidyverse*

As of this writing, there are more than 3000 objects in the R base packages, and more than 15,000 other packages available on CRAN, most containing dozens of objects of their own. This represents a huge amount of functionality, and nobody could be expected to remember it all. The best we can hope for is that people should be able to discover it, using the help system and other resources, as well as judicious guesses about where to look. Guessing is made easier when consistent principles are followed as code is written. For example, names should reflect the purpose of packages and functions. Guessing is made harder by inconsistency, for example when names are poorly chosen, or conventions for forming names are inconsistent.

Due to the way it was written, base R is quite inconsistent in its naming conventions. As discussed back in Section 1.3, it started out trying for consistency with S. It has had dozens of contributors since then, and fashions in computing have changed, so it includes many different styles of naming. Just looking at function names in base packages that contain the word `add`, we see `add_datalist`, `add.scope`, `add1`, `addGrob`, `addmargins`, `grid.add`, and `tkadd`, among others. Knowing that you want to add something to something else isn't enough to guess the name: does "add" come first or last? Is it separated by an underscore, a dot, or nothing? How are the parts capitalized? There are also inconsistencies in names of similar function arguments, ordering of arguments, and types of values returned from functions.

Most of us will never write code anywhere near the complexity of R, but many of us will work on projects that are complex enough to exceed our ability to memorize all of the details, and will work on teams where others besides ourselves contribute code that we need to understand. In these situations it is important to think about consistency in our programming.

In this chapter, we will look at the *tidyverse*, a collection of R packages designed to follow a consistent design philosophy. We will start with a presentation of the philosophy, then study several *tidyverse* packages in some detail to see how it works in practice. On the way, we'll also learn how to use a useful and popular collection of packages. The packages can be loaded individually, or as a group by running

```
library(tidyverse)

## -- Attaching packages --------- tidyverse 1.3.0 --
## v tibble  3.0.3     v dplyr  1.0.2
## v tidyr   1.1.2     v stringr 1.4.0
## v readr   1.4.0     v forcats 0.5.0
## v purrr   0.3.4
## -- Conflicts ---------- tidyverse_conflicts() --
## x tidyr::extract()    masks magrittr::extract()
## x dplyr::filter()     masks stats::filter()
## x dplyr::lag()        masks stats::lag()
## x purrr::set_names() masks magrittr::set_names()
```

Each of them has one or more vignettes giving more detail than we can give. You can browse the vignettes for the packages we discuss using

```
tidyversepkgs <- c("tidyverse", "tibble", "readr", "stringr", "dplyr")
browseVignettes(tidyversepkgs)
```

After introducing each package, we will include a short discussion of the packages from the point of view of their design. If you're only interested in learning about the packages, you can skip this, and come back to it later when you are thinking about designing your own complex project.

5.1 | The *tidyverse* principles

Hadley Wickham is the principal author behind the *tidyverse*, to which many others have contributed. He has written down his design principles in *The tidy tools manifesto*, which is included as a vignette (part of the documentation) in the `tidyverse` package. You can read the full document by running

```
vignette("manifesto", package = "tidyverse")
```

after installing the `tidyverse` package. We'll summarize the key points here. The main points are quoted from the vignette; the italicized comments are ours.

1. Re-use existing data structures.
   R supports many different ways of storing data. We should place a high value on consistency: focus on a small number of structures that are already familiar to users, rather than inventing new ones. He recommends using data frames for rectangular data sets and simple vectors for smaller ones. More on this in Section 5.2.

2. Compose simple functions with the pipe.
   "The pipe" is the `%>%` pipe operator that we discussed in Section 4.2.5. Rather than writing complex functions that do a lot, Wickham recommends breaking down complex operations into simple sequential ones. Write functions for those simple operations that follow the conventions that work with the `%>%` operator, and let the user put together

those steps into easy-to-understand chains of transformations. This goes further than top-down design, discussed in Section 4.5.1: whereas top-down design suggests breaking up a problem into smaller pieces, this principle says to make each of those pieces a small transformation that can be done in a pipe.

3. Embrace functional programming.
We mentioned functional programming in the introduction to Chapter 4.

4. Design for humans.
Computational efficiency should be a secondary concern to usability.

5.1.1 Discussion

In our opinion, principle 4 is the most important of the principles, and should apply to almost any project. Princple 1 is also important to simplify coding. The other two principles are a matter of style, and setting a consistent style is important. You could choose different design styles than using pipes and functional programming, but do pick a style and stick to it.

5.2 | The tibble package: a data frame improvement

The first *tidyverse* principle recommends using data frames for most rectangular data sets. However, the data frames in base R have a few defaults that can cause confusion:

- In R versions earlier than 4.0.0, character vectors are automatically changed to factors.
- Names are changed to legal R variable names, e.g. spaces are replaced with dots:

```
data.frame("Annual income" = 100000)

##   Annual.income
## 1         1e+05
```

- Printing very large data frames takes up a lot of space in the console.
- Taking a subset of a data frame sometimes produces a data frame, and sometimes produces a vector:

```
df1 <- data.frame(x = 1:2, y = 2:1)
df1[, 1:2]

##   x y
## 1 1 2
## 2 2 1

df1[, 1]

## [1] 1 2
```

Each of these issues has a workaround, but rather than requiring it to be used, the `tibble` package introduces a new kind of data frame called a *tibble* that fixes them by default: character vectors and names are left as is, printing defaults to a summary, and subsetting produces another tibble. Besides those changes, the `tibble()` function has other differences from `data.frame()`:

- The arguments must all be the same length, or length 1; recycling of other lengths is assumed to be an error.
- The arguments are evaluated in order, and earlier arguments can be used in the definition of later ones. For example,

```
tibble(x = 1:2, y = x + 1)

## # A tibble: 2 x 2
##       x     y
##   <int> <dbl>
## 1     1     2
## 2     2     3
```

5.2.1 Discussion

In our opinion, almost all of these changes to data frames are improvements. They reduce some common user errors with data frames. The only one we question is the last one, the sequential processing of arguments to `tibble()`. While this adds convenience, it creates inconsistency, and so is a poor design. Most other functions in R evaluate arguments in the frame of the caller, so `y = x + 1` would ignore the earlier argument x, and would search for x in the current environment. Watch out if you name tibble columns with the same names as other variables, because behavior depends on the order of arguments to `tibble()`:

```
x <- c(100, 200)
tibble(x = 1:2, y = x + 1)

## # A tibble: 2 x 2
##       x     y
##   <int> <dbl>
## 1     1     2
## 2     2     3

tibble(y = x + 1, x = 1:2)

## # A tibble: 2 x 2
##       y     x
##   <dbl> <int>
## 1   101     1
## 2   201     2
```

The `data.frame()` function would give the same y column in both cases, basing the value on the global variable x.

5.3 | The `readr` package: reading data in the *tidyverse*

One task that is common in statistical computations is reading data from a file. We discussed the base function `read.table()` in Section 2.10.5; in this section we'll describe the functions in the `readr` package.

The main goal of the `readr` package is to allow the user to read a file and output a tibble. This involves three steps:

1. The file needs to be converted to a rectangular matrix of strings.
2. The type of each column needs to be determined.
3. Each column needs to be converted into the appropriate type.

Functions like `read_csv()` do the first step, and call other functions for the other two steps. The user can specify the types of columns using strings like `"nnn"` to indicate three numeric values, or can give `col_*()` functions to implicitly specify the type, or `readr` can guess at the types using the `guess_parser()` function. The final conversion step is performed by a number of `col_*()` functions. For example, `col_number()` takes strings like `"$1,000.00"` as input and outputs numeric values like `1000`.

The `readr` package has several nice features. It can read from a variety of sources besides files, including reading directly from a character vector. If an error occurs in reading, it will report the error and carry on. For example,

```
data <- "x,y,z
         1,2,3
         4,5,6
         7,B,9"
read_csv(data)

## # A tibble: 3 x 3
##       x y        z
##   <dbl> <chr> <dbl>
## 1     1 2        3
## 2     4 5        6
## 3     7 B        9
```

We see that the middle column is read as character (because of the B in the third row of data). We could force it to read numbers in several ways, including

```
read_csv(data, col_types = "nnn")

## Warning: 1 parsing failure.
## row col expected actual      file
##   3   y a number      B literal data

## # A tibble: 3 x 3
```

```
##         x       y       z
##     <dbl>   <dbl>   <dbl>
## 1       1       2       3
## 2       4       5       6
## 3       7      NA       9
```

and then we will get a nice report about the error.

The package also contains some functions such as `write_csv()` to write files. This is actually an easier task than reading them, and the main benefit of those functions in `readr` is that they are somewhat faster than the base R functions.

5.3.1 Discussion

The `readr` package breaks functionality down into small pieces and puts them together in a consistent way to do what we want. It's a good example of designing for humans: the computer has to do a lot of work (e.g. to produce the informative error messages), but it is tremendously helpful to the user. We recommend it!

5.4 | The `stringr` package for manipulating strings

When we read data from a file, often it needs further manipulation to be useful. For example, we may read some phone numbers in one format and others in a different format, and need to make them consistent so they can be compared. Or we may have leading or trailing spaces on strings that are invisible when printed and cause problems later.

The `stringr` package is a collection of functions to deal with problems like these. Its vignette classifies the functions into four groups:

1. Working with individual characters within longer strings.
2. Adding and removing white space.
3. Operations that depend on the conventions in different languages, such as sorting strings.
4. Pattern matching.

Example 5.1

We may have a data frame `df` with a column `phone` containing North American phone numbers. One conventional way to display these is `nnn-nnn-nnnn` where each `n` is a single digit, however many other conventions are in use, and our data frame has a mix of different styles. We would like to standardize them. Some are displayed with a leading `+1`, others use spaces instead of hyphens between the groups of numbers, and others use no spacing at all.

```
df
```

```
## # A tibble: 5 x 1
##   phone
##   <chr>
## 1 705 555 0100
## 2 +1 519 555 0101
## 3 4165550102
## 4 514 555-0103
## 5 011-800-555-0104
```

Our strategy to standardize the numbers is as follows:

1. Remove all non-digits.
2. If 11 digits are left and the first is a 1, remove it too.
3. If anything other than 10 digits are left, it's an error and should give NA; otherwise reformat to the standard format.

We can implement this strategy using `stringr` functions as follows:

```
phone <- df$phone %>%
        str_remove_all("[^0-9]") %>%
        str_replace("1(..........)", "\\1") %>%
        `[<-`(., str_length(.) != 10, NA) %>%
        `str_sub<-`(7, 6, value = "-") %>%
        `str_sub<-`(4, 3, value = "-")
phone
```

```
## [1] "705-555-0100" "519-555-0101" "416-555-0102" "514-555-0103"
## [5] NA
```

Understanding the code

We use pipes, because `stringr` is a *tidyverse* package that has good support for pipes. The first step in the pipe extracts the column of data. The second removes all digits: the pattern `[^0-9]` is a "regular expression" that is read as "a single character that is not in the range 0 to 9." The third replacement uses a different regular expression `1(..........)`, which is read as "the character 1 followed by a grouping of 10 characters"; we replace that with what was found in the grouping.

The last three steps in the pipe look strange, because they are using replacement functions. The fourth step corresponds to the R code

```
temp[str_length(temp) != 10] <- NA
```

except that a dot is used instead of `temp`. Replacements like this are done with functions whose names end in the characters `<-`; such names need to be quoted to be legal R code. Thus the fourth step calls the function `` `[<-` `` to replace bad entries with NA, and the fifth and sixth steps call `` `str_sub<-` `` to substitute the hyphen into the appropriate places in the strings.

5.4.1 Discussion

Handling strings is a very important and sometimes difficult task in statistical computing. The `stringr` package makes it rather less difficult by a good consistent design. The need to use replacement functions within the pipe is a little awkward, but otherwise the package follows the *tidyverse* principles quite well.

5.5 | The `dplyr` package for manipulating data sets

Whereas `stringr` dealt with manipulations of string variables, the `dplyr` package deals with manipulations of data frames.

There are two groups of functions in `dplyr`. The first group works on a single data frame at a time and is discussed in `vignette("dplyr")`. We'll concentrate on that group in this book. The second group works on pairs of data frames, and is described in `vignette("two-table")`. It uses database concepts that are beyond our scope.

The functions in `dplyr` are designed to work in `magrittr` pipes. They are intended to be thought of as verbs: do this, then do that, etc., and are named that way. The `"dplyr"` vignette describes them this way:

- `filter()` selects cases based on their values.
  For example,

```
mpg %>% filter(cyl == 5)

## # A tibble: 4 x 11
##   manufacturer model displ year   cyl trans drv    cty   hwy fl
##   <chr>        <chr> <dbl> <int> <int> <chr> <chr> <int> <int> <chr>
## 1 volkswagen   jetta   2.5  2008     5 auto~ f        21    29 r
## 2 volkswagen   jetta   2.5  2008     5 manu~ f        21    29 r
## 3 volkswagen   new ~   2.5  2008     5 manu~ f        20    28 r
## 4 volkswagen   new ~   2.5  2008     5 auto~ f        20    29 r
## # ... with 1 more variable: class <chr>
```

  shows us the four cars in the `mpg` data frame that have a five-cylinder engine.
- `arrange()` sorts the rows of a data frame.
  We can sort the cars into ascending city mileage, with ties broken by highway mileage, using

```
options(tibble.print_min = 3)
mpg %>% arrange(cty, hwy)

## # A tibble: 234 x 11
##   manufacturer model displ year   cyl trans drv    cty   hwy fl
##   <chr>        <chr> <dbl> <int> <int> <chr> <chr> <int> <int> <chr>
## 1 dodge        dako~   4.7  2008     8 auto~ 4         9    12 e
## 2 dodge        dura~   4.7  2008     8 auto~ 4         9    12 e
## 3 dodge        ram ~   4.7  2008     8 auto~ 4         9    12 e
## # ... with 231 more rows, and 1 more variable: class <chr>
```

Here we set the `tibble.print_min` option to 3 to limit printing in these examples.

If we had wanted descending order, we would use the `desc()` helper function:

```
mpg %>% arrange(desc(cty), desc(hwy))

## # A tibble: 234 x 11
##   manufacturer model displ year   cyl trans drv    cty   hwy fl
##   <chr>        <chr> <dbl> <int> <int> <chr> <chr> <int> <int> <chr>
## 1 volkswagen   new ~   1.9  1999     4 manu~ f        35    44 d
## 2 volkswagen   jetta   1.9  1999     4 manu~ f        33    44 d
## 3 volkswagen   new ~   1.9  1999     4 auto~ f        29    41 d
## # ... with 231 more rows, and 1 more variable: class <chr>
```

- `select()` selects variables based on their names.
  We could use

```
mpg %>% select(manufacturer, model, cty, hwy)

## # A tibble: 234 x 4
##   manufacturer model   cty   hwy
##   <chr>        <chr> <int> <int>
## 1 audi         a4       18    29
## 2 audi         a4       21    29
## 3 audi         a4       20    31
## # ... with 231 more rows
```

if we were only interested in those four columns. We can rename columns as we select them, e.g.

```
mpg %>% select(manufacturer, model, City = cty, Highway = hwy)

## # A tibble: 234 x 4
##   manufacturer model  City Highway
##   <chr>        <chr> <int>   <int>
## 1 audi         a4       18      29
## 2 audi         a4       21      29
## 3 audi         a4       20      31
## # ... with 231 more rows
```

or use the `rename()` function to rename columns without selection.

- `mutate()` computes variables that may be functions of existing variables; `transmute()` also drops all old variables. As we saw with `tibble()` in Section 5.2, these functions operate sequentially, so later changes can refer to earlier ones.

  For example, to change units from miles per gallon to litres per 100 km, we could use

```
lper100km <- mpg %>% mutate(cty = 235.215/cty, hwy = 235.215/hwy)
lper100km

## # A tibble: 234 x 11
```

```
##    manufacturer model displ year   cyl trans drv   cty   hwy fl
##    <chr>        <chr> <dbl> <int> <int> <chr> <chr> <dbl> <dbl> <chr>
## 1 audi          a4     1.8  1999     4 auto~ f     13.1  8.11 p
## 2 audi          a4     1.8  1999     4 manu~ f     11.2  8.11 p
## 3 audi          a4     2    2008     4 manu~ f     11.8  7.59 p
## # ... with 231 more rows, and 1 more variable: class <chr>
```

- summarize() (or with alternate spelling, summarise()) applies functions to groups of values. The group_by() function defines the groups it works with.

  For example, to find the mean litres per 100 km by number of cylinders, we could use

```
lper100km %>% group_by(cyl) %>%
  summarize(cty = mean(cty), hwy = mean(hwy))

## 'summarise()' ungrouping output (override with
'.groups' argument)

## # A tibble: 4 x 3
##     cyl   cty   hwy
##   <int> <dbl> <dbl>
## 1     4  11.5  8.36
## 2     5  11.5  8.18
## 3     6  14.7 10.6
## 4     8  19.1 13.8
```

- sample_n() and sample_frac() sample values, possibly from within groups.

  Here is a random vehicle for each cylinder count:

```
lper100km %>% group_by(cyl) %>% sample_n(1)

## # A tibble: 4 x 11
## # Groups:   cyl [4]
##    manufacturer model displ year   cyl trans drv   cty   hwy fl
##    <chr>        <chr> <dbl> <int> <int> <chr> <chr> <dbl> <dbl> <chr>
## 1 honda         civic  1.8  2008     4 auto~ f     9.80  6.53 c
## 2 volkswagen    new ~  2.5  2008     5 manu~ f     11.8  8.40 r
## 3 dodge         dako~  3.7  2008     6 manu~ 4     15.7 12.4  r
## 4 chevrolet     c150~  5.3  2008     8 auto~ r     21.4 15.7  e
## # ... with 1 more variable: class <chr>
```

5.5.1 Discussion

We have already mentioned our misgivings about sequential processing of arguments in tibble(); these also apply to mutate() and transmute(). Other than that, we find dplyr to be a good, very consistent design.

5.6 | Other *tidyverse* packages

The *tidyverse* project includes dozens of R packages besides the ones we've discussed in this book. Other core *tidyverse* packages include:

- `tidyr`: tools for rearranging data sets into the standard "tidy" format of one case per row. Data may arrive with multiple observations per row, stored in different columns; these functions help you to fix that.
- `forcats`: functions for working with factors. These allow entries in tables and plots to be easily merged and reordered.
- `purrr`: functions implementing functional programming in a consistent way. If you are interested in exploring that style of programming, you can read about `purrr` in `https://purrr.tidyverse.org`.

The `www.tidyverse.org` website is an evolving source of information on the *tidyverse* project. If you have enjoyed this chapter, go there and discover other interesting *tidyverse* packages.

6

Simulation

Much of statistics relies on being able to evaluate expectations of random variables, and finding quantiles of distributions.[1] For example:

- In hypothesis testing, the *p*-value of a sample is defined as the probability of observing data at least as extreme as the sample in hand, given that the null hypothesis is true. This is the expected value of a random variable defined to be 0 when a sample is less extreme, and 1 otherwise.
- The bias of an estimator is defined to be the expected value of the estimator minus the true value that it is estimating.
- Confidence intervals are based on quantiles of the distribution of a pivotal quantity, e.g. $(\bar{X} - \mu)/(s/\sqrt{n})$.

In simple cases we may evaluate these quantities analytically, or use large sample approximations. However, in other cases we need computer-based methods to approximate them.

In this chapter, you will be introduced to Monte Carlo simulation. This introduction will include basic ideas of random (or more properly, *pseudorandom*) number generation. You will then see how to simulate random variables from several of the common probability distributions. Next, we will show you how simulation can be used in some surprising ways: to model natural processes and to evaluate integrals. The final topics of the chapter on Markov chains, as well as rejection and importance sampling will give you a hint as to what more advanced methods are like.

[1] See Appendix A if you need a review of random variables and their properties.

6.1 | Monte Carlo simulation

One of the most general computer-based methods for approximating properties of random variables is the Monte Carlo method.

To approximate the mean $\mu = E(X)$ using the Monte Carlo method, we generate m independent and identically distributed (i.i.d.) copies of X, namely $X_1, \ldots, X_m$, and use the sample mean $\bar{X} = (1/m) \sum X_i$ as an estimate of $E(X)$. For large values of m, $\bar{X}$ gives a good approximation[2] to $E(X)$.

[2] This follows from the law of large numbers.

Furthermore, if m is large the distribution of the sample mean, $\bar{X}$, can be approximated[3] by a normal distribution with mean μ and variance σ^2/m. Here σ^2 is the variance $\text{Var}(X)$, which can be approximated by the sample variance $s^2 = [1/(m-1)] \sum (X_i - \bar{X})^2$. This allows us to construct approximate confidence intervals for μ. For example, $\bar{X} \pm 1.96s/\sqrt{m}$ will contain μ approximately 95% of the time.

The remainder of this chapter describes methods for simulating the generation of random variables on a computer. We will describe deterministic methods of generating values, which are then treated as though they are random. It is useful to think of two participants in this process: the programmer hiding behind a curtain knows that the algorithms are deterministic and predictable, but the user of those numbers is unaware of the mechanisms used to compute them, so to that user, the numbers appear random and unpredictable. In practice, both participants may be the same person! To distinguish this scheme from true random numbers which really are unpredictable, we will call our simulated random numbers *pseudorandom numbers* in the remainder of the chapter.

[3] This is an example of a central limit theorem.

6.2 | Generation of pseudorandom numbers

We begin our discussion of simulation with a brief exploration of the mechanics of pseudorandom number generation. In particular, we will describe one of the simplest methods for *simulating* independent uniform random variables on the interval [0,1].

A multiplicative congruential random number generator produces a sequence of pseudorandom numbers, $u_0, u_1, u_2, \ldots$, which appear similar to independent uniform random variables on the interval [0,1].

Let m be a large integer, and let b be another integer which is smaller than m. The value of b is often chosen to be near the square root of m. Different values of b and m give rise to pseudorandom number generators of varying quality. There are various criteria available for choosing good values of these parameters, but it is always important to test the resulting generator to ensure that it is providing reasonable results.

To begin, an integer x_0 is chosen between 1 and m. x_0 is called the seed. We discuss strategies for choosing x_0 below.

Once the seed has been chosen, the generator proceeds as follows:

$$x_1 = b\, x_0 \pmod{m},$$
$$u_1 = x_1/m.$$

u_1 is the first pseudorandom number, taking some value between 0 and 1. The second pseudorandom number is then obtained in the same manner:

$$x_2 = b\, x_1 \pmod{m},$$
$$u_2 = x_2/m.$$

u_2 is another pseudorandom number. If m and b are chosen properly and are not disclosed to the user, it is difficult to predict the value of u_2, given the value of u_1 only. In other words, for most practical purposes u_2 is approximately independent of u_1. The method continues according to the following formulas:

$$x_n = b \, x_{n-1} \pmod{m},$$

$$u_n = x_n/m.$$

This method produces numbers which are entirely deterministic, but to an observer who doesn't know the formula above, the numbers appear to be random and unpredictable, at least in the short term.

Example 6.1

Take $m = 7$ and $b = 3$. Also, take $x_0 = 2$. Then

$$
\begin{aligned}
x_1 &= 3 \times 2 \pmod{7} = 6, & u_1 &= 0.857, \\
x_2 &= 3 \times 6 \pmod{7} = 4, & u_2 &= 0.571, \\
x_3 &= 3 \times 4 \pmod{7} = 5, & u_3 &= 0.714, \\
x_4 &= 3 \times 5 \pmod{7} = 1, & u_4 &= 0.143, \\
x_5 &= 3 \times 1 \pmod{7} = 3, & u_5 &= 0.429, \\
x_6 &= 3 \times 3 \pmod{7} = 2, & u_6 &= 0.286.
\end{aligned}
$$

It should be clear that the iteration will set $x_7 = x_1$ and cycle x_i through the same sequence of integers, so the corresponding sequence u_i will also be cyclic. An observer might not easily be able to predict u_2 from u_1, but since $u_{i+6} = u_i$ for all $i > 0$, longer sequences are very easy to predict. In order to produce an unpredictable sequence, it is desirable to have a very large cycle length so that it is unlikely that any observer will ever see a whole cycle. The cycle length cannot be any larger than m, so m would normally be taken to be very large.

Care must be taken in the choice of b and m to ensure that the cycle length is actually m. Note, for example, what happens when $b = 171$ and $m = 29241$. Start with $x_0 = 3$, say.

$$x_1 = 171 \times 3 = 513,$$

$$x_2 = 171 \times 513 \pmod{29241} = 0.$$

All remaining x_n values will be 0. To avoid this kind of problem, we should choose m so that it is not divisible by b; thus, prime values of m will be preferred. The next example gives a generator with somewhat better behavior.

Example 6.2

The following lines produce 50 pseudorandom numbers based on the multiplicative congruential generator:

$$x_n = 171 \, x_{n-1} \pmod{30269},$$

$$u_n = x_n/30269,$$

with initial seed $x_0 = 27218$.

```
random.number <- numeric(50) # this will store the
                              # pseudorandom output
random.seed <- 27218
for (j in 1:50) {
    random.seed <- (171 * random.seed) %% 30269
    random.number[j] <- random.seed / 30269
}
```

The results, stored in the vector `random.number`, are as follows. Note that the vector elements range between 0 and 1. These are the pseudorandom numbers, $u_1, u_2, \ldots, u_{50}$.

```
random.number

##  [1] 0.76385080 0.61848756 0.76137302 0.19478675 0.30853348 0.75922561
##  [7] 0.82757937 0.51607255 0.24840596 0.47741914 0.63867323 0.21312234
## [13] 0.44391952 0.91023820 0.65073177 0.27513297 0.04773861 0.16330239
## [19] 0.92470845 0.12514454 0.39971588 0.35141564 0.09207440 0.74472232
## [25] 0.34751726 0.42545178 0.75225478 0.63556774 0.68208398 0.63636063
## [31] 0.81766824 0.82126929 0.43704780 0.73517460 0.71485678 0.24051009
## [37] 0.12722587 0.75562457 0.21180085 0.21794575 0.26872378 0.95176583
## [43] 0.75195745 0.58472364 0.98774324 0.90409330 0.59995375 0.59209092
## [49] 0.24754700 0.33053619
```

A similar kind of operation (though using a different formula, and with a *much* longer cycle) is used internally by R to produce pseudorandom numbers automatically with the function `runif()`.

Syntax
`runif(n, min = a, max = b)`

Execution of this command produces n pseudorandom uniform numbers on the interval $[a, b]$. The default values are $a = 0$ and $b = 1$. The seed is selected internally.

Example 6.3
Generate 5 uniform pseudorandom numbers on the interval $[0, 1]$, and 10 uniform such numbers on the interval $[-3, -1]$.

```
runif(5)

## [1] 0.9502223 0.3357378 0.1330718 0.4901114 0.0607455

runif(10, min = -3, max = -1)

##  [1] -2.284105 -2.545768 -2.199852 -1.126908 -1.324746 -2.744848
##  [7] -1.549739 -1.445740 -2.834744 -1.372574
```

If you execute the above code yourself, you will almost certainly obtain different results than those displayed in our output. This is because the starting seed that you will use will be different from the one that was selected when we ran our code.

There are two different strategies for choosing the starting seed x_0. If the goal is to make an unpredictable sequence, then a random value is desirable. For example, the computer might determine the current time of day to the nearest millisecond, then base the starting seed on the number of milliseconds past the start of the minute. To avoid predictability, this external randomization should only be done once, after which the formula above should be used for updates. For example, if the computer clock were used as above before generating *every* u_i, on a fast computer there would be long sequences of identical values that were generated within a millisecond of each other.

The second strategy for choosing x_0 is to use a fixed, non-random value, e.g. $x_0 = 1$. This makes the sequence of u_i values predictable and repeatable. This would be useful when debugging a program that uses random numbers, or in other situations where repeatability is needed. The way to do this in R is to use the set.seed() function.

For example,

```
set.seed(32789)   # this ensures that your output will match ours
runif(5)

## [1] 0.3575211 0.3537589 0.2672321 0.9969302 0.1317401
```

Exercises

1 Generate 20 pseudorandom numbers using

$$x_n = 172\, x_{n-1} \pmod{30307}$$

with initial seed $x_0 = 17218$.

2 Generate 20 pseudorandom numbers using the multiplicative congruential generator with $b = 171$ and $m = 32767$ with an initial seed of 2018.

3 Use the runif() function (with set.seed(32078)) to generate 10 pseudorandom numbers from
   (a) the uniform $(0, 1)$ distribution.
   (b) the uniform $(3, 7)$ distribution.
   (c) the uniform $(-2, 2)$ distribution.

4 Generate 1000 uniform pseudorandom variates using the runif() function, assigning them to a vector called U. Use set.seed(19908).
   (a) Compute the average, variance, and standard deviation of the numbers in U.
   (b) Compare your results with the true mean, variance, and standard deviation.
   (c) Compute the proportion of the values of U that are less than 0.6, and compare with the probability that a uniform random variable U is less than 0.6.

(d) Estimate the expected value of $1/(U+1)$.

(e) Construct a histogram of the values of U, and of 1/(U+1).

5 Simulate 10000 independent observations on a uniformly distributed random variable on the interval [3.7,5.8].

(a) Estimate the mean, variance, and standard deviation of such a uniform random variable and compare your estimates with the true values.

(b) Estimate the probability that such a random variable is greater than 4.0. Compare with the true value.

6 Simulate 10000 values of a uniform $(0, 1)$ random variable, U_1, using runif(), and simulate another set of 10000 values of a uniform $(0, 1)$ random variable U_2. Assign these vectors to U1 and U2, respectively. Since the values in U1 and U2 are approximately independent, we can view U_1 and U_2 as independent uniform $(0, 1)$ random variables.

(a) Estimate $E[U_1 + U_2]$. Compare with the true value, and compare with an estimate of $E[U_1] + E[U_2]$.

(b) Estimate $\text{Var}(U_1 + U_2)$ and $\text{Var}(U_1) + \text{Var}(U_2)$. Are they equal? Should the true values be equal?

(c) Estimate $P(U_1 + U_2 \le 1.5)$.

(d) Estimate $P(\sqrt{U_1} + \sqrt{U_2}) \le 1.5)$.

7 Suppose U_1, U_2, and U_3 are independent uniform random variables on the interval $(0, 1)$. Use simulation to estimate the following quantities.

(a) $E[U_1 + U_2 + U_3]$.

(b) $\text{Var}(U_1 + U_2 + U_3)$ and $\text{Var}(U_1) + \text{Var}(U_2) + \text{Var}(U_3)$.

(c) $E[\sqrt{U_1 + U_2 + U_3}]$.

(d) $P(\sqrt{U_1} + \sqrt{U_2} + \sqrt{U_3} \ge 0.8)$.

8 Use the round() function together with runif() to generate 1000 pseudorandom integers which take values from 1 through 10, assigning these values to a vector called discreteunif. Use the table() function to check whether the observed frequencies for each value are close to what you expect. If they are not close, how should you modify your procedure?

9 The sample() function allows you to take a simple random sample from a vector of values. For example, sample(c(3,5,7), size = 2, replace = FALSE) will yield a vector of two values taken (without replacement) from the set {3,5,7}. Use the sample() function to generate 50 pseudorandom integers from 1 through 100,

(a) sampled without replacement,

(b) sampled with replacement.

10 The following code simulates the sum (X) and difference (Y) of two uniform random variables $(U_1$ and $U_2)$. A scatterplot of Y versus X is then displayed and the correlation between X and Y is estimated.

```
U2 <- runif(1000)
U1 <- runif(1000)
X <- U1 + U2
Y <- U1 - U2
plot(Y ~ X)
cor(X,Y)          # this calculates the sample correlation
```

The correlation gives a measure of *linear* dependence between two random variables. A value near 0 indicates almost no such dependence, while a value near -1 or 1 indicates the existence of a linear relationship.

Execute the above code and use the output to answer the following questions.

(a) Do you think that X and Y are linearly dependent?

(b) Do you think that X and Y are stochastically independent? (To answer this, look carefully at the scatterplot.)

(c) Do you think that U_1 and U_2 are linearly dependent? (Perform an appropriate calculation to check.)

(d) Do you think that U_1 and U_2 are stochastically independent? (Obtain an appropriate plot to check.)

6.3 | Simulation of other random variables

6.3.1 Bernoulli random variables

A Bernoulli trial is an experiment in which there are only two possible outcomes. For example, a light bulb may work or not work; these are the only possibilities. Each outcome ("work" or "not work") has a probability associated with it; the sum of these two probabilities must be 1.

Example 6.4

Consider a student who guesses on a multiple choice test question which has five options; the student may guess correctly with probability 0.2 and incorrectly with probability 0.8. (The possible outcome of a guess is to either be correct or to be incorrect.)

Suppose we would like to know how well such a student would do on a multiple choice test consisting of 20 questions. We can get an idea by using simulation.

Each question corresponds to an independent Bernoulli trial with probability of success equal to 0.2. We can simulate the correctness of the student for each question by generating an independent uniform random number. If this number is less than 0.2, we say that the student guessed correctly; otherwise, we say that the student guessed incorrectly.

This will work, because the probability that a uniform random variable is less than 0.2 is exactly 0.2, while the probability that a uniform random variable exceeds 0.2 is exactly 0.8, which is the same as the probability that the student guesses incorrectly. Thus, the uniform random number generator is simulating the student. R can do this as follows:

```
set.seed(23207) # use this to obtain our output
guesses <- runif(20)
correct.answers <- (guesses < 0.2)
correct.answers

##  [1] FALSE FALSE FALSE FALSE  TRUE  TRUE  TRUE FALSE  TRUE  TRUE FALSE
## [12] FALSE FALSE FALSE FALSE FALSE FALSE FALSE  TRUE
```

The vector `correct.answers` is a logical vector which contains the results of the simulated student's guesses; a `TRUE` value corresponds to a correct guess, while a `FALSE` corresponds to an incorrect guess. The total number of correct guesses can be calculated.

```
table(correct.answers)

## correct.answers
## FALSE   TRUE
##    14      6
```

Our simulated student would score 6/20.

In the preceding example, we could associate the values "1" and "0" with the outcomes from a Bernoulli trial. This defines the Bernoulli random variable: a random variable which takes the value 1 with probability p, and 0 with probability $1 - p$.

The expected value of a Bernoulli random variable is p and its theoretical variance is $p(1 - p)$. In the above example, a student would expect to guess correctly 20% of the time; our simulated student was a little bit lucky, obtaining a mark of 30%.

Exercises

1 Write an R function which simulates the outcomes of a student guessing at a True-False test consisting of n questions.

   (a) Use the function to simulate one student guessing the answers to a test with 10 questions; calculate the number of correct answers for this student.

   (b) Simulate the number of correct answers for a student who guesses at a test with 1000 questions.

2 Suppose a class of 100 writes a 20-question True-False test, and everyone in the class guesses at the answers.

   (a) Use simulation to estimate the average mark on the test as well as the standard deviation of the marks.

   (b) Estimate the proportion of students who would obtain a mark of 30% or higher.

3 Write an R function which simulates 500 light bulbs, each of which has probability 0.99 of working. Using simulation, estimate the expected value and variance of the random variable X, which is 1 if the light bulb works and 0 if the light bulb does not work. What are the theoretical values?

4 Write an R function which simulates a binomial random variable with $n = 25$ and $p = 0.4$. (This is a sum of 25 independent Bernoulli (p) random variables.) By generating 100 of these binomial random variables, estimate the mean and variance of such a binomial random variable. (Compare with the theoretical values: 10, 6.)

6.3.2 Binomial random variables

Let X denote the sum of m independent Bernoulli random variables, each having probability p. X is called a binomial random variable; it represents the number of "successes" in m Bernoulli trials.

A binomial random variable can take values in the set $\{0, 1, 2, \ldots, m\}$. The probability of a binomial random variable X taking on any one of these values is governed by the binomial distribution:

$$P(X = x) = \binom{m}{x} p^x (1 - p)^{m-x}, \quad x = 0, 1, 2, \ldots, m.$$

These probabilities can be computed using the dbinom() function.

Syntax
```
dbinom(x, size, prob)
```

Here, size and prob are the binomial parameters m and p, respectively, while x denotes the number of "successes." The output from this function is the value of $P(X = x)$.

Example 6.5
Compute the probability of getting four heads in six tosses of a fair coin.

```
dbinom(x = 4, size = 6, prob = 0.5)

## [1] 0.234375
```

Thus, $P(X = 4) = 0.234$, when X is a binomial random variable with $m = 6$ and $p = 0.5$.

Cumulative probabilities of the form $P(X \leq x)$ can be computed using pbinom(); this function takes the same arguments as dbinom(). For example, we can calculate $P(X \leq 4)$ where X is the number of heads obtained in six tosses of a fair coin as:

```
pbinom(4, 6, 0.5)

## [1] 0.890625
```

The function qbinom() gives the quantiles for the binomial distribution. The 89th percentile of the distribution of X (as defined above) is:

```
qbinom(0.89, 6, 0.5)

## [1] 4
```

The expected value (or mean) of a binomial random variable is mp and the variance is $mp(1 - p)$.

The rbinom() function can be used to generate binomial pseudorandom numbers.

Syntax
```
rbinom(n, size, prob)
```

Here, size and prob are the binomial parameters, while n is the number of variates generated.

Example 6.6

Suppose 10% of the water heater dip tubes produced by a machine are defective, and suppose 15 tubes are produced each hour. Each tube is independent of all other tubes. This process is judged to be out of control when more than five defective tubes are produced in any single hour. Simulate the number of defective tubes produced by the machine for each hour over a 24-hour period, and determine if any process should have been judged out of control at any point in that simulation run.

Since 15 tubes are produced each hour and each tube has a 0.1 probability of being defective, independent of the state of the other tubes, the number of defectives produced in one hour is a binomial random variable with $m = 15$ and $p = 0.1$. To simulate the number of defectives for each hour in a 24-hour period, we need to generate 24 binomial random numbers. We then identify all instances in which the number of defectives exceeds 5. One such simulation run is:

```
defectives <- rbinom(24, 15, 0.1)
defectives

## [1] 0 1 1 0 1 1 2 5 0 0 1 1 3 3 0 2 2 0 1 0 1 1 4 2

any(defectives > 5)

## [1] FALSE
```

Exercises

1 Suppose the proportion defective is 0.15 for a manufacturing operation. Simulate the number of defectives for each hour of a 24-hour period, assuming 25 units are produced each hour. Check if the number of defectives ever exceeds 5. Repeat, assuming $p = 0.2$ and then $p = 0.25$.

2 Simulate 10000 binomial pseudorandom numbers with parameters 20 and 0.3, assigning them to a vector called binsim. Let X be a Binomial(20, 0.3) random variable. Use the simulated numbers to estimate

(a) $P(X \leq 5)$.
(b) $P(X = 5)$.
(c) $E[X]$.
(d) $\text{Var}(X)$.
(e) The 95th percentile of X. (You may use the quantile() function.)
(f) The 99th percentile of X.
(g) The 99.9999th quantile of X.

In each case, compare your estimates with the true values. What is required to estimate extreme quantities accurately?

3 Use simulation to estimate the mean and variance of a binomial random variable with $n = 18$ and $p = 0.76$. Compare with the theoretical values.

4 Consider the following function which is designed to simulate binomial pseudorandom variates using the so-called *inversion* method.

```
ranbin <- function(n, size, prob) {
    cumpois <- pbinom(0:(size - 1), size, prob)
    singlenumber <- function() {
        x <- runif(1)
        N <- sum(x > cumpois)
        N
    }
    replicate(n, singlenumber())
}
```

(a) Study this function carefully and write documentation for it.[4] Note, particularly, what the operations in the `singlenumber()` function are for.

(b) Use `ranbin()` to simulate vectors of length 1000, 10000, and 100000 from the binomial distribution with size parameter 10 and probability parameter 0.4. Use the `microbenchmark()` function to compare the execution times for these simulations with the corresponding execution times when `rbinom()` is used.

5 The following function simulates binomial pseudorandom numbers by summing up the corresponding independent Bernoulli random variables.

```
ranbin2 <- function(n, size, prob) {
    singlenumber <- function(size, prob) {
        x <- runif(size)
        N <- sum(x < prob)
        N
    }
    replicate(n, singlenumber(size, prob))
}
```

(a) Study this function carefully and write documentation for it. Note, particularly, what the operations in the `singlenumber()` function are for.

(b) Use `ranbin2()` to simulate vectors of length 10000 from the binomial distribution with size parameters 10, 100, and 1000, and probability parameter 0.4. Use the `microbenchmark()` function to compare the execution times for these simulations with the corresponding execution times when `rbinom()` is used. Compare with execution times from the `ranbin()` function created in the previous exercise.

6 The generator in the previous exercise required `size` uniform pseudorandom numbers to be generated for each binomial number generated. The following generator is based on the same principle as the previous

[4] The `replicate()` function allows us to repeatedly call `singlenumber()`, assigning n results to a vector. See `help(replicate)` for more information.

one, but only requires one uniform pseudorandom number to be generated for each binomial number generated.

```
ranbin3 <- function(n, size, prob) {
    singlenumber <- function(size, prob) {
        k <- 0
        U <- runif(1)
        X <- numeric(size)
        while (k < size) {
            k <- k + 1
            if (U <= prob) {
                X[k] <- 1
                U <- U / prob
            } else {
                X[k] <- 0
                U <- (U - prob)/(1 - prob)
            }
        }
        return(sum(X))
    }
    replicate(n, singlenumber(size, prob))
}
```

(a) Use the `ranbin3()` function to generate 100 pseudorandom numbers from binomial distributions with parameters
   (i) `size` = 20 and `prob` = 0.4.
   (ii) `size` = 500 and `prob` = 0.7.
(b) What is the conditional distribution of U/p, given that $U < p$?
(c) What is the conditional distribution of $(U - p)/(1 - p)$, given that $U > p$?
(d) Use the answers to the above questions to provide documentation for the `ranbin3()` function.

7 One version of the central limit theorem says that if X is a binomial random variable with parameters m and p, and

$$Z = \frac{X - mp}{\sqrt{mp(1 - p)}},$$

then Z is approximately standard normal, and the approximation improves as m gets large.

The following code simulates a large number of such Z values for values of m in the set $\{1, 2, \ldots, 100\}$ and plots a normal QQ plot in each case.

```
for (m in 1:100) {
    z <- (rbinom(20000, size = m, prob = 0.4) - m * 0.4) /
        sqrt(m * 0.4 * 0.6)
    qqnorm(z, ylim = c(-4, 4), main = paste("QQ-plot, m = ", m))
    qqline(z)
}
```

(a) Execute the code and observe how the distribution of Z changes as m increases.

(b) Modify the code so that a similar "movie" is produced for the cases where $p = 0.3, 0.2, 0.1, 0.05$, respectively. How large must m be before you see a reasonably straight line in the QQ plot? Is $m = 100$ satisfactorily large in all cases?

6.3.3 Poisson random variables

The Poisson distribution is the limit of a sequence of binomial distributions with parameters n and p_n, where n is increasing to infinity, and p_n is decreasing to 0, but where the expected value (or mean) np_n converges to a constant λ. The variance $np_n(1 - p_n)$ converges to this same constant. Thus, the mean and variance of a Poisson random variable are both equal to λ. This parameter is sometimes referred to as a *rate*.

Poisson random variables arise in a number of different ways. They are often used as a crude model for count data. Examples of count data are the numbers of earthquakes in a region in a given year, or the number of individuals who arrive at a bank teller in a given hour. The limit comes from dividing the time period into n independent intervals, on which the count is either 0 or 1. The Poisson random variable is the total count.

The possible values that a Poisson random variable X could take are the nonnegative integers $\{0, 1, 2, \ldots\}$. The probability of taking on any of these values is

$$P(X = x) = \frac{e^{-x}\lambda^x}{x!}, \quad x = 0, 1, 2, \ldots.$$

These probabilities can be evaluated using the dpois() function.

Syntax
```
dpois(x, lambda)
```

Here, lambda is the Poisson rate parameter, while x is the number of Poisson events. The output from the function is the value of $P(X = x)$.

Example 6.7
According to the Poisson model, the probability of three arrivals at an automatic bank teller in the next minute, where the average number of arrivals per minute is 0.5, is

```
dpois(x = 3, lambda = 0.5)

## [1] 0.01263606
```

Therefore, $P(X = 3) = 0.0126$, if X is a Poisson random variable with mean 0.5.

Cumulative probabilities of the form $P(X \leq x)$ can be calculated using ppois(), and Poisson quantiles can be computed using qpois().

We can generate Poisson random numbers using the rpois() function.

Syntax

```
rpois(n, lambda)
```

The parameter `n` is the number of variates produced, and `lambda` is as above.

Example 6.8

Suppose traffic accidents occur at an intersection with a mean rate of 3.7 per year. Simulate the annual number of accidents for a 10-year period, assuming a Poisson model.

```
rpois(10, 3.7)
## [1] 6 7 2 3 5 7 6 2 4 4
```

Poisson processes

A Poisson process is a simple model of the collection of events that occur during an interval of time. A way of thinking about a Poisson process is to think of a random collection of points on a line or in the plane (or in higher dimensions, if necessary).

The homogeneous Poisson process has the following properties:

1. The distribution of the number of points in a set is Poisson with rate proportional to the size of the set.
2. The numbers of points in non-overlapping sets are independent of each other.

In particular, for a Poisson process with rate λ the number of points on an interval $[0, T]$ is Poisson distributed with mean λT. One way to simulate this is as follows.

1. Generate N as a Poisson pseudorandom number with parameter λT.
2. Generate N independent uniform pseudorandom numbers on the interval $[0, T]$.

Example 6.9

Simulate points of a homogeneous Poisson process having rate 1.5 on the interval $[0, 10]$.

```
N <- rpois(1, 1.5 * 10)
P <- runif(N, max = 10)
sort(P)

##  [1] 0.0321442 0.1173187 0.2542297 2.4376206 3.9358325 4.0503778
##  [7] 4.5093112 5.2883388 7.4392293 8.4700712 8.7615109 8.8157830
## [13] 9.3580064
```

Exercises

1 Simulate the number of accidents for each year for 15 years, when the average rate is 2.8 accidents per year, assuming a Poisson model for numbers of accidents each year.

2 Simulate the number of surface defects in the finish of a sports car for 20 cars, where the mean rate is 1.2 defects per car.

3 Estimate the mean and variance of a Poisson random variable whose mean is 7.2 by simulating 10000 Poisson pseudorandom numbers. Compare with the theoretical values.

4 Simulate vectors of 10000 pseudorandom Poisson variates with mean 5, 10, 15, and 20, assigning the results to P5, P10, P15, and P20, respectively.

   (a) Estimate $E[\sqrt{X}]$ and $\mathrm{Var}(\sqrt{X})$, where X is Poisson with rates $\lambda = 5, 10, 15$, and 20.

   (b) Noting that the variance of X increases with the mean of X, when X is a Poisson random variable, what is the effect of taking a square root of X on the relationship between the variance and the mean? (Statisticians often take square roots of count data to "stabilize the variance"; do you understand what this means?)

5 Conduct a simulation experiment to check the reasonableness of the assertion that the distribution of the number of points from a rate 1.5 Poisson process which fall in the interval $[4, 5]$ is Poisson with mean 1.5 by the following simulation. First, simulate a large number of realizations of the Poisson process on the interval $[0, 10]$. Then count the number of points in $[4, 5]$ for each realization. Compare this set of counts with simulated Poisson values using a QQ plot. We supply the code for this below, and leave it to you to execute it and look at the resulting graph.

```
poissonproc <- function() {
    N <- rpois(1, 1.5 * 10)
    P <- runif(N, max = 10)
    return(sum( 4 <= P & P <= 5 ))
}
counts <- replicate(10000, poissonproc())
qqplot(counts, rpois(10000, 1.5))
abline(0, 1) # the points lie reasonably close to this line
```

6 One version of the central limit theorem says that if X is a Poisson random variable with parameter λ, and

$$Z = \frac{X - \lambda}{\sqrt{\lambda}},$$

then Z is approximately standard normal, and the approximation improves as λ gets large.

The following code simulates a large number of such Z values for values of λ in the set $\{1, 3, \ldots, 99\}$ and plots a normal QQ plot in each case.

```
for (m in seq(1, 100, 2)) {
    z <- (rpois(20000, lambda = m) - m) / sqrt(m)
    qqnorm(z, ylim = c(-4, 4), main = "QQ-plot")
    qqline(z)
    mtext(bquote(lambda == .(m)), 3)   # this creates a subtitle which
                                        # mixes mathematical and numerical notation
}
```

(a) Execute the code and observe how the distribution of Z changes as λ increases.

(b) How large must λ be before you see a reasonably straight line in the QQ plot?

7 Simulate 10000 realizations of a Poisson process with rate 2.5 on the interval $[0, 2]$.

(a) In each case, count the number of points in the subintervals $[0, 1]$ and $[1, 2]$.

(b) Are the counts in part (a) reasonably approximated by Poisson distributions with rate 2.5?

(c) Using an appropriate scatterplot, make a judgment as to whether it is reasonable to assume that the number of points in the interval $[0, 1]$ is independent of the number in $[1, 2]$. (In order for the scatterplot to be useful, it will be necessary to use the `jitter()` function.)

8 The times of onset of rain can be approximately modeled as a Poisson process. For example, the onset of rain during the months of July and August at the Winnipeg International Airport is fairly well modeled by such a process with rate 0.023 onsets/hour. Use this model to simulate times of the onset of rain at the Winnipeg airport for a two-month period. Identify at least one way in which the Poisson process could fail as a model for the times at which rain starts in a location.

9 Poisson processes can be defined in dimensions higher than 1. Such models are used in fields such as ecology when comparing observed locations of say, tree saplings, with what would result from a "completely random" process.

In a homogeneous 2-dimensional Poisson process, the distribution of points in a region is Poisson with rate proportional to its area, and the numbers of points in non-overlapping regions are independent of each other. Use the following code to plot a 2-dimensional Poisson process of points having rate $\lambda = 2$ per unit area, in the square $[0, 10] \times [0, 10]$.

```
lambda <- 2
regionlength <- 10
regionwidth <- 10
N <- rpois(1, lambda*regionlength*regionwidth)
U1 <- runif(N, min=0, max=regionwidth)
U2 <- runif(N, min=0, max=regionlength)
```

As usual, you can use the `plot()` function to display the spatial locations of the points.

```
plot(U1, U2)
```

Modify the code so that it is a Poisson process with rate $\lambda = 4$ per unit area, and plot the result, comparing the number of points with the $\lambda = 2$ case.

10 Referring to the previous exercise, suppose tree saplings are observed in a 15 square meter region at a rate of 0.25 per square meter. Under the assumption that the sapling locations follow a homogeneous Poisson process, simulate a single realization and plot the resulting point pattern. From what you know about tree saplings, identify at least one problem with the Poisson process as a model for this phenomenon.

6.3.4 Exponential random numbers

Exponential random variables are used as simple models for such things as failure times of mechanical or electronic components, or for the time it takes a server to complete service to a customer. The exponential distribution is characterized by a constant *failure rate*, denoted by λ.

T has an exponential distribution with rate $\lambda > 0$ if

$$P(T \leq t) = 1 - e^{-\lambda t}$$

for any nonnegative t. The pexp() function can be used to evaluate this function.

Syntax
```
pexp(q, rate)
```

The output from this is the value of $P(T \leq q)$, where T is an exponential random variable with parameter rate.

Example 6.10

Suppose the service time at a bank teller can be modeled as an exponential random variable with rate 3 per minute. Then the probability of a customer being served in less than 1 minute is

```
pexp(1, rate = 3)

## [1] 0.9502129
```

Thus, $P(X \leq 1) = 0.95$, when X is an exponential random variable with rate 3.

Differentiating the right-hand side of the distribution function with respect to t gives the exponential probability density function:

$$f(t) = \lambda e^{-\lambda t}.$$

The dexp() function can be used to evaluate this. It takes the same arguments as the pexp() function. The qexp() function can be used to obtain quantiles of the exponential distribution.

The expected value of an exponential random variable is $1/\lambda$, and the variance is $1/\lambda^2$.

A simple way to simulate exponential pseudorandom variates is based on the *inversion* method. For an exponential random variable $F(x) = 1 - e^{-\lambda x}$, so $F^{-1}(x) = -\frac{\log(1-U)}{\lambda}$. Therefore, for any $x \in (0, 1)$, we have

$$P(F(T) \leq x) = P(T \leq F^{-1}(x)) = F(F^{-1}(x)) = x.$$

Thus, $F(T)$ is a uniform random variable on the interval $(0, 1)$. Since we know how to generate uniform pseudorandom variates, we can obtain exponential variates by applying the inverse transformation $F^{-1}(x)$ to them.

That is, generate a uniform pseudorandom variable U on $[0,1]$, and set

$$1 - e^{-\lambda T} = U.$$

Solving this for T, we have

$$T = -\frac{\log(1 - U)}{\lambda}.$$

T has an exponential distribution with rate λ.

The R function `rexp()` can be used to generate n random exponential variates.

Syntax
```
rexp(n, rate)
```

Example 6.11
A bank has a single teller who is facing a lineup of 10 customers. The time for each customer to be served is exponentially distributed with rate 3 per minute. We can simulate the service times (in minutes) for the 10 customers.

```
servicetimes <- rexp(10, rate = 3)
servicetimes

##  [1] 0.25415279 0.79177402 0.24280817 0.07887371 0.10738250 0.16583246
##  [7] 0.83294959 0.09676131 0.16938459 0.53317718
```

The total time until these 10 simulated customers will complete service is around 3 minutes and 16 seconds:

```
sum(servicetimes)

## [1] 3.273096
```

Another way to simulate a Poisson process
It can be shown that the points of a homogeneous Poisson process with rate λ on the line are separated by independent exponentially distributed

random variables which have mean $1/\lambda$. This leads to another simple way of simulating a Poisson process on the line.

Example 6.12
Simulate the first 25 points of a Poisson 1.5 process, starting from 0.

```
X <- rexp(25, rate = 1.5)
cumsum(X)
```

```
##  [1]  1.406436  1.608897  1.800167  3.044730  3.160853  3.640911
##  [7]  4.827413  5.229759  6.542869  6.596817  7.305832  8.134470
## [13] 10.704220 11.412163 11.515945 11.642972 12.277173 12.505261
## [19] 15.205137 15.548352 16.727192 17.381278 17.678511 18.457350
## [25] 18.658113
```

Exercises

1 Simulate 50000 exponential random numbers having rate 3.
  (a) Find the proportion of these numbers which are less than 1. Compare with the probability that an exponential random variable with rate 3 will be less than 1.
  (b) Compute the average of these numbers. Compare with the expected value.
  (c) Calculate the variance of this sample, and compare with the theoretical value.

2 Suppose that a certain type of battery has a lifetime which is exponentially distributed with mean 55 hours. Use simulation to estimate the average and variance of the lifetime for this type of battery. Compare with the theoretical values.

3 A simple electronic device consists of two components which have failure times which may be modeled as independent exponential random variables. The first component has a mean time to failure of 3 months, and the second has a mean time to failure of 6 months. The electronic device will fail when either of the components fails. Use simulation to estimate the mean and variance of the time to failure for the device.

4 Re-do the calculation in the previous question under the assumption that the device will fail only when both components fail.

5 Simulate 10000 realizations of a Poisson process with rate 2.5, using the method described in this section. Check that the distribution of the number of points in the interval $[0, 2]$ is reasonably close to a Poisson distribution with mean 5.

6.3.5 Normal random variables
A normal random variable X has a probability density function given by

$$f(x) = \frac{1}{\sigma\sqrt{2\pi}} e^{-\frac{(x-\mu)^2}{2\sigma^2}},$$

where μ is the expected value of X, and σ^2 denotes the variance of X. The *standard normal* random variable has mean $\mu = 0$ and standard deviation $\sigma = 1$.

The normal density function can be evaluated using the `dnorm()` function, the distribution function can be evaluated using `pnorm()`, and the quantiles of the normal distribution can be obtained using `qnorm()`. For example, the 95th percentile of the normal distribution with mean 2.7 and standard deviation 3.3 is:

```
qnorm(0.95, mean = 2.7, sd = 3.3)

## [1] 8.128017
```

Normal pseudorandom variables can be generated using the `rnorm()` function in R.

Syntax
```
rnorm(n, mean, sd)
```

This produces n normal pseudorandom variates which have mean `mean` and standard deviation `sd`.

Example 6.13
We can simulate 10 independent normal variates with a mean of -3 and standard deviation of 0.5 using

```
rnorm(10, -3, 0.5)

##   [1] -3.520803 -3.130006 -2.682143 -2.330936 -3.158297 -3.293808
##   [7] -3.171530 -2.815075 -2.783860 -2.899138
```

We can simulate random numbers from certain conditional distributions by first simulating according to an unconditional distribution, and then rejecting those numbers which do not satisfy the specified condition.

Example 6.14
Simulate x from the standard normal distribution, conditional on the event that $0 < x < 3$. We will simulate from the entire normal distribution and then accept only those values which lie between 0 and 3.

We can simulate a large number of such variates as follows:

```
x <- rnorm(100000)          # simulate from the standard normal
x <- x[(0 < x) & (x < 3)]   # reject all x's outside (0,3)
hist(x, probability=TRUE)   # show the simulated values
```

Figure 6.1 shows how the histogram tracks the rescaled normal density over the interval $(0, 3)$.

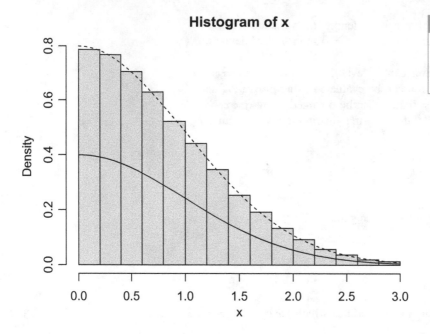

Histogram of x

Fig. 6.1 Histogram of simulated values with the standard normal density (solid curve) and the rescaled normal density (dashed curve) overlaid.

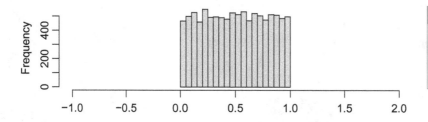

Fig. 6.2 Histogram of 10000 values of $e^{-(Z_1^2+Z_2^2)/2}$ where Z_1 and Z_2 are simulated independent standard normal random variates.

6.3.6 Generating normal variates using the Box–Müller transformation

Because the normal CDF and quantile functions cannot be written in closed form, it is not possible to find a convenient formula that converts a single uniform random variable into a normal random variable. However, there is a simple formula that converts pairs of independent uniform random variables into pairs of independent normal random variables.

If Z_1 and Z_2 are independent normal random variables, and we set $D = \sqrt{Z_1^2 + Z_2^2}$, then it can be shown that $\exp(-D^2/2)$ has a uniform distribution on $[0, 1]$. This can be checked by simulation as follows. Simulate a large number of pairs of independent standard normal variates Z_1 and Z_2, and plot the histogram of the calculated values of $\exp[-(Z_1^2 + Z_2^2)/2]$. The result should approximate a rectangle located on the interval $[0, 1]$. Figure 6.2 displays a such a histogram, resulting from the following code:

```
Z1 <- rnorm(10000)
Z2 <- rnorm(10000)
hist(exp(-(Z1^2 + Z2^2)/2), main="", xlim=c(-1, 2))
```

Indeed, we see that $e^{-D^2/2}$ follows a uniform distribution on $[0, 1]$. Therefore, we can identify $e^{-D^2/2}$ with a uniform random variable U:

$$U = e^{-D^2/2}.$$

We can invert this transformation, i.e. solve this equation for D in terms of U, to see that

$$D = \sqrt{-2\log(U)}.$$

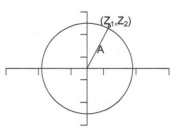

Fig. 6.3 Location of a pair of independent standard normal variates on a circle of given radius (i.e. the length of the segment A).

Another observation about the (Z_1, Z_2) pair is that when plotted as a point on the plane, the location of the point must be a distance $D = \sqrt{Z_1^2 + Z_2^2}$ from the origin. This means that the point must be located on a circle which is centered at the origin. The joint density of (z_1, z_2) is $f(z_1, z_2) = (1/2\pi) \exp(-z_1^2/2 - z_2^2/2)$ which is constant on the circle, so they are equally likely to be located anywhere on it (Figure 6.3). In other words, the angle between the segment A and the horizontal axis follows a uniform distribution on the interval $[0, 2\pi]$. Thus if V has a uniform distribution on $[0, 2\pi]$, we can generate the (Z_1, Z_2) pair using $Z_1 = D\cos(V)$ and $Z_2 = D\sin(V)$.

These observations provide us with the Box–Müller approach to converting uniform random numbers into standard normal random numbers:

```
U <- runif(n) # generate n uniform[0,1] values
D <- sqrt(-2*log(U)) # calculate the distance
V <- runif(n, 0, 2*pi) #generate uniform[0,2pi] values
Z1 <- D*cos(V)
Z2 <- D*sin(V)
```

The result is two independent sets of independent standard normal variates. Figure 6.4 shows histograms of simulated samples of 100000 Z_1 and Z_2. As expected, the distribution shapes match the standard normal distribution closely.

Generating normal random variates with the Box–Müller transformation is an option for the `rnorm()` function. In order to use this option, type

```
RNGkind(normal.kind = "Box-Muller")
```

prior to invoking your call to `rnorm()`. This option can give a slight improvement in speed over the default method. On the other hand, the default method gives a slightly better approximation to the normal distribution when computed using standard computer arithmetic. You would only notice these differences if you needed to simulate billions of numbers. Run

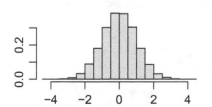

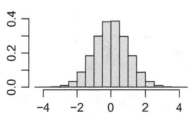

Fig. 6.4 Histograms of Z_1 and Z_2 variates obtained by the Box–Müller transformation method.

```
RNGkind(normal.kind = "default")
```

to return to the standard generator.

6.3.7 All built-in distributions

There are many standard distributions built in to R. These follow a general naming convention: rXXXX generates random values, dXXXX gives the density or probability function, pXXXX gives the cumulative distribution function, and qXXXX gives the quantiles. Table 6.1 lists many of the univariate continuous distributions, and Table 6.2 lists many of the univariate discrete distributions. For simplicity, the normalizing constants in the densities and probability functions have been omitted.

Exercises

1 Simulate 100 realizations of a normal random variable having mean 51 and standard deviation 5.2. Estimate the mean and standard deviation of your simulated sample and compare with the theoretical values.

2 Simulate 1000 realizations of a standard normal random variable Z, and use your simulated sample to estimate
  (a) $P(Z > 2.5)$.
  (b) $P(0 < Z < 1.645)$.
  (c) $P(1.2 < Z < 1.45)$.
  (d) $P(-1.2 < Z < 1.3)$.
  Compare with the theoretical values.

Table 6.1 | *Continuous distributions built in to R.*

Name	rXXXX	Parameters	Range	Mean	Kernel of Density
Beta	rbeta	shape1 = α shape2 = β	$0 < x < 1$	$\dfrac{\alpha}{\alpha + \beta}$	$x^{\alpha-1}(1-x)^{\beta-1}$
Cauchy	rcauchy	location = l scale = s	$-\infty < x < \infty$		$\dfrac{1}{(1 + (x-l)/s)^2}$
Chi-square	rchisq	df = ν	$x > 0$	ν	$x^{\nu/2-1}e^{-x/2}$
Exponential	rexp	rate = λ	$x > 0$	$1/\lambda$	$\exp(-\lambda x)$
F	rf	df1 = ν_1 df2 = ν_2	$x > 0$	$\dfrac{\nu_2}{\nu_2 - 2}$	$\dfrac{x^{\nu_1/2-1}}{(\nu_1 x + \nu_2)^{(\nu_1+\nu_2)/2}}$
Gamma	rgamma	shape = α rate = β	$x > 0$	$\dfrac{\alpha}{\beta}$	$x^{\alpha-1}e^{-\beta x}$
Logistic	rlogis	location = m scale = s	$-\infty < x < \infty$	m	$\dfrac{\exp\left(\frac{x-m}{s}\right)}{\left[1 + \exp\left(\frac{x-m}{s}\right)\right]^2}$
Lognormal	rlognorm	meanlog = μ sdlog = σ	$x > 0$	$e^{\mu+\sigma^2/2}$	$\dfrac{1}{x}\exp\left(-\dfrac{(\log x - \mu)^2}{2\sigma^2}\right)$
Normal	rnorm	mean = μ sd = σ	$-\infty < x < \infty$	μ	$\exp\left(-\dfrac{(x-\mu)^2}{2\sigma^2}\right)$
Student's t	rt	df = ν	$-\infty < x < \infty$	0	$(1 + x^2/\nu)^{-(n+1)/2}$
Uniform	runif	min = a max = b	$a < x < b$	$\dfrac{a+b}{2}$	1
Weibull	rweibull	shape = a scale = b	$x > 0$	$b\Gamma(1 + 1/a)$	$x^{a-1}\exp\left[-\left(\dfrac{x}{b}\right)^a\right]$

Table 6.2 | *Discrete distributions built in to R.*

Name	rXXXX	Parameters	Range	Mean	Kernel of Probability
Binomial	rbinom	$\text{size} = n$ $\text{prob} = p$	$x = 0, \ldots, n$	np	$\binom{n}{x} p^x (1-p)^{n-x}$
Geometric	rgeom	$\text{prob} = p$	$x = 0, 1, \ldots$	$\dfrac{1-p}{p}$	$(1-p)^x$
Hypergeometric	rhyper	m, n, k	$x = \max(0, k-n), \ldots,$ $\min(m, k)$	$\dfrac{km}{m+n}$	$\binom{m}{x}\binom{n}{k-x}$
Negative binomial	rnbinom	$\text{size} = n$ $\text{prob} = p$	$x = 0, 1, \ldots$	$n\dfrac{1-p}{p}$	$\binom{x+n-1}{x}(1-p)^x$
Poisson	rpois	$\text{lambda} = \lambda$	$x = 0, 1, \ldots$	λ	$\dfrac{\lambda^x}{x!}$

3 Simulate from the conditional distribution of a normal random variable X with mean 3 and variance 16, given that $|X| > 2$.

4 Using the fact that a χ^2 random variable on 1 degree of freedom has the same distribution as the square of a standard normal random variable, simulate 100 independent realizations of such a χ^2 random variable, and estimate its mean and variance. (Compare with the theoretical values: 1, 2.)

5 A χ^2 random variable on n degrees of freedom has the same distribution as the sum of n independent standard normal random variables. Simulate a χ^2 random variable on 8 degrees of freedom, and estimate its mean and variance. (Compare with the theoretical values: 8, 16.)

6 What is the default method used in `rnorm()` to generate normal random variates? Hint: read the documentation on the function `RNGkind`. Use `microbenchmark()` to compare timings for the Box–Müller method with the default method when applied to the function

```
test <- function() for (i in 1:10) x <- rnorm(100000000)
```

7 Suppose Y has an exponential distribution with scale parameter b^a (i.e. rate parameter $\lambda = b^{-a}$).

(a) It can be shown that if $X = Y^{1/a}$, then X is a Weibull random variable with shape parameter a and scale parameter b. Use this fact to derive a method of simulating a sample of Weibull random variates, given a sample of exponential random variates.

(b) Write a function that takes n, a, and b as input and which returns n Weibull random variates having shape parameter a and scale parameter b.

6.4 | Multivariate random number generation

Most interesting problems in statistics and applied probability don't involve just one random value, they will involve several values that are related. R has a few multivariate distributions built in, but in many cases users need to construct their own simulations. There are many techniques for doing this. We will describe just one: sequential conditional generation.

The idea of this technique is that even if $X = (X_1, X_2, \ldots, X_p)$ has a complicated p-dimensional distribution, X_1 will have a 1-dimensional marginal distribution. So we start by simulating just X_1, then simulate X_2 from its conditional distribution given X_1, and X_3 conditional on X_1 and X_2, and so on. If it is difficult to calculate marginal and conditional distributions then this might not be feasible, but in a surprising number of cases, it is not.

Example 6.15

A model commonly used in financial engineering says that the price of a stock X_{t+1} at the close of trading on day $t+1$ is equal to the closing price X_t on the previous day, multiplied by a value whose logarithm has a normal distribution. The multipliers are independent from day to day.

Suppose a stock starts at \$100.00 per share, and we expect a 1% change in price from one day to the next. What would be the joint distribution of the prices over the next five days? What is the probability that it remains above \$100 on all five days?

We can simulate this by starting with $X_0 = 100$, and multiplying by $\exp(Z_t)$, where Z_t, $t = 1, \ldots, 5$ are independent normal random variables with mean 0 and standard deviation of $\log(1.01)$. We do this in a `replicate()` loop to get 1000 examples of the simulation:

```
X <- numeric(6)
X[1] <- 100
results <- replicate(1000, {
  for (t in 1:5)
    X[t + 1]  <- X[t] * exp(rnorm(1, mean = 0, sd = log(1.01)))
  X
})
str(results)

##   num [1:6, 1:1000] 100 100.6 100.8 99.8 100.8 ...
```

We see that they have been returned in a matrix with 6 rows and 1000 columns. How many of those cases have all values greater than 100?

```
table(apply(results, 2, function(x) all(x[2:6] > 100)))

##
## FALSE   TRUE
##   757    243
```

We see that it happens about a quarter of the time.

Exercises

1 We can use the method of this section to simulate data coming from the bivariate probability model of Example 3.11. The probability density function given in the example can be factored as

$$f_{X_1,X_2}(x_1,x_2) = f_{X_2|X_1}(x_1,x_2)f_{X_1}(x_1),$$

where the function $f_{X_2|X_1}(x_1,x_2)$ gives the conditional probability density of X_2, given X_1, and $f_{X_1}(x_1)$ denotes the marginal density of X_1. The marginal density of X_1 is, in fact, a Weibull model with parameters $a = \alpha_1$ and $b = \beta_2^{1/\alpha_1}$, and the conditional density of X_2 given X_1 is Weibull with $a = \alpha_2$ and $b = (\beta_0 + \beta_1 x_1)^{1/\alpha_2}$.

(a) Write a function which takes as input n and a five-component vector par (which contains slots for the five α and β parameters) and returns n pairs of simulated values from the bivariate density by first simulating X_1, from its Weibull marginal distribution, and then simulating X_2 from its Weibull conditional distribution, given X_1.

(b) Test your simulator by generating 366 bivariate pairs, using the parameter values specified in Example 3.11. Reproduce the plot shown in Figure 3.23, but use your simulated data in place of the real data.

6.5 | Markov chain simulation

Markov chains are sequences of random variables $X_0, X_1, \ldots$ where the distribution of X_{t+1}, conditional on all previous values, depends only on X_t. They are commonly used in modeling systems with short memories, such as the stock market where the price tomorrow is modeled to depend only on the price today, biological systems where the genome of the offspring depends only on the genome of the parents, etc. When X_t is a discrete random variable with a finite number of states $1, \ldots, n$, it is convenient to represent the conditional distributions in an $n \times n$ matrix P, where entry P_{ij} holds the conditional probability that $X_{t+1} = j$ given that $X_t = i$. Because probabilities sum to 1, we have row sums $\sum_{j=1}^{n} P_{ij} = 1$ for all $i = 1, \ldots, n$.

Simulation of such Markov chains in R is easy using the sequential conditional simulation method that was described in the previous section. The value of X_{t+1} is simply the value drawn by

```
sample(1:n, size = 1, prob = P[X[t], ])
```

An interesting fact about Markov chains is that they have an *invariant distribution*, i.e. a distribution $P(X_t = i) = \pi_i$ such that if X_t is drawn from the invariant distribution and updated using the P matrix, then the marginal distribution of X_{t+1} will also be the invariant distribution. (For some P, there will be more than one invariant distribution, but there is always at least one.) Even more interesting is the fact that for *some* P matrices, if X_0 is drawn from *any* distribution, then the marginal distribution of X_t for large t approximates the invariant distribution. This is used in methods called Markov chain Monte Carlo (or MCMC) to draw values with distribution close to π_i even when π_i can't be calculated directly. We'll see MCMC again in Section 6.7.4.

Example 6.16

Consider a model of a disease with three stages. Stage 1 is healthy, stage 2 is mild disease, and stage 3 is severe disease. Healthy individuals remain healthy with probability 0.99 and develop mild disease with probability 0.01. Individuals with mild disease are cured and become healthy with probability 0.5, remain with mild disease with probability 0.4, and progress to serious disease with probability 0.1. Finally, those with severe disease stay in that state with probability 0.75, and improve to mild disease with probability 0.25.

This describes a Markov chain with three states, and

$$P = \begin{bmatrix} 0.99 & 0.01 & 0.00 \\ 0.50 & 0.40 & 0.10 \\ 0.00 & 0.25 & 0.75 \end{bmatrix}.$$

We will simulate two individuals for 10000 steps: one who starts healthy, and one who starts with severe disease:

```
P <- matrix(c(0.99, 0.01,   0,
              0.5,  0.4,     0.1,
              0,    0.25,    0.75), 3, 3, byrow = TRUE)
healthy <- numeric(10000)
healthy[1] <- 1
for (t in 1:9999)
  healthy[t + 1] <- sample(1:3, size = 1, prob = P[healthy[t], ])
table(healthy)

## healthy
##    1    2    3
## 9698  221   81

sick <- numeric(10000)
sick[1] <- 3
for (t in 1:9999)
  sick[t + 1] <- sample(1:3, size = 1, prob = P[sick[t], ])
table(sick)

## sick
##    1    2    3
## 9712  213   75
```

We see that the two individuals have very similar distributions of states over the 10000 steps. In fact, their distribution is close to the (unique) invariant distribution for *P*, which can be shown by other means (e.g. see Chapter Exercise 1 in Chapter 7) to be approximately $(0.973, 0.020, 0.008)$.

6.6 | Monte Carlo integration

Suppose $g(x)$ is any function that is integrable on the interval $[a, b]$. The integral

$$\int_a^b g(x)dx$$

gives the area of the region with $a < x < b$ and y between 0 and $g(x)$ (where negative values count towards negative areas).

Monte Carlo integration uses simulation to obtain approximations to these integrals. It relies on the law of large numbers. This law says that a sample mean from a large random sample will tend to be close to the expected value of the distribution being sampled. If we can express an integral as an expected value, we can approximate it by a sample mean.

For example, let $U_1, U_2, \ldots, U_n$ be independent uniform random variables on the interval $[a, b]$. These have density $f(u) = 1/(b - a)$ on that interval. Then

$$E[g(U_i)] = \int_a^b g(u)\frac{1}{b - a}du,$$

so the original integral $\int_a^b g(x)dx$ can be approximated by $b - a$ times a sample mean of $g(U_i)$.

Example 6.17
To approximate the integral $\int_0^1 x^4 dx$, use the following lines:

```
u <- runif(100000)
mean(u^4)
```

```
## [1] 0.2005908
```

Compare the exact answer 0.2 which can easily be computed in this case.

Example 6.18
To approximate the integral $\int_2^5 \sin(x)dx$, use the following lines:

```
u <- runif(100000, min = 2, max = 5)
mean(sin(u))*(5-2)
```

```
## [1] -0.6851379
```

The true value can be shown to be -0.700.

Multiple integration

Now let $V_1, V_2, \ldots, V_n$ be an additional set of independent uniform random variables on the interval $[0,1]$, and suppose $g(x,y)$ is now an integrable function of the two variables x and y. The law of large numbers says that

$$\lim_{n\to\infty} \sum_{i=1}^{n} g(U_i, V_i)/n = \int_0^1 \int_0^1 g(x,y)dxdy$$

with probability 1.

So we can approximate the integral $\int_0^1 \int_0^1 g(x,y)dxdy$ by generating two sets of independent uniform pseudorandom variates, computing $g(U_i, V_i)$ for each one, and taking the average.

Example 6.19

Approximate the integral $\int_3^{10} \int_1^7 \sin(x-y)dxdy$ using the following:

```
U <- runif(100000, min = 1, max = 7)
V <- runif(100000, min = 3, max = 10)
mean(sin(U - V))*42

## [1] 0.07989664
```

The factor of $42 = (7-1)(10-3)$ compensates for the joint density of U and V being $f(u,v) = 1/42$.

The uniform density is by no means the only density that can be used in Monte Carlo integration. If the density of X is $f(x)$, then $E[g(X)/f(X)] = \int [g(x)/f(x)]f(x)dx = \int g(x)dx$ so we can approximate the latter by sample averages of $g(X)/f(X)$.

Example 6.20

To approximate the integral $\int_1^\infty \exp(-x^2)dx$, write it instead as $\int_0^\infty \exp[-(x+1)^2]dx$, and use an exponential distribution for X:

```
X <- rexp(100000)
mean( exp( -(X + 1)^2 ) / dexp(X) )

## [1] 0.140112
```

The true value of this integral is 0.1394.

Monte Carlo integration is not always successful: sometimes the ratio $g(X)/f(X)$ varies so much that the sample mean doesn't converge. Try to choose $f(x)$ so this ratio is roughly constant, and avoid situations where $g(x)/f(x)$ can be arbitrarily large.

Exercises

1 Use Monte Carlo integration to estimate the following integrals. Compare with the exact answer, if known.

$$\int_0^1 x\,dx, \quad \int_1^3 x^2\,dx, \quad \int_0^\pi \sin(x)\,dx, \quad \int_1^\pi e^x\,dx, \quad \int_0^\infty e^{-x}\,dx,$$

$$\int_0^\infty e^{-x^3}\,dx, \quad \int_0^3 \sin(e^x)\,dx, \quad \int_0^1 \frac{1}{\sqrt{2\pi}}e^{-x^2/2}\,dx,$$

$$\int_0^2 \frac{1}{\sqrt{2\pi}}e^{-x^2/2}\,dx, \quad \int_0^3 \frac{1}{\sqrt{2\pi}}e^{-x^2/2}\,dx.$$

2 Use Monte Carlo integration to estimate the following double integrals.

$$\int_0^1 \int_0^1 \cos(x-y)\,dx\,dy, \quad \int_0^1 \int_0^1 e^{-(y+x)^2}(x+y)^2\,dx\,dy,$$

$$\int_0^3 \int_0^1 \cos(x-y)\,dx\,dy, \quad \int_0^5 \int_0^2 e^{-(y+x)^2}(x+y)^2\,dx\,dy.$$

6.7 | Advanced simulation methods

The simulation methods discussed so far will only work for particular types of probability densities or distributions. General purpose simulation methods can be used to draw pseudorandom samples from a wide variety of distributions.

Example 6.21

Suppose X is a Binomial(n,p) random variable with n known, but where the value of p is not known precisely; all that is known is that it is near 0.5. Given the data value $X = x$, we want to estimate p.

The maximum likelihood estimator for p is $\widehat{p} = \frac{x}{n}$, but this ignores our prior knowledge, i.e. the fact that p is really near 0.5.

If we convert our prior knowledge to a density, e.g., $p \sim N(0.5, \sigma = 0.1)$, Bayes' theorem[5] lets us calculate the conditional density of p, given $X = x$ as:

$$f(p \mid X = x) \propto \exp\left(\frac{-(p-0.5)^2}{2(0.1)^2}\right)p^x(1-p)^{n-x}, \quad 0 < p < 1.$$

It is quite difficult to work out the constant that makes this a standard density integrating to 1, but numerical approximations (e.g. using Monte Carlo integration) are possible.

[5] We'll discuss this reasoning in more detail in Example 6.25.

The goal of the remainder of this section is to present simulation methods which can be used to generate pseudorandom numbers from a density like the one in the above example. Three simulation methods are commonly used:

- rejection sampling
- importance sampling
- Markov chain Monte Carlo.

6.7.1 Rejection sampling

The idea of rejection sampling was used in Section 6.3.5 to sample from a conditional distribution: sample from a convenient distribution, and select a subsample to achieve the target distribution. We will show how to use rejection sampling to draw a random sample from a univariate density or probability function $g(x)$, using a sequence of two examples.

Our first example demonstrates the simplest version of rejection sampling.

Example 6.22

Simulate pseudorandom variates from the triangular density function

$$g(x) = \begin{cases} 1 - |1 - x|, & 0 \leq x < 2 \\ 0, & \text{otherwise} \end{cases}$$

The graph of the density function is displayed in the left panel of Figure 6.5. If we could draw points uniformly from the triangular region below the density, the x-coordinate would be distributed with density $g(x)$. The right-hand panel of this figure shows that the graph where the density is nonzero can be entirely contained in a rectangle of height 1 and width 2. A subset of uniformly distributed points in the rectangle will be uniformly distributed in the triangular area under the triangular density. Thus, a strategy for simulating values from the triangular density is:

1. Simulate a point (U_1, U_2) uniformly in the rectangle.
2. If (U_1, U_2) is located within the triangular region, accept U_1 as a pseudorandom variate; otherwise, reject it, and return to step 1.

Since the triangular density occupies half of the area of the rectangle, we would expect to sample roughly two uniform points from the rectangle for every point we accept from the triangular distribution.

In vectorized form, the steps are:

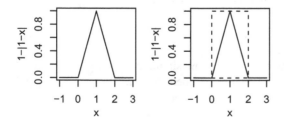

Fig. 6.5 The graph of the triangular density function on $(0, 2)$, together with a dashed rectangle in the right-hand panel.

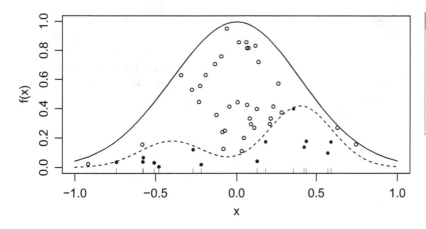

Fig. 6.6 Density $f(x)$ (solid line) and $kg(x)$ (dashed line). The points are uniformly distributed below $f(x)$; those above $kg(x)$ (open dots) are rejected, while those below (solid dots) are accepted. The tick marks show the output values of X.

```
U1 <- runif(100000, max=2)
U2 <- runif(100000)
X <- U1[U2 < (1 - abs(1 - U1))]
```

The vector X will contain approximately 50000 simulated values from the triangular distribution.

To accommodate situations where the density $g(x)$ might be nonzero on larger (possibly infinite) regions, and to increase the potential for computational efficiency, a more general form of rejection sampling is possible. Find a constant k, and density $f(x)$ from which we know how to sample, and for which $kg(x) \le f(x)$ for all x.

Then we draw points uniformly below $kg(x)$ by taking a subsample of those drawn below $f(x)$ (see Figure 6.6):

```
repeat {
    draw X ~ f(X) , U ~ unif(0,1)
    if U * f(X) < k * g(X)
        break
}
output X
```

Example 6.23
Simulate from the density $g(x) = Ce^{-x^{1.5}}$ for $x \ge 0$. The constant C is the unknown normalizing constant for this density. Even though we don't know C, since $0.5e^{-x^{1.5}} \le e^{-x}$, we can use rejection sampling with $k = 0.5/C$:

```
kg <- function(x) 0.5*exp(-(x^1.5))
X <- rexp(100000)
U <- runif(100000)
                                    # accept only those X
X <- X[ U*dexp(X) < kg(X) ]  # for which Uf(X) < kg(X)
```

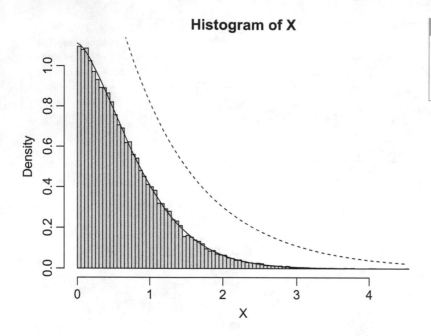

Histogram of X

Fig. 6.7 Histogram of a sample from $g(x) = Ce^{-x^{1.5}}$. The approximate density $g(x)$ is shown with the solid line, and $f(x)/k$ is shown dashed.

The vector X now contains a large number of pseudorandom numbers from the required density. We can plot a histogram of these numbers as follows:

```
hist(X, freq = FALSE, breaks="Scott")
```

We have chosen the relative frequency version of the histogram in order to overlay the theoretical density. The problem is that we don't know C to make $g(x)$ a density function. We could use Monte Carlo integration to find it, or more simply we can use the fact that we expect to accept a proportion k of the sampled points. The resulting graph is shown in Figure 6.7.

Exercises

1 Write a function to generate standard normal pseudorandom numbers on the interval $[-4, 4]$, using `runif()` and the rejection method. Can you modify the function so that it can generate standard normal pseudorandom numbers on the entire real line?

2 The following function returns normal pseudorandom numbers:

```
rannorm <- function(n, mean = 0, sd = 1){
    singlenumber <- function() {
        repeat{
            U <- runif(1)
            U2 <- sign(runif(1, min = -1))      # value is +1 or -1
            Y <- rexp(1) * U2          # Y is a double exponential r.v.
```

```
            if (U < dnorm(Y) / exp(-abs(Y))) break
        }
        return(Y)
    }
    replicate(n, singlenumber()) * sd + mean
}
```

(a) Use this function to generate a vector of 10000 normal pseudoran-
    dom numbers with mean 8 and standard deviation 2.
(b) Obtain a QQ plot to check the accuracy of this generator.
(c) Use the `curve()` function to draw the graph of the standard normal
    density on the interval $[0,4]$. Use the `add = TRUE` parameter to
    overlay the exponential density on the same interval to verify that
    the rejection method has been implemented appropriately.

3 Consider the following two methods for simulating from the discrete
distribution with values $0, 1, 2, 3, 4, 5$ which take respective probabilities
$0.2, 0.3, 0.1, 0.15, 0.05, 0.2$.

  The first method is an inversion method:

```
probs <- c(0.2, 0.3, 0.1, 0.15, 0.05, 0.2)
randiscrete1 <- function(n, probs) {
    cumprobs <- cumsum(probs)
    singlenumber <- function() {
        x <- runif(1)
        N <- sum(x > cumprobs)
        N
    }
    replicate(n, singlenumber())
}
```

The second method is a rejection method:

```
randiscrete2 <- function(n, probs) {
    singlenumber <- function() {
        repeat{
            U <- runif(2, min=c(-0.5, 0), max=c(length(probs) - 0.5,
                        max(probs)))
            if (U[2] < probs[round(U[1]) + 1]) break
        }
        return(round(U[1]))
    }
    replicate(n, singlenumber())
}
```

Execute both functions using $n = 100$, 1000, and 10000. Use
`microbenchmark()` to determine which method is faster.

4 Repeat the above exercise using the probability distribution on the
integers $\{0, 1, 2, \ldots, 99\}$ defined by

```
set.seed(91626)
probs <- runif(100)
probs <- probs / sum(probs)
```

When is rejection sampling preferred to the inversion method for discrete distributions?

6.7.2 Rejection sampling for bivariate distributions

In dimensions higher than 1, it is not usually possible to work out convenient expressions for quantiles. Therefore, alternative simulation methods to the inverse CDF transform method are needed. This is where the rejection method continues to be very useful. We illustrate the method with a single example here.

Example 6.24

Suppose $\theta > 1$, $k(\theta)$ is some unknown positive-valued function of θ, and

$$f_{X,Y}(x,y) = k(\theta)e^{-(xy+\theta(x+y))}, \quad \text{for } x \geq 0, y \geq 0$$

and 0, otherwise.

The function $f_{X,Y}(x,y)$ will be a proper probability density function as long as $k(\theta)$ is chosen to satisfy the condition that the double integral of $f_{X,Y}(x,y)$ over all nonnegative x and y is 1. Even though we cannot analytically determine $k(\theta)$, we can be certain that such a function exists if the everywhere positive function $e^{-(xy+\theta(x+y))}$ is bounded by a nonnegative function that integrates to a finite value. To see this requires a few steps. First, note that if $\alpha \geq 2$ and $\beta \geq 2$, then

$$\alpha\beta \geq \alpha + \beta$$

since $\alpha\beta > 2\beta$ and $\alpha\beta > 2\alpha$, and upon adding these inequalities, it follows that $2\alpha\beta > 2\alpha + 2\beta$. Next, note that, with the identification $\alpha = x+2$ and $\beta = y+2$, the previous result allows us to deduce the following:

$$xy + \theta(x+y) = (x+2)(y+2) + (\theta-2)(x+y) - 4$$
$$\geq x+2+y+2 + (\theta-2)(x+y) - 4 = (\theta-1)(x+y).$$

Therefore,

$$e^{-(xy+\theta(x+y))} \leq e^{-(\theta-1)x}e^{-(\theta-1)y}.$$

Integrating the right-hand side of this inquality over all $x \in [0,\infty)$ and $y \in [0,\infty)$ gives $1/(\theta-1)^2$ which is a finite value for $\theta > 1$. This implies that the double integral of $e^{-(xy+\theta(x+y))}$ over the same quadrant must be some positive value that is even less than $1/(\theta-1)^2$; by setting $k(\theta)$ to the reciprocal of this value, we can guarantee that the double integral of $f_{X,Y}(x,y)$ is 1.

Rejection sampling can be used to simulate pairs of random variables from the model discussed here. The arguments given in the previous paragraph imply that

$$f_{X,Y}(x,y) \leq \frac{k}{(\theta-1)^2}d_X(x)d_Y(y),$$

where $d_X(x)$ and $d_Y(y)$ are exponential PDFs with respective rates $\theta - 1$. Thus, we can bound the required PDF by a PDF formed as the product of two exponential PDFs: that is, we will simulate pairs of independent exponential random variables.

The fact that we do not know k is immaterial here, since it is the ratio of $f_{X,Y}(x,y)$ to $d_X(x)d_Y(y)$ that matters when accepting or rejecting a proposed (x,y) pair. More precisely, in order to accept a (x,y) pair, we require

$$\frac{f_{X,Y}(x,y)}{d_X(x)d_Y(y)} \leq \frac{U}{(\theta - 1)^2}$$

where U is sampled from the uniform distribution on $[0,1]$. The inline function `rejectStep()` in the code below implements this rejection procedure.

```
rbexp <- function(n, theta = 2) {
    nremaining <- n
    rejectStep <- function(n, theta) {
        X <- rexp(n, rate = theta - 1)
        Y <- rexp(n, rate = theta - 1)
        V <- runif(n)*dexp(X, rate = theta - 1)*
                     dexp(Y, rate = theta - 1)/(theta-1)^2
        ACCEPT <- V <= exp(-(X*Y + theta*(X+Y)))
        X <- X[ACCEPT]; Y <- Y[ACCEPT]
        cbind(X, Y)
    }
    XY <- cbind(c(), c())
    while (nremaining > 0) {
        XY <- rbind(XY, rejectStep(nremaining, theta = theta))
        nObs <- nrow(XY)
        nremaining <- n - nObs
    }
    XY[1:n, ]
}
```

The `while()` loop is used because only a fraction of the n proposed pairs are initially accepted. If the procedure stopped at that point, the user who had requested n pairs would be disappointed. Instead, the procedure is repeated until the full set of random pairs has been accepted.

Output from the function is in the form of an $n \times 2$ matrix. The following is a result when $n = 4$:

```
rbexp(4, 2)

##                 X          Y
## [1,] 0.08219298 0.49990201
## [2,] 0.35414994 0.09815176
## [3,] 0.02637586 0.40989352
## [4,] 0.72166780 0.95687900
```

Exercises

1 The `rbexp()` function in this section will usually call `rejectStep()` several times in order to accumulate n accepted values. Perhaps it would be more efficient to ask for `2*nremaining` each time, so that fewer calls will be needed, even though this might generate more than we need.

   (a) Use `microbenchmark()` to find which whole number multiple of `nremaining` is most efficient when n = 1000. Try using multiples `1:10` of `nremaining`.

   (b) Repeat for n = 4. Is the same multiple still the best?

6.7.3 Importance sampling

A weighted average is an average in which observations are individually weighted. That is, instead of the usual sample average formula $\bar{x} = (1/n) \sum_{i=1}^{n} x_i$ we incorporate weights $w_1, \ldots, w_n$ and use $\bar{x}_w = \sum_{i=1}^{n} w_i x_i / \sum_{i=1}^{n} w_i$. The usual sample average can be seen to be a weighted average with all weights equal.

Importance sampling is a technique to generate both the sample and the weights randomly, in such a way that weighted averages approximate expected values with respect to a target density function $g(x)$. As with rejection sampling, we start by sampling from some other more convenient density $f(x)$:

1. Choose a convenient density $f(x)$ (which we know how to draw samples from).

2. Draw $(x_1, \ldots, x_n)$ as a sample from $f(x)$.

3. Calculate weights $w_i = g(x_i)/f(x_i)$.

We may now approximate the expectation of a function $h(X)$ where $X \sim g(x)$ using averages of $h(x_i)$ weighted by w_i.

One way to see why this works is to notice that w_i is proportional to the probability that a rejection sampler would accept x_i as a draw from $g(x)$. Given x_i, the contribution $w_i h(x_i) / \sum_{i=1}^{n} w_i$ in the weighted average formula is exactly the expected contribution from this draw to a sample mean if we were using rejection sampling. We know rejection sampling works, so importance sampling must work too. It may even be more efficient, in that we don't throw away information from rejected draws. In addition, it is not necessary to find the constant k as in rejection sampling. Neither $g(x_i)$ nor $f(x_i)$ need be normalized densities: dividing by the sum of the weights automatically provides the appropriate scaling.

On the other hand, working with weighted samples is more difficult than working with simple random samples, so in many cases rejection sampling would be preferred.

We illustrate these issues by continuing with the example from the previous section. We may approximate the mean and variance of the density $g(x)$ from that section using the `weighted.mean` function:

```
X <- rexp(100000)
W <- g(X)/dexp(X)
mean <- weighted.mean(X, W)
mean
```

```
## [1] 0.6579773
```

```
weighted.mean( (X - mean)^2, W )   # The variance as E[ (X - Xbar)^2 ]
```

```
## [1] 0.3036141
```

Exercises

1 Write a function which generates a weighted sample of Binomial(m, p) pseudorandom numbers using importance sampling. Compare the weighted average to the theoretical mean.

6.7.4 The Metropolis–Hastings algorithm

Sometimes when we are given a probability function or probability density function $g(x)$ we don't have enough information for rejection sampling or successful importance sampling. Onc powerful use of MCMC allows us to approximate samples by constructing a Markov chain where $g(x)$ is the unique invariant distribution.

This sounds hard, but in fact there are several general techniques for doing so that are fairly easy to program. One of them is known as the Metropolis–Hastings algorithm.

Let's assume that we have drawn $X_t = x_t$ from the target distribution $g(x)$. We want to draw X_{t+1} from the conditional distribution that defines the Markov chain. This might be a discrete or continuous distribution; in this description we'll assume it is a continuous distribution, but the discussion is very similar for discrete ones. We'll write the probability density function for the update as $\pi(x|x_t)$. In order that $g(x)$ is the invariant distribution, we want the resulting marginal distribution of X_{t+1} to also be $g(x)$.

Calculating marginal distributions usually involves doing an integral, but here there's a trick: if we can guarantee that the joint distribution of (X_t, X_{t+1}) is a symmetric distribution, then its two marginal distributions will have to be the same. So all we need to do is to construct $\pi(x|x_t)$ so that the resulting joint distribution is symmetric.

The joint distribution is simply

$$\pi(x_t, x_{t+1}) = g(x_t)\pi(x_{t+1}|x_t)$$

using the sequential sampling argument mentioned earlier. Making this symmetric in x_t, x_{t+1} requires

$$g(x_t)\pi(x_{t+1}|x_t) = g(x_{t+1})\pi(x_t|x_{t+1})$$

or

$$\frac{\pi(x_{t+1}|x_t)}{\pi(x_t|x_{t+1})} = \frac{g(x_{t+1})}{g(x_t)}.$$

It turns out there are lots of choices for $\pi(x_{t+1}|x_t)$ that solve this equation. For example, start with almost any conditional distribution $p(x_{t+1}|x_t)$ (we'll call this the "proposal distribution"). If the ratio $p(x_{t+1}|x_t)/p(x_t|x_{t+1})$ is too big (i.e. bigger than $g(x_{t+1})/g(x_t)$), we "shave off" some of the density from x_{t+1} and move it to x_t.

From a simulation point of view, a simple way to shave off probability is to simulate a proposal Y with density $p(y|x_t)$, and if it is in the zone where the ratio is too big, we randomly decide whether to keep it or not. If we keep it, then $X_{t+1} = Y$. If we don't, then use $X_{t+1} = x_t$ instead. (By moving to x_t we increase the probability of the diagonal $X_{t+1} = X_t$ of the joint distribution: this doesn't create any new asymmetry.) How do we make that random decision? We compute a uniform $(0,1)$ variable U, and compare it to a value called the Metropolis ratio.

To summarize, here is how the Metropolis–Hastings algorithm simulates X_{t+1} given that $X_t = x_t$:

1. Simulate $Y \sim p(y|x_t)$ giving value y, and $U \sim \text{Uniform}(0,1)$ giving u.
2. Compute the Metropolis ratio

$$\alpha(x_t, y) = \frac{g(y)/p(y|x_t)}{g(x_t)/p(x_t|y)}.$$

3. If $u < \alpha(x_t, y)$ then $X_{t+1} = y$, otherwise $X_{t+1} = x_t$.

Some careful calculation should convince you that when X_{t+1} is simulated as shown above, the symmetry equation will be satisfied.

One special choice of proposal is called the "Metropolis algorithm," where Y is chosen to be X_t plus a random step chosen from a symmetric distribution, for example a normal distribution with mean 0. In that case, $p(y|x_t) = p(x_t|y)$, and the Metropolis ratio simplifies to $g(y)/g(x_t)$. We will always accept a proposal to jump to a location with higher density, and sometimes accept a proposal to jump to a lower density.

Does this actually work? Not always, but it does in a really wide variety of problems. Some care needs to be taken in choosing the proposal distribution: if it tries to jump too far almost all proposals will be rejected. If it doesn't jump far enough they'll mostly be accepted, but in both cases X_{t+1} will end up close to X_t, and it will take a very long time for the Markov chain to converge to its invariant distribution.

Some invariant distributions are particularly elusive. For example, if there are widely separated islands of probability, the chain may not propose to jump between them within the time you have available for your simulation, and you may never see X_t values in one of the islands. However, in many, many situations the Metropolis and Metropolis–Hastings algorithms provide ways to get samples that work quite well.

Example 6.25
The Bayesian approach to statistics is based on the idea that we can summarize our knowledge about unknown things in a probability distribution.

For example, if you stand a coin on its edge (Figure 6.8) and then bang the table until it falls down (Figure 6.9), it will show heads with probability

Fig. 6.8 Coins standing up.

θ. But θ might not be $1/2$, because coins are not necessarily made with perfect symmetry, so they might favor falling with heads showing over falling with tails showing, or *vice versa*.

We might guess that it will be close to $1/2$, and summarize our uncertainty by saying that θ is believed to come from a distribution with mean 0.5 and standard deviation of 0.1. (Pick different values depending on your own knowledge about the value of θ.) We can be even more specific and pick a normal distribution with those parameters. It's not an ideal choice, because that says $\theta < 0$ or $\theta > 1$ are possible, but they are very unlikely (less than one chance in a million), so it can serve as a good approximation to our beliefs.

Because this is based on our prior knowledge about coins, we call this our "prior distribution" for θ.

Now we might choose a coin and carry out an experiment, standing it on edge, and banging the table dozens (or thousands) of times. Or we might take a whole bag of coins, stand them all up, and bang the table once to see how they all fall, on the assumption that they all follow the same rules. Suppose we have observed heads showing x times out of n coins falling. How should that affect our belief?

If the true probability of seeing heads is θ, then x should be a single draw from a binomial distribution, with size n and probability θ. The probability function for x given θ is

Fig. 6.9 Coins fallen down.

$$\binom{n}{x}\theta^x(1-\theta)^{n-x}$$

(see Table 6.2). Using our rule for sequential calculation of probabilities, this means that the joint distribution for θ and x is proportional to

$$\exp\left(-\frac{(\theta-\mu)^2}{2\sigma^2}\right)\binom{n}{x}\theta^x(1-\theta)^{n-x},$$

where $\mu = 0.5$ and $\sigma = 0.1$. But we've observed x! So what we can do now is compute the conditional distribution of θ given x. We're now thinking of x as a constant, so we only need to keep terms that involve θ, and we find the density is proportional to

$$\exp\left(-\frac{(\theta-\mu)^2}{2\sigma^2}\right)\theta^x(1-\theta)^{n-x}.$$

This is only valid for $0 < \theta < 1$; outside that range, the conditional density is zero. (This is called the "posterior distribution" for θ, because it shows what we should believe after observing some data.)

The density kernel given above is not a standard density, you won't find it in Table 6.1. But we can plot it and try sampling from it approximately, using the Metropolis algorithm, in order to study its properties.

We carried out this experiment with multiple coins in one of our classes. We tipped $n = 200$ coins, and observed $x = 54$ heads. We can plot the prior and posterior density kernels as follows (Figure 6.10):

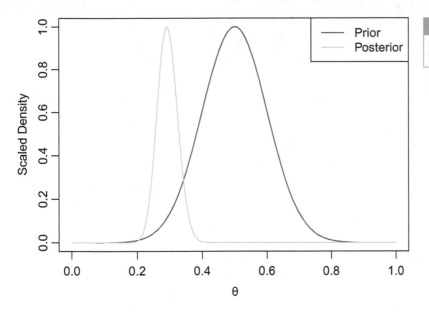

```
theta <- seq(0, 1, length.out = 200)
prior <- dnorm(theta, mean = 0.5, sd = 0.1)
prior <- prior/max(prior)
n <- 200
x <- 54
posterior <- prior * theta^x * (1 - theta)^(n - x)
posterior <- posterior/max(posterior)
plot(theta, prior, type = "l", col = "blue",
     xlab = expression(theta), ylab = "Scaled Density")
lines(theta, posterior, col = "green")
legend("topright", legend = c("Prior", "Posterior"), lty = 1,
       col = c("blue", "green"))
```

In this code we rescale both densities to have a maximum value of one: this is easier than integrating the posterior to give an area of one. Since the Metropolis algorithm uses the ratio $g(y)/g(x_t)$, such scaling makes no difference to the sampling.

To sample from the posterior using the Metropolis algorithm, we need a starting value x_0, and a symmetric distribution for the proposed steps. We'll use $x_0 = 0.5$ and Normal$(0, 0.1)$ steps to start. To see how this performs, we'll generate X_1 to X_{100} and plot the results.

```
logg <- function(theta) {
  dnorm(theta, mean = 0.5, sd = 0.1, log = TRUE) +
    x*log(theta) + (n - x)*log(1-theta)
}
N <- 100
xt <- numeric(N + 1)
xt[1] <- 0.5
sd <- 0.1
```

```
steps <- rnorm(N, 0, sd)
u <- runif(N)
for (i in 1:N) {
  y <- xt[i] + steps[i]
  if (y <= 0 || y >= 1 || log(u[i]) > logg(y) - logg(xt[i]))
    xt[i + 1] <- xt[i]
  else
    xt[i + 1] <- y
}
plot(0:N, xt, type = "l", ylab = expression(x[t]), xlab = "t")
```

The plot is shown in Figure 6.11.

Understanding the code

Since R does indexing of vectors starting at 1, we put x_0 into xt[1], and generate new values in xt[2] up to xt[N + 1]. We also take the difference of log densities rather than the ratio of densities to avoid overflow or underflow in the calculation of $g(y)/g(x_t)$.

When we examine the output of our short simulation, we see that the first few observations (up to about $t = 10$) look too large: this is called the "burn-in" period, and those values should be discarded. After that it appears to settle down, moving around in the posterior successfully. To estimate the mean and standard deviation of the posterior distribution, we can take the sample values of simulations after $t = 10$. We'll get better values with a larger sample, so we'll repeat the calculations with $N = 10000$, giving estimates mean $= 0.293$ and s.d. $= 0.031$. We see that our knowledge about θ has improved (the standard deviation of the posterior is much less than that of the prior), and our estimate of its location has moved substantially away from 0.5.

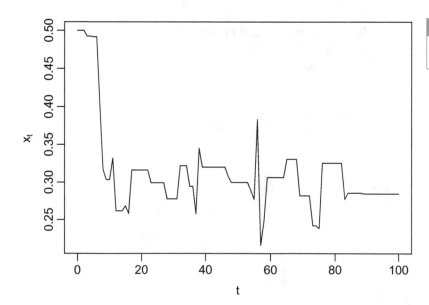

Fig. 6.11 One hundred steps of the Metropolis algorithm targeting the posterior density.

Chapter exercises

1 Write a function which simulates two people (Ann and Bob) playing table tennis. (Assume that the first person to reach 21 points wins the game.)

   (a) Begin with the assumption that each player successively hits the ball with probability p_{Ann} and p_{Bob}, respectively. Find the probability that Ann will win for various values of these probabilities.

   (b) Add more features such as ability to serve, to smash the ball, or spin the ball. Use your imagination.

2 (Adapted from *Elementary Probability Theory with Stochastic Processes* by K. L. Chung, Springer, 1975.) The following model has been used for the study of contagion. Suppose that there are N persons some of whom are sick with influenza. The following assumptions are made:

- when a sick person meets a healthy one, the chance is α that the latter will be infected;
- all encounters are between two persons;
- all possible encounters in pairs are equally likely;
- one such encounter occurs in every unit of time.

   (a) Write a function which simulates this model for various values of N (say, 10000) and α (say, between 0.001 and 0.1). Monitor the history of this process, assuming that one individual is infected at the beginning.

   (b) Suppose that initially only one individual is infected. What is the expected length of time until 1000 people are infected?

   (c) Now add the assumption that each infected person has a 0.01 chance of recovering at each time unit. Monitor several histories of this new process, and compare them with the histories of the old process.

   (d) Re-do with the assumption that the time between encounters is an exponential random variable with mean 5 minutes.

   (e) Re-do assuming that the time between encounters is the absolute value of a normal random variable with a mean of 5 minutes and a standard deviation of 1 minute.

3 Simulate the following simple model of auto insurance claims:

- Claims arise according to a Poisson process at a rate of 100 per year.
- Each claim is a random size following a gamma distribution with shape and rate parameters both equal to 2. This distribution has mean 1 and variance 1/2. Claims must be paid by the insurance company as soon as they arise.
- The insurance company earns premiums at a rate of 105 per year, spread evenly over the year (i.e. at time t measured in years, the total premium received is $105t$).

Write R code to do the following:

   (a) Simulate the times and amounts of all the claims that would occur in one year. Draw a graph of the total amount of money that the insurance company would have through the year, starting from zero: it should increase smoothly with the premiums, and drop at each claim time.

(b) Repeat the simulation 1000 times, and estimate the following quantities:
  i. The expected minimum amount of money that the insurance company would have.
  ii. The expected final amount of money that the insurance company would have.

4 Let $f(x) = (\sin x)^2$ for $0 < x < 2\pi$.

(a) Graph the function.

(b) Use Monte Carlo integration to find the area under $f(x)$ on the range $0 < x < 2\pi$, and to find a 95% confidence interval for the area.

(c) Use trigonometry or calculus to find the same area exactly. Did the confidence interval cover the true value?

(d) Write a function called `rsin2` which generates random values from the density $f(x)/k$, $0 < x < 2\pi$, where k is the area found above. The function should take a single argument specifying how many samples are required, e.g. `rsin2(10)` would return a vector of 10 samples from this distribution. Use the rejection method to draw the samples. Plot a histogram based on 1000 samples.

(e) Use your function to draw a sample of 1,000,000 samples, and calculate a 95% confidence interval for the mean. (By symmetry, the true mean must be π. Did your confidence interval cover the true value?)

5 The `NLP` package in R does "natural language processing," operations involving words in human languages like English. One task is to split text into separate words and punctuation symbols. In this exercise we will simulate some new text based on the patterns in an existing source of text, the novel *Pride and Prejudice* by Jane Austen.

(a) Install the `NLP` and `janeaustenr` packages if you don't already have them.

(b) The whole text of *Pride and Prejudice* is stored in `janeaustenr::prideprejudice`. You can convert the first chapter into the form used by `NLP` using

```
library(NLP)

##
## Attaching package: 'NLP'
## The following object is masked from 'package:ggplot2':
##
##     annotate

library(janeaustenr)
chap1 <- as.String(prideprejudice[10:120])
```

and can extract the words with punctuation (the "tokens") using

```
tokens <- chap1[whitespace_tokenizer(chap1)]
tokens[1:12]

##  [1] "It"            "is"             "a"       "truth"
##  [5] "universally"   "acknowledged," "that"    "a"
##  [9] "single"        "man"            "in"      "possession"
```

(c) Use `table(tokens)` to display the frequency of words and punctuation. Sample 20 tokens from Chapter 1 with the same frequency as in the original text using this code:

```
tab <- table(tokens)
paste(sample(names(tab), 20, replace = TRUE, prob = tab),
      collapse = " ")
```

The output will be nonsense, since English text is not a bag of independent words. But is it a Markov chain? Write two functions: first, a function that takes a vector like `tokens` and produces a list `transitions`, where for every token `transitions[[token]]` contains the frequencies of tokens that follow it. Second, write a function that samples from the Markov chain that uses these frequencies to define transition probabilities. Run both functions and see if you get intelligible text.

(d) Can you do this using triplets of words instead of just pairs?

6 A simple generalization of a homogeneous Poisson process is a Poisson cluster process. According to this model, a Poisson distributed number, N, of clusters, each having a Poisson distributed number of points, is constructed in a two-stage process. At the first stage, N points of a homogeneous Poisson process are generated: the cluster *centers*. At the second stage, the $M(i)$ points of the ith cluster are generated according to a bivariate normal distribution with mean at the location of the ith cluster center, and with given standard deviations in each direction. A model similar to this was proposed long ago for clusters of galaxies.[6]

[6] Neyman, J. and Scott, E. L. (1952) A theory of the spatial distribution of galaxies. *Astrophysical Journal* **116** 144–163.

The following code simulates a Poisson cluster process with a mean of 15 clusters, having 40 points on average, on a 1000×1000 region. Cluster radii are based on a normal distribution with standard deviation 20. Execute the code, and observe the resulting point pattern.

```
N <- rpois(1, 15)    # N cluster centers
U1 <- runif(N, min = 0, max = 1000)
U2 <- runif(N, min = 0, max = 1000)
# (U1, U2) are the coordinates of the cluster centers

M <- rpois(N, 40)    # Numbers of points in each cluster
x <- vector("list", N) # create a list with N empty components
y <- vector("list", N)
for (i in 1:N) {
  x[[i]] <- rnorm(M[i], mean = U1[i], sd = 20)
  y[[i]] <- rnorm(M[i], mean = U2[i], sd = 20)
}
clusters <- data.frame(x = unlist(x), y = unlist(y))
plot(clusters)  # visualize the result
```

Note the use of the `vector()` function in creating an empty `list()` object.

(a) Observe what happens when the expected number of clusters is increased to 25.

(b) What happens to the point pattern when you change the normal random variables defining the clusters so that they have standard deviation sd = 40?... sd = 5?

(c) Experiment with elliptical clusters, by using a smaller standard deviation in the x direction than in the y direction. Does the resulting point pattern match your expectations?

(d) Use the rexp() function in the above code to generate clusters which are of random size and shape.

Computational linear algebra

Linear algebra deals with vector spaces and linear operations on them. In mathematics, we usually represent vectors as column vectors of numbers, and linear operations as matrices. Applying a linear operation to a vector becomes multiplication of a column vector by a matrix, and composition of operations is matrix multiplication.

One of the most important applications of linear algebra is in solving systems of linear equations. For example, we represent the system

$$3x_1 - 4x_2 = 6,$$
$$x_1 + 2x_2 = -3$$

as

$$Ax = b,$$

where

$$A = \begin{bmatrix} 3 & -4 \\ 1 & 2 \end{bmatrix}, \quad x = \begin{bmatrix} x_1 \\ x_2 \end{bmatrix}, \quad b = \begin{bmatrix} 6 \\ -3 \end{bmatrix}$$

and solve it as

$$x = A^{-1}b = \begin{bmatrix} 0.2 & 0.4 \\ -0.1 & 0.3 \end{bmatrix} \begin{bmatrix} 6 \\ -3 \end{bmatrix} = \begin{bmatrix} 0 \\ -1.5 \end{bmatrix}.$$

Linear algebra is also extensively used in statistics in linear regression, smoothing, simulation, and so on. We will touch on some of these applications in this book, but most of them are beyond our scope.

From a computational point of view, many of the issues in linear algebra come down to solving systems of linear equations efficiently and accurately. In order to assess accuracy we need to understand properties of the matrices; this understanding is valuable in itself. Efficiency often means formulating problems differently than we would from a strict mathematical point of view. For example, as we will see below, we would not normally solve $Ax = b$ using the mathematical solution $x = A^{-1}b$: computationally, this is both inefficient and inaccurate.

In this chapter, we will present several approaches to this problem, and illustrate them with R code. R incorporates routines for linear algebra computations from the *LAPACK*[1] library. This is a well-tested, well-trusted library, and R is an excellent platform for computational linear algebra. However, as with all numerical computation, understanding the underlying theory is essential in order to obtain reliable results.

[1] Anderson, E., Bai, Z., Bischof, C. *et al.* (1999) LAPACK Users' Guide. Third Edition. SIAM. Available on-line at www.netlib.org/lapack/lug/lapack_lug.html.

7.1 Vectors and matrices in R

Numeric "vector" and "matrix" objects in R are a close match to mathematical vectors and matrices. (R also allows other types of data in its vectors and matrices, but that won't concern us here.) R normally makes no distinction between column vectors and row vectors, though it does allow matrices with one column or one row when this distinction is important.

Numeric matrices in R are printed as rectangular arrays of numbers, but are stored internally as vectors with dimension attributes. For the purpose of computational linear algebra, the internal storage can usually be ignored.

7.1.1 Constructing matrix objects

Matrices can be constructed using the functions `matrix()`, `cbind()` or `rbind()`.

Syntax

```
matrix(data, nrow, ncol)   # data is a vector of nrow*ncol values
cbind(d1, d2, ..., dm)     # d1, ..., dm are vectors (columns)
rbind(d1, d2, ..., dn)     # d1, ..., dn are vectors (rows)
```

Example 7.1
Hilbert matrices are often studied in numerical linear algebra because they are easy to construct but have surprising properties.

```
H3 <- matrix(c(1, 1/2, 1/3, 1/2, 1/3, 1/4, 1/3, 1/4, 1/5), nrow = 3)
H3

##           [,1]      [,2]      [,3]
## [1,] 1.0000000 0.5000000 0.3333333
## [2,] 0.5000000 0.3333333 0.2500000
## [3,] 0.3333333 0.2500000 0.2000000
```

Here `H3` is the 3×3 Hilbert matrix, where entry (i,j) is $1/(i+j-1)$. Note that `ncol` is not required in the command that created it, since the `data` argument has been assigned a vector consisting of nine elements; it is clear that if there are three rows there must also be three columns.

We could also construct this matrix by binding columns together as follows:

```
1/cbind(seq(1, 3), seq(2, 4), seq(3, 5))
```

```
##             [,1]       [,2]       [,3]
## [1,] 1.0000000 0.5000000 0.3333333
## [2,] 0.5000000 0.3333333 0.2500000
## [3,] 0.3333333 0.2500000 0.2000000
```

In this example, `rbind()` would give the same result, because of symmetry.

Matrices are not necessarily square.

Example 7.2
For some simple non-square examples, consider

```
matrix(seq(1, 12), nrow = 3)
```

```
##       [,1] [,2] [,3] [,4]
## [1,]    1    4    7   10
## [2,]    2    5    8   11
## [3,]    3    6    9   12
```

and

```
x <- seq(1, 3)
x2 <- x^2
X <- cbind(x, x2)
X
```

```
##      x x2
## [1,] 1  1
## [2,] 2  4
## [3,] 3  9
```

The matrix X, above, could also have been constructed as

```
X <- matrix(c(1, 2, 3, 1, 4, 9), ncol = 2)
```

though it will print differently, because we haven't entered any column names.

Exercises

1 Use the `matrix()`, `seq()`, and `rep()` functions to construct the following 5×5 *Hankel* matrix:

$$A = \begin{bmatrix} 1 & 2 & 3 & 4 & 5 \\ 2 & 3 & 4 & 5 & 6 \\ 3 & 4 & 5 & 6 & 7 \\ 4 & 5 & 6 & 7 & 8 \\ 5 & 6 & 7 & 8 & 9 \end{bmatrix}.$$

Convert the code into a function which can be used to construct matrices of dimension $n \times n$ which have the same pattern. Use the function to output 10×10 and 12×12 Hankel matrices.

2 Use rbind() to stack the vectors [0.1 0.5 0.0 0.4], [0.2 0.3 0.5 0.0], [0.3 0.0 0.5 0.2], and [0.2 0.3 0.2 0.3] into a 4×4 matrix. Assign the result to an object called P.

3 Use cbind() to construct the 7×3 matrix:

$$W = \begin{bmatrix} 1 & 2 & 4 \\ 1 & 3 & 7 \\ 1 & 4 & 5 \\ 1 & 5 & 6 \\ 1 & 6 & 7 \\ 1 & 7 & 5 \\ 1 & 8 & 3 \end{bmatrix}.$$

7.1.2 Accessing matrix elements; row and column names

Indexing of matrix elements is the same as for data frames: the (i, j) element is located in the ith row and jth column. For example, the $(3, 2)$ element of X is 9. We can access this element using

```
X[3, 2]

## x2
##  9
```

We can access the ith row using X[i,], and the jth column using X[, j]. For example,

```
X[3,]

##  x x2
##  3  9

X[, 2]

## [1] 1 4 9
```

When we do this, the result is usually a vector, with no dimension information kept. If we want to maintain the result as a row or column vector, we use the optional drop = FALSE argument when we index:

```
X[3, , drop = FALSE]

##       x x2
## [1,] 3  9

X[, 2, drop = FALSE]

##      x2
## [1,]  1
## [2,]  4
## [3,]  9
```

As X shows, it is possible for the rows and/or columns of a matrix to have individual names. For example,

```
colnames(X)

## [1] "x"   "x2"
```

In this example, the rows do not have names:

```
rownames(X)

## NULL
```

We can assign names using

```
rownames(X) <- c("obs1", "obs2", "obs3")
X

##        x x2
## obs1 1   1
## obs2 2   4
## obs3 3   9
```

Internally, R stores matrices and data frames quite differently. Matrices are stored as a single vector of values with an associated dimension attribute, while data frames are stored as lists of columns. Because of this, the $ extraction function does not work for matrices. For example,

```
X$x

## Error in X$x: $ operator is invalid for atomic vectors
```

However, it is possible to use the row or column names to access rows or columns as in the following example:

```
X[, "x"]

## obs1 obs2 obs3
##    1    2    3
```

Exercises

1 Construct the *stochastic matrix* that appears below.

```
        clear cloudy
clear    0.8    0.2
cloudy   0.3    0.7
```

A stochastic matrix has the properties that all entries are nonnegative and the rows sum to 1, i.e. it describes transition probabilities for a Markov chain of the type introduced in Section 6.5. In this example, we might be thinking of the weather on a sequence of days; if it is clear today, the probability of a clear day tomorrow is 0.8, and if it is cloudy today, the probability of a clear day tomorrow is 0.3. Using the methods of Section 6.5, simulate a month of weather using these transitions.[2]

2 Construct the two vectors of heights (in cm) and weights (in kg) for five individuals:

```
height <- c(172, 168, 167, 175, 180)
weight <- c(62, 64, 51, 71, 69)
```

Bind these vectors into a matrix, and modify the result to obtain:

```
        height weight
Neil       172     62
Cindy      168     64
Pardeep    167     51
Deepak     175     71
Hao        180     69
```

3 Refer to the previous exercise. Pardeep's height is really 162 cm, Hao's height is really 181 cm and his weight is really 68 kg. Correct the matrix accordingly.

7.1.3 Matrix properties

The dimension of a matrix is its number of rows and its number of columns. For example,

```
dim(X)
```

```
## [1] 3 2
```

Recall that the determinant of a 2×2 matrix $\begin{bmatrix} a & b \\ c & d \end{bmatrix}$ can be calculated as $ad - bc$. For larger square matrices, the calculation becomes more complicated. It can be found in R using the `det()` function, as in

```
det(H3)
```

```
## [1] 0.000462963
```

The diagonal elements can be obtained using the `diag()` function, as in

```
diag(X)
```

```
## [1] 1 4
```

```
diag(H3)
```

```
## [1] 1.0000000 0.3333333 0.2000000
```

We can then compute the trace (the sum of the diagonal entries) using a home-made function such as

```
trace <- function(data) sum(diag(data))
```

[2] The transition matrix here is, in fact, based on weather data from Winnipeg International Airport for the summer of 1960.

Applying this function to our matrices constructed in Examples 7.1 and 7.2, we obtain

```
trace(X)

## [1] 5

trace(H3)

## [1] 1.533333
```

The `diag()` function can also be used to turn a vector into a square diagonal matrix whose diagonal elements correspond to the entries of the given vector. For example,

```
diag(diag(H3))

##         [,1]        [,2] [,3]
## [1,]     1 0.0000000  0.0
## [2,]     0 0.3333333  0.0
## [3,]     0 0.0000000  0.2
```

The `t()` function is used to calculate the matrix transpose $X^\top$:

```
t(X)

##     obs1 obs2 obs3
## x      1    2    3
## x2     1    4    9
```

Exercises

1 Verify that $\det(A) = \det(A^\top)$ by experimenting with several matrices A.

2 A matrix A is said to be *skew-symmetric* if

$$A^\top = -A.$$

Construct a 3×3 skew-symmetric matrix and verify that its determinant is 0. What is the trace of your matrix?

7.1.4 Triangular matrices

The functions `lower.tri()` and `upper.tri()` can be used to obtain the lower and upper triangular parts of matrices. The output of the functions is a matrix of logical elements, with TRUE representing the relevant triangular elements. For example,

```
lower.tri(H3)

##         [,1]   [,2]  [,3]
## [1,] FALSE FALSE FALSE
## [2,]  TRUE FALSE FALSE
## [3,]  TRUE  TRUE FALSE
```

We can obtain the lower triangular matrix whose nonzero elements match the lower triangular elements of H3 by using

```
Hnew <- H3
Hnew[upper.tri(H3, diag = TRUE)]  <- 0  # diag = TRUE causes all
                                        # diagonal elements to be
                                        # included
Hnew
##           [,1] [,2] [,3]
## [1,] 0.0000000 0.00    0
## [2,] 0.5000000 0.00    0
## [3,] 0.3333333 0.25    0
```

Exercises

1 Obtain a matrix which has the same upper triangular part as H3 (including the diagonal) but is 0 below the diagonal.

2 Check the output from

```
Hnew[lower.tri(H3)]
```

Is it what you expected?

3 With X as defined in Example 7.2, what difference would you expect between X[3, 2] and X[3, 2, drop = FALSE]? Use R to calculate the dimension of each of these expressions.

7.1.5 Matrix arithmetic

Multiplication of a matrix by a scalar constant is the same as multiplication of a vector by a constant. For example, using the X matrix from the previous section, we can multiply each element by 2 as in

```
Y <- 2 * X
Y
##      x x2
## obs1 2  2
## obs2 4  8
## obs3 6 18
```

Elementwise addition of matrices also proceeds as for vectors. For example,

```
Y + X
##      x x2
## obs1 3  3
## obs2 6 12
## obs3 9 27
```

When adding matrices, always ensure that the dimensions match properly. If they do not match correctly, an error message will appear, as in arrays

```
t(Y) + X
```

```
## Error in t(Y) + X: non-conformable arrays
```

In this example, $Y^\top$ is a 2 × 3 matrix while X is 3 × 2.

The command X * Y performs elementwise multiplication. Note that this differs from the usual form of matrix multiplication that we will discuss in Section 7.2. For example,

```
X * Y
```

```
##          x   x2
## obs1   2    2
## obs2   8   32
## obs3  18  162
```

Again, in order for this kind of multiplication to work, the dimensions of the matrices must match.

7.2 | Matrix multiplication and inversion

If A and B are matrices, then the matrix product AB is the matrix representing the composition of the two operations: first apply B, then apply A to the result. For matrix multiplication to be a properly defined operation, the matrices to be multiplied must *conform*. That is, the number of columns of the first matrix must match the number of rows of the second matrix. The resulting matrix AB will have its row dimension taken from A and its column dimension taken from B.

In R, this form of matrix multiplication can be performed using the operator %*%, for example

```
t(Y) %*% X
```

```
##       x   x2
## x    28   72
## x2   72  196
```

From the previous section we saw that t(Y) has three columns and X has three rows, so we can perform the multiplication $Y^\top X$. The result is a 2 × 2 matrix, since t(Y) has two rows and X has two columns.

If we failed to transpose Y, we would obtain an error, as in

```
Y %*% X
```

```
## Error in Y %*% X: non-conformable arguments
```

The `crossprod()` function is a somewhat more efficient way to calculate Y^TX:

```
crossprod(Y, X)

##     x   x2
## x   28  72
## x2  72  196
```

Note that the first argument of `crossprod()` is transposed automatically. The reason this is more efficient than `t(Y) %*% X` is that the latter needs to make a new object `t(Y)` before performing the multiplication. If Y is a large matrix, this will consume a lot of memory and noticeable computation time. The `crossprod(Y, X)` function call can access the elements of `Y` directly, since the (i,j) element of Y^T is simply the (j,i) element of Y.

Exercises

1 Compute $1.5X$, using the matrix X that was defined at the end of Section 7.1.1.

2 Use the `crossprod()` function to compute X^TX and XX^T. Note the dimensions of the resulting products.

3 Consider the following code which compares the times for computing the product of two matrices (A and B) and a vector v:

$$ABv.$$

```
library(microbenchmark)
A <- matrix(rep(1, 1000000), nrow = 1000)  # a matrix of 1's
B <- A
v <- rep(1, 1000)     # a vector of 1's
microbenchmark(A %*% B %*% v,
               (A %*% B) %*% v,
               A %*% (B %*% v), times = 10)

## Unit: milliseconds
##              expr        min         lq       mean     median
##    A %*% B %*% v 770.040205 775.592270 781.965270 778.427518
##  (A %*% B) %*% v 770.608633 771.788267 778.398599 778.298938
##  A %*% (B %*% v)   2.795341   2.835159   2.877357   2.853293
##          uq        max neval cld
## 789.380235 797.052404    10   b
## 782.547556 792.678882    10   b
##   2.936859   3.025221    10   a
```

(a) Is there a mathematical difference between ABv, $(AB)v$, and $A(Bv)$?

(b) Explain why the third calculation takes less time than the other calculations.

(c) Can you explain the behavior that you observe upon running the following calculations?

```
library(microbenchmark)
A <- matrix(rep(1, 1000000), nrow = 1000)   # a matrix of 1's
B <- diag(1000)        # 1000 x 1000 identity matrix
v <- rep(1, 1000)      # a vector of 1's
microbenchmark( A %*% B %*% v,
               (A %*% B) %*% v,
                A %*% (B %*% v), times = 10)
```

7.2.1 Matrix inversion

The inverse of a square $n \times n$ matrix A, denoted by A^{-1}, is the solution to the matrix equation $AA^{-1} = I$, where I is the $n \times n$ identity matrix. We can view this as n separate systems of linear equations in n unknowns, whose solutions are the columns of A^{-1}. For example, with

$$A = \begin{bmatrix} 3 & -4 \\ 1 & 2 \end{bmatrix}$$

the matrix equation

$$\begin{bmatrix} 3 & -4 \\ 1 & 2 \end{bmatrix} \begin{bmatrix} b_{11} & b_{12} \\ b_{21} & b_{22} \end{bmatrix} = \begin{bmatrix} 1 & 0 \\ 0 & 1 \end{bmatrix}$$

is equivalent to the two equations:

$$\begin{bmatrix} 3 & -4 \\ 1 & 2 \end{bmatrix} \begin{bmatrix} b_{11} \\ b_{21} \end{bmatrix} = \begin{bmatrix} 1 \\ 0 \end{bmatrix}$$

and

$$\begin{bmatrix} 3 & -4 \\ 1 & 2 \end{bmatrix} \begin{bmatrix} b_{12} \\ b_{22} \end{bmatrix} = \begin{bmatrix} 0 \\ 1 \end{bmatrix}.$$

The usual computational approach to finding A^{-1} involves solving these two equations.

However, this is not always a good idea! Often the reason we are trying to find A^{-1} is so that we can solve a system $Ax = b$ with the solution $x = A^{-1}b$. It doesn't make sense from a computational point of view to solve n systems of linear equations in order to obtain a result which will be used as the solution to one system. If we know how to solve systems, we should use that knowledge to solve $Ax = b$ directly. Furthermore, using A^{-1} may give a worse approximation to the final result than the direct approach, because there are so many more operations involved, giving opportunities for much more rounding error to creep into our results.

7.2.2 The *LU* decomposition

The general strategy for solving a system of equations $Ax = b$ is to break down the problem into simpler ones. This often involves rewriting the matrix A in a special form; one such form is called the *LU* decomposition.

In the LU decomposition, we write A as a product of two matrices L and U. The matrix L is lower triangular with unit values on the diagonal, i.e.

$$L = \begin{bmatrix} 1 & 0 & \cdots & 0 \\ l_{21} & 1 & \ddots & \vdots \\ \vdots & & \ddots & 0 \\ l_{n1} & l_{n2} & \cdots & 1 \end{bmatrix}.$$

U is upper triangular, i.e.

$$U = \begin{bmatrix} u_{11} & u_{12} & \cdots & u_{1n} \\ 0 & u_{22} & \cdots & u_{2n} \\ \vdots & \ddots & \ddots & \vdots \\ 0 & \cdots & 0 & u_{nn} \end{bmatrix}.$$

It turns out that this factorization of A is quite easy to find by stepping through the entries one by one. For example, if

$$A = \begin{bmatrix} 2 & 4 & 3 \\ 6 & 16 & 10 \\ 4 & 12 & 9 \end{bmatrix}$$

the calculations would proceed as follows, where we write the entries of A as a_{ij}. We make repeated use of the relation

$$a_{ij} = \sum_{k=1}^{3} l_{ik} u_{kj}$$

and take advantage of knowing the 0's and 1's in L and U:

1. $a_{11} = 2 = l_{11} \times u_{11} = 1 \times u_{11}$, so $u_{11} = 2$.
2. $a_{21} = 6 = l_{21} \times u_{11} = l_{21} \times 2$, so $l_{21} = 3$.
3. $a_{31} = 4 = l_{31} \times u_{11} = l_{31} \times 2$, so $l_{31} = 2$.
4. $a_{12} = 4 = l_{11} \times u_{12}$, so $u_{12} = 4$.
5. $a_{22} = 16 = l_{21} \times u_{12} + l_{22} \times u_{22} = 3 \times 4 + 1 \times u_{22}$, so $u_{22} = 4$.
6. $a_{32} = 12 = l_{31} \times u_{12} + l_{32} \times u_{22} = 2 \times 4 + l_{32} \times 4$, so $l_{32} = 1$.
7. $a_{13} = 3 = l_{11} \times u_{13} = 1 \times u_{13}$, so $u_{13} = 3$.
8. $a_{23} = 10 = l_{21} \times u_{13} + l_{22} \times u_{23} = 3 \times 3 + 1 \times u_{23}$, so $u_{23} = 1$.
9. $a_{33} = 9 = l_{31} \times u_{13} + l_{32} \times u_{23} + l_{33} \times u_{33} = 2 \times 3 + 1 \times 1 + 1 \times u_{33}$, so $u_{33} = 2$.

Once we have L and U in hand, solving the system of equations $Ax = b$ is easy. We write the system as $L(Ux) = b$, set $y = Ux$, and solve $Ly = b$ for y first. Because L is lower triangular, this is straightforward using a procedure known as *forward substitution*. Continuing the example above, with $b = [-1, -2, -7]^{\top}$, and setting $y = [y_1, y_2, y_3]^{\top}$, we make use of the relation

$$b_i = \sum_{j=1}^{3} l_{ij} y_j$$

to calculate:

10. $b_1 = -1 = l_{11} \times y_1 = 1 \times y_1$, so $y_1 = -1$.

11. $b_2 = -2 = l_{21} \times y_1 + l_{22} \times y_2 = 3 \times (-1) + 1 \times y_2$, so $y_2 = 1$.

12. $b_3 = -7 = l_{31} \times y_1 + l_{32} \times y_2 + l_{33} \times y_3 = 2 \times (-1) + 1 \times 1 + 1 \times y_3$, so $y_3 = -6$.

Finally, we solve $Ux = y$. This time the fact that U is upper triangular means solving for the entries in reverse order is easy, using a procedure called *back substitution*:

13. $y_3 = -6 = u_{33} \times x_3 = 2 \times x_3$, so $x_3 = -3$.

14. $y_2 = 1 = u_{22} \times x_2 + u_{23} \times x_3 = 4 \times x_2 + 1 \times (-3)$, so $x_2 = 1$.

15. $y_1 = -1 = u_{11} \times x_1 + u_{12} \times x_2 + u_{13} \times x_3 = 2 \times x_1 + 4 \times 1 + 3 \times (-3)$, so $x_1 = 2$.

By processing these steps successively, the problem of solving $Ax = b$ has been reduced to solving 15 successive linear equations, each with just one unknown. The procedure is easily automated. In fact, the default method used in R for solving linear equations is based on this technique; the only substantial difference is that the ordering of the columns is rearranged before factoring so that rounding error is minimized.

7.2.3 Matrix inversion in R

In R, matrices are inverted and linear systems of equations are solved using the `solve()` or `qr.solve()` functions. `solve()` uses a method based on the *LU* decomposition; `qr.solve()` is based on the *QR* decomposition that is described in Section 7.4.3.

As an example, we compute the inverse of the 3×3 Hilbert matrix introduced in Section 7.1.

```
H3inv <- solve(H3)
H3inv

##      [,1] [,2] [,3]
## [1,]    9  -36   30
## [2,]  -36  192 -180
## [3,]   30 -180  180
```

To verify that this is the inverse of `H3`, we can check that the product of `H3inv` and `H3` is the 3×3 identity.

```
H3inv %*% H3

##                [,1]          [,2]          [,3]
## [1,]  1.000000e+00  0.000000e+00 -8.881784e-16
## [2,]  7.105427e-15  1.000000e+00  0.000000e+00
## [3,] -1.421085e-14 -7.105427e-15  1.000000e+00
```

The diagonal elements are all 1's, but five of the off-diagonal elements are non-zero. Scientific notation is used for these elements; they are all computed to be of the order of 10^{-14} or smaller. They are "numerically" close to 0. H3inv is not the exact inverse of H3, but it is believable that it is very close.

Exercises

1 Compute the inverse of $X^\top X$, using the matrix X that was defined at the end of Section 7.1.1. Verify your result using crossprod().
2 Can you compute the inverse of $XX^\top$? Why is there a problem?
3 The general $n \times n$ Hilbert matrix has (i,j) element given by $1/(i+j-1)$.
   (a) Write a function which gives the $n \times n$ Hilbert matrix as its output, for any positive integer n.
   (b) Are all of the Hilbert matrices invertible?
   (c) Use solve() and qr.solve() to compute the inverse of the Hilbert matrices, up to $n = 10$. Is there a problem?

7.2.4 Solving linear systems

The function solve(A, b) gives the solution to systems of equations of the form $Ax = b$.

For example, let us find x such that $H_3x = b$ where H_3 is the 3×3 Hilbert matrix and $b = [1\ 2\ 3]^\top$.

```
b <- c(1, 2, 3)
x <- solve(H3, b)
x
```

```
## [1]    27 -192   210
```

In other words, the solution vector is $x = [27, -192, 210]^\top$.

Exercises

1 Let $[x_1, x_2, x_3, x_4, x_5, x_6]^\top = [10, 11, 12, 13, 14, 15]^\top$. Find the coefficients of the quintic polynomial $f(x)$ for which $[f(x_1), f(x_2), f(x_3), f(x_4), f(x_5), f(x_6)]^\top = [25, 16, 26, 19, 21, 20]^\top$. Hint: the quintic polynomial $f(x) = a_0 + a_1x + a_2x^2 + a_3x^3 + a_4x^4 + a_5x^5$ can be viewed as the matrix product of the row vector $[1, x, x^2, x^3, x^4, x^5]$ with the column vector $[a_0, a_1, a_2, a_3, a_4, a_5]^\top$. Work out the matrix version of this to give $[f(x_1), f(x_2), f(x_3), f(x_4), f(x_5), f(x_6)]^\top$.

7.3 | Eigenvalues and eigenvectors

Eigenvalues and eigenvectors can be computed using the function eigen(). For example,

```
eigen(H3)
```

```
## eigen() decomposition
## $values
## [1] 1.40831893 0.12232707 0.00268734
```

```
##
## $vectors
##             [,1]         [,2]         [,3]
## [1,]  0.8270449   0.5474484   0.1276593
## [2,]  0.4598639  -0.5282902  -0.7137469
## [3,]  0.3232984  -0.6490067   0.6886715
```

To see what this output means, let x_1 denote the first column of the $vectors output, i.e. $[0.827\ 0.460\ 0.323]^\top$. This is the first eigenvector, and it corresponds to the eigenvalue 1.408. Thus,

$$H_3 x_1 = 1.408 x_1.$$

Denoting the second and third columns of $vectors by x_2 and x_3, we have

$$H_3 x_2 = 0.122 x_2$$

and

$$H_3 x_3 = 0.00269 x_3.$$

Exercises

1 Calculate the matrix $H = X(X^\top X)^{-1} X^\top$, where X was as defined in Example 7.2.
2 Calculate the eigenvalues and eigenvectors of H.
3 Calculate the trace of the matrix H, and compare with the sum of the eigenvalues.
4 Calculate the determinant of the matrix H, and compare with the product of the eigenvalues.
5 Using the definition, verify that the columns of X are eigenvectors of H.
6 Obtain the 6×6 Hilbert matrix, and compute its eigenvalues and eigenvectors. Compute the inverse of the matrix. Is there a relation between the eigenvalues of the inverse and the eigenvalues of the original matrix? Is there supposed to be a relationship?
   Repeat the above analysis on the 7×7 Hilbert matrix.

7.4 Other matrix decompositions

7.4.1 The singular value decomposition of a matrix

The singular value decomposition of a square matrix A consists of three square matrices, U, D, and V. The matrix D is a diagonal matrix. The relation among these matrices is

$$A = UDV^\top.$$

The matrices U and V are said to be *orthogonal*, which means that $U^{-1} = U^\top$ and $V^{-1} = V^\top$.

The singular value decomposition of a matrix is often used to obtain accurate solutions to linear systems of equations.

The elements of D are called the singular values of A. Note that $A^\top A = V^{-1}D^2V$. This is a "similarity transformation" which tells us that the squares of the singular values of A are the eigenvalues of $A^\top A$.

The singular value decomposition can be obtained using the function svd(). For example, the singular value decomposition of the 3×3 Hilbert matrix H_3 is

```
H3.svd <- svd(H3)
H3.svd

## $d
## [1] 1.40831893 0.12232707 0.00268734
##
## $u
##              [,1]        [,2]        [,3]
## [1,] -0.8270449  0.5474484  0.1276593
## [2,] -0.4598639 -0.5282902 -0.7137469
## [3,] -0.3232984 -0.6490067  0.6886715
##
## $v
##              [,1]        [,2]        [,3]
## [1,] -0.8270449  0.5474484  0.1276593
## [2,] -0.4598639 -0.5282902 -0.7137469
## [3,] -0.3232984 -0.6490067  0.6886715
```

We can verify that these components can be multiplied in the appropriate way to reconstruct H_3.

```
H3.svd$u %*% diag(H3.svd$d) %*% t(H3.svd$v)

##              [,1]        [,2]        [,3]
## [1,] 1.0000000 0.5000000 0.3333333
## [2,] 0.5000000 0.3333333 0.2500000
## [3,] 0.3333333 0.2500000 0.2000000
```

Because of the properties of the U, V, and D matrices, the singular value decomposition provides a simple way to compute a matrix inverse. For example, $H_3^{-1} = VD^{-1}U^\top$ and can be recalculated as

```
H3.svd$v %*% diag(1/H3.svd$d) %*% t(H3.svd$u)

##        [,1] [,2] [,3]
## [1,]     9  -36   30
## [2,]   -36  192 -180
## [3,]    30 -180  180
```

7.4.2 The Choleski decomposition of a positive definite matrix

If a matrix A is positive definite, it possesses a square root. In fact, there are usually several matrices B such that $B^2 = A$. The Choleski decomposition is similar, but the idea is to find an upper triangular matrix U such that $U^\top U = A$. The function chol() accomplishes this task.

For example, we can compute the Choleski decomposition of the 3×3 Hilbert matrix.

```
H3.chol <- chol(H3)
H3.chol                           # This is U, the upper triangular matrix

##          [,1]         [,2]         [,3]
## [1,]     1 0.5000000 0.3333333
## [2,]     0 0.2886751 0.2886751
## [3,]     0 0.0000000 0.0745356

crossprod(H3.chol, H3.chol)   # Multiplying t(U) %*% U to recover H3

##              [,1]         [,2]         [,3]
## [1,] 1.0000000 0.5000000 0.3333333
## [2,] 0.5000000 0.3333333 0.2500000
## [3,] 0.3333333 0.2500000 0.2000000
```

Once the Choleski decomposition of a matrix $A = U^\top U$ has been obtained, we can compute the inverse of A using the fact that $A^{-1} = U^{-1}U^{-\top}$ (where $U^{-\top}$ is a short way to write the transpose of U^{-1}). This computation is much more stable than direct calculation of A^{-1} by Gaussian elimination. The function `chol2inv()` does this calculation. For example, we can compute the inverse of H3 as

```
chol2inv(H3.chol)

##          [,1] [,2] [,3]
## [1,]      9  -36   30
## [2,]    -36  192 -180
## [3,]     30 -180  180
```

Once the Choleski decomposition has been obtained, we can compute solutions to linear systems of the form

$$Ax = b.$$

If $A = U^\top U$, then we see that $Ux = U^{-\top}b$. Therefore, the solution x can be obtained in a two-step procedure:

1. Solve $U^\top y = b$ for y. The solution will satisfy $y = U^{-\top}b$.
2. Solve $Ux = y$.

The first system is lower triangular, so forward substitution can be used to solve it. The function `forwardsolve()` can be used for this.

The second system is upper triangular, so back substitution using function `backsolve()` can be used.

For the problem $H_3 x = b$, where $b = [1\ 2\ 3]^\top$, we can proceed as follows:

```
b <- seq(1, 3)
y <- forwardsolve(t(H3.chol), b)
backsolve(H3.chol, y)                         # the solution x

## [1]     27 -192    210
```

7.4.3 The QR decomposition of a matrix

Another way of decomposing a matrix A is via the QR decomposition

$$A = QR,$$

where Q is an orthogonal matrix, and R is an upper triangular matrix. This decomposition can be applied even if A is not square. Again, this decomposition can be used to obtain accurate solutions to linear systems of equations.

For example, suppose we want to solve

$$Ax = b$$

for x, given the $n \times n$ matrix A and n-vector b. If we compute the QR decomposition of A first, we can write

$$QRx = b.$$

Multiplying through by $Q^\top$ on the left gives

$$Rx = Q^\top b.$$

This is an easier system to solve, because R is an upper triangular matrix. Note that $Q^\top b$ is an easily calculated n-vector.

To obtain the decomposition, we use the qr() function. For example,

```
H3.qr <- qr(H3)
H3.qr

## $qr
##                [,1]        [,2]         [,3]
## [1,] -1.1666667 -0.6428571 -0.450000000
## [2,]  0.4285714 -0.1017143 -0.105337032
## [3,]  0.2857143  0.7292564  0.003901372
##
## $rank
## [1] 3
##
## $qraux
## [1] 1.857142857 1.684240553 0.003901372
##
## $pivot
## [1] 1 2 3
##
## attr(,"class")
## [1] "qr"
```

The output is an object of class qr.

The functions qr.Q() and qr.R() can be applied to this object to obtain the explicit Q and R matrices. For our example, we have

```
Q <- qr.Q(H3.qr)
Q
```

```
##             [,1]       [,2]       [,3]
## [1,] -0.8571429  0.5016049  0.1170411
## [2,] -0.4285714 -0.5684856 -0.7022469
## [3,] -0.2857143 -0.6520864  0.7022469
```

```
R <- qr.R(H3.qr)
R
```

```
##             [,1]       [,2]          [,3]
## [1,] -1.166667 -0.6428571 -0.450000000
## [2,]  0.000000 -0.1017143 -0.105337032
## [3,]  0.000000  0.0000000  0.003901372
```

We can recover H_3 by multiplying Q by R:

```
Q %*% R
```

```
##             [,1]      [,2]      [,3]
## [1,] 1.0000000 0.5000000 0.3333333
## [2,] 0.5000000 0.3333333 0.2500000
## [3,] 0.3333333 0.2500000 0.2000000
```

Again, the inverse of H_3 can be obtained from $R^{-1}Q^\top$. Since R is upper triangular, this inverse can be computed quickly, in principle. In the following, we compute R^{-1} in a computationally inefficient way, simply to demonstrate that the decomposition can be used to get at the inverse of a matrix.

```
qr.solve(R) %*% t(Q)
```

```
##        [,1]  [,2]  [,3]
## [1,]     9   -36    30
## [2,]   -36   192  -180
## [3,]    30  -180   180
```

Orthogonal transformations preserve Euclidean distance

Consider the 2×2 orthogonal matrix

$$Q = \frac{1}{\sqrt{2}} \begin{bmatrix} 1 & -1 \\ 1 & 1 \end{bmatrix}$$

and vectors $x = [3\ 4]^\top$ and $y = [5\ 8]^\top$:

```
x <- c(3, 4)
y <- c(5, 8)
Q <- matrix(c(1, 1, -1, 1), nrow = 2)/sqrt(2)
```

The (Euclidean) distance between x and y can be calculated as

```
sqrt(t(x - y) %*% (x - y))
##          [,1]
## [1,]  4.472136
```

and the distance between Qx and Qy is the same:

```
sqrt(t(Q %*% x - Q %*% y) %*% (Q %*% x - Q %*% y))
##          [,1]
## [1,]  4.472136
```

This result is not an accident. It is true in general that the Euclidean distance between any two vectors x and y is the same as the Euclidean distance between Qx and Qy when Q is an orthogonal matrix.

Solving over-determined systems

Suppose

$$A = \begin{bmatrix} 1 & 2 \\ 1 & 5 \\ 1 & 8 \\ 1 & 9 \\ 1 & 11 \end{bmatrix}$$

and $y = [4\ 8\ 12\ 15\ 21]^\top$. How can we find a point x (in two dimensions) which minimizes the Euclidean distance between y and Ax?

Before solving the problem, you can gain some intuition by trying particular values of x, for example $x = [3\ 7]^\top$:

```
A <- matrix(c(rep(1, 5), 2, 5, 8, 9, 11), nrow = 5)
y <- c(4, 8, 12, 15, 21)
x <- c(3, 7)
sqrt(t(y - A %*% x) %*% (y - A %*% x))

##          [,1]
## [1,]  96.74709
```

From above, we have that the distance between y and Ax is the same as $Q^\top y$ and $Q^\top Ax$ for any orthogonal matrix Q. If Q is the matrix of the QR decomposition of A, then

$$Q^\top Ax = Q^\top QRx = Rx.$$

Therefore, we can solve the problem by finding the vector x which minimizes the distance between Rx and $Q^\top y$. This turns out to be a simpler problem than we started with.

Finding the QR decomposition of A, and pre-multiplying both A and y by $Q^\top$, we obtain

```
A.QR <- qr(A)
Q <- qr.Q(A.QR, complete = TRUE)
R <- qr.R(A.QR, complete = TRUE)
QTy <- t(Q) %*% y
QTy
```

```
##               [,1]
## [1,] -26.8328157
## [2,]  12.7279221
## [3,]  -2.3487875
## [4,]  -1.2429967
## [5,]   0.9685849
```

```
R
```

```
##              [,1]         [,2]
## [1,] -2.236068 -15.652476
## [2,]  0.000000   7.071068
## [3,]  0.000000   0.000000
## [4,]  0.000000   0.000000
## [5,]  0.000000   0.000000
```

Notice what happens when we calculate Rx for any two-dimensional x, such as the one suggested above:

```
R %*% x
```

```
##             [,1]
## [1,] -116.27553
## [2,]   49.49747
## [3,]    0.00000
## [4,]    0.00000
## [5,]    0.00000
```

The last three elements of x are always 0, because the last three rows of R are all 0's. It doesn't matter what x is; this will always happen. Thus, even the x-vector which makes Rx as close as possible to $Q^\top y$ will result in the last three elements of Rx being 0's. Therefore, we can only control the top two elements of Rx through our choice of the elements of the vector x. We can choose x so that the first two elements of Rx exactly match the first two elements of $Q^\top y$. This choice minimizes the distance between Rx and $Q^\top y$ and hence, between Ax and y.

The qr.solve() function performs the computation directly:

```
x <- qr.solve(A, y)
x
```

```
## [1] -0.6  1.8
```

As a check, we can verify that the first two elements of Rx match the first two elements of $Q^\top y$ calculated above.

```
R %*% x

##               [,1]
## [1,]  -26.83282
## [2,]   12.72792
## [3,]    0.00000
## [4,]    0.00000
## [5,]    0.00000
```

Exercises

1 Calculate the singular value decomposition of the 4×4 Hilbert matrix. Use this to numerically calculate its inverse.

2 Find a square root of the 4×4 Hilbert matrix.

3 Find the point x in two dimensions which minimizes the distance between $y = [7\,3\,5\,4\,8]^\top$ and Ax where

$$A = \begin{bmatrix} 1 & 2 \\ 1 & 3 \\ 1 & 4 \\ 1 & 5 \\ 1 & 6 \end{bmatrix}.$$

4 Find the point x in three dimensions which minimizes the distance between $y = [7\,3\,5\,4\,8]^\top$ and Ax where

$$A = \begin{bmatrix} 1 & 2 & 4 \\ 1 & 3 & 3 \\ 1 & 4 & 5 \\ 1 & 5 & 3 \\ 1 & 6 & 2 \end{bmatrix}.$$

7.5 | Other matrix operations

The function `outer()` is sometimes useful in statistical calculations. It can be used to perform an operation on all possible pairs of elements coming from two vectors.

A simple example involves computing all quotients among pairs of elements of the sequence running from 1 through 5.

```
x1 <- seq(1, 5)
outer(x1, x1, "/")      # or outer(x1, x1, function(x, y) {x / y})

##        [,1] [,2]      [,3] [,4] [,5]
## [1,]      1  0.5 0.3333333 0.25  0.2
## [2,]      2  1.0 0.6666667 0.50  0.4
## [3,]      3  1.5 1.0000000 0.75  0.6
## [4,]      4  2.0 1.3333333 1.00  0.8
## [5,]      5  2.5 1.6666667 1.25  1.0
```

Replacing the division operation with the subtraction operator gives all pairwise differences.

```
outer(x1, x1, "-")

##      [,1] [,2] [,3] [,4] [,5]
## [1,]    0   -1   -2   -3   -4
## [2,]    1    0   -1   -2   -3
## [3,]    2    1    0   -1   -2
## [4,]    3    2    1    0   -1
## [5,]    4    3    2    1    0
```

The third argument can be any function that takes two vector arguments. The second argument can differ from the first. For example,

```
y <- seq(5, 10)
outer(x1, y, "+")

##      [,1] [,2] [,3] [,4] [,5] [,6]
## [1,]    6    7    8    9   10   11
## [2,]    7    8    9   10   11   12
## [3,]    8    9   10   11   12   13
## [4,]    9   10   11   12   13   14
## [5,]   10   11   12   13   14   15
```

7.5.1 Kronecker products

The function `kronecker()` can be used to compute the Kronecker product of two matrices and other more general products. See the `help()` file for more information.

7.5.2 `apply()`

In statistical applications, it is sometimes necessary to apply the same function to each of the rows of a matrix, or to each of the columns. A `for()` loop could be used, but it is sometimes more efficient computationally to use the `apply()` function.

There are three arguments. The first specifies the matrix. The second specifies whether the operation is to be applied to rows (`1`) or columns (`2`). The third argument specifies the function which should be applied.

A simple example is to compute the sum of the rows of H_3.

```
apply(H3, 1, sum)

## [1] 1.8333333 1.0833333 0.7833333
```

Chapter exercises

1 Consider the following *circulant* matrix.

$$P = \begin{bmatrix} 0.1 & 0.2 & 0.3 & 0.4 \\ 0.4 & 0.1 & 0.2 & 0.3 \\ 0.3 & 0.4 & 0.1 & 0.2 \\ 0.2 & 0.3 & 0.4 & 0.1 \end{bmatrix}.$$

(a) P is an example of a stochastic matrix. Use the `apply()` function to verify that the row sums add to 1.

(b) Compute P^n for $n = 2, 3, 5, 10$. Is a pattern emerging?

(c) Find a nonnegative row vector x whose elements sum to 1 and which satisfies

$$xP = x.$$

Do you see any connection between P^{10} and x?

(d) Using the methods of Section 6.5, generate a pseudorandom sequence of numbers $y_1, \ldots, y_{10000}$ with $y_1 = 1$ and the remainder from the Markov chain with transition matrix P.

(e) Use the `table()` function to determine the relative frequency distribution of the four possible values in the y vector. Compare this distribution with the *invariant distribution* x calculated earlier.

2 Repeat the previous exercise using the matrix

$$P = \begin{bmatrix} 0.1 & 0.2 & 0.3 & 0.4 & 0.0 & 0.0 & 0.0 \\ 0.1 & 0.1 & 0.1 & 0.1 & 0.1 & 0.1 & 0.4 \\ 0.2 & 0.2 & 0.2 & 0.2 & 0.2 & 0.0 & 0.0 \\ 0.3 & 0.3 & 0.3 & 0.1 & 0.0 & 0.0 & 0.0 \\ 0.3 & 0.3 & 0.3 & 0.1 & 0.0 & 0.0 & 0.0 \\ 0.3 & 0.3 & 0.3 & 0.1 & 0.0 & 0.0 & 0.0 \\ 0.3 & 0.3 & 0.3 & 0.1 & 0.0 & 0.0 & 0.0 \end{bmatrix}.$$

3 An insurance company has four types of policies, which we will label A, B, C, and D.

- They have a total of 245,921 policies.
- The annual income from each policy is $10 for type A, $30 for type B, $50 for type C, and $100 for type D.
- The total annual income for all policies is $7,304,620.
- The claims on the different types of policy arise at different rates. The expected number of type A claims on a single policy is 0.1 claims per year, type B 0.15 claims per year, type C 0.03 claims per year, and type D 0.5 claims per year.
- The total expected number of claims for the company is 34,390.48 per year.
- The expected size of the claims is different for each policy type. For type A, it is $50, for type B it is $180, for type C it is $1500, and for type D it is $250.
- The expected total claim amount is $6,864,693. This is the sum over all policies of the expected size of claim times the expected number of claims in a year.

Use R to do the following:

(a) Find the total number of each type of policy.

(b) Find the total income and total expected claim size for each type of policy.

(c) Assuming that claims arise in a Poisson process, and each claim amount follows a Gamma distribution with shape parameter 2 and the means listed above, use simulation to estimate the following:

  (i) The variance in the total claim amount.

    (ii) The probability that the total claim amount will exceed the total annual income from these policies.

    Write a function to do these calculations, and do it once for the overall company income and claims, and once for each of the four types of policy.

4 The function `kappa()` can be used to compute the condition number of a given matrix (the ratio of the largest to smallest non-zero singular values). This gives an idea as to how bad certain numerical calculations will be when applied to the matrix. Large values of the condition number indicate poor numerical properties; in particular, accuracy in the numerical calculation of the inverse of a matrix with a large condition number will be poor. Calculate the respective condition numbers for the 3×3, 5×5, and 7×7 Hilbert matrices. Interpret the results.

Numerical optimization

In many areas of statistics and applied mathematics one has to solve the following problem: given a function $f(\cdot)$, which value of x makes $f(x)$ as large or as small as possible?

For example, in financial modeling $f(x)$ might be the expected return from a portfolio, with x being a vector holding the amounts invested in each of a number of possible securities. There might be constraints on x (e.g. the amount to invest must be positive, the total amount invested must be fixed, etc.).

In statistical modeling, we may want to find a set of parameters for a model which minimize the expected prediction errors for the model. Here x would be the parameters and $f(\cdot)$ would be a measure of the prediction error.

Knowing how to do minimization is sufficient. If we want to maximize $f(x)$, we simply change the sign and minimize $-f(x)$. We call both operations "numerical optimization." Use of derivatives and simple algebra often lead to the solution of such problems, but not nearly always. Because of the wide range of possibilities for functions $f(\cdot)$ and parameters x, this is a rich area of computing.

8.1 | The golden section search method

The golden section search method is a simple way of finding the minimizer of a single-variable function which has a single minimum on the interval $[a,b]$.

Consider minimizing the function

$$f(x) = |x - 3.5| + (x - 2)^2$$

on the interval $[0,5]$. This function is not differentiable at $x = 3.5$, so some care must be taken to find the minimizer. We can write an R function to evaluate $f(x)$ as follows:

```
f <- function(x) {
    abs(x - 3.5) + (x - 2)^2
}
```

To check that this function has a single minimum in the interval we use the `curve()` function to plot it:

```
curve(f, from = 1, to = 5)
```

The curve is displayed in Figure 8.1, where we can see that the minimizer is located near $x = 2.5$.

The golden section search method is an iterative method, which may be outlined as follows:

1. Start with the interval $[a, b]$, known to contain the minimizer.
2. Repeatedly shrink it, finding smaller and smaller intervals $[a', b']$ which still contain the minimizer.
3. Stop when $b' - a'$ is small enough, i.e. when the interval length is less than a pre-set tolerance.

When the search stops, the midpoint of the final interval will serve as a good approximation to the true minimizer, with a maximum error of $(b' - a')/2$.

The shrinkage step 2 begins by evaluating the function at two points $x_1 < x_2$ in the interior of the interval $[a, b]$. (How the points are chosen will be described below.) Because we have assumed that there is a unique minimum, we know that if $f(x_1) > f(x_2)$, then the minimum must lie to the right of x_1, i.e. in the interval $[a', b'] = [x_1, b]$. If $f(x_1) < f(x_2)$, the minimum must lie in $[a', b'] = [a, x_2]$ (see Figure 8.2). (What if the values are exactly equal? Convince yourself that we can choose either update.) Then new values of $x_1, f(x_1), x_2$, and $f(x_2)$ are computed, and the method is repeated until the tolerance criterion is satisfied.

The choice of the points between a and b makes use of properties of the golden ratio $\phi = (\sqrt{5} + 1)/2$. The golden ratio (which we saw in Chapter 3 in the context of Fibonacci numbers) has a number of interesting algebraic properties. We make use of the fact that $1/\phi = \phi - 1$ and $1/\phi^2 = 1 - 1/\phi$ in the following. (Some authors call the value $\Phi = 1/\phi$ the "silver ratio," but we'll stick with ϕ in our formulas.)

We locate the interior points at $x_1 = b - (b - a)/\phi$ and $x_2 = a + (b - a)/\phi$. The reason for this choice is as follows. After one iteration of the search, it is possible that we will throw away a and replace it with $a' = x_1$. Then the new value to use as x_1 will be

$$
\begin{aligned}
x_1' &= b - (b - a')/\phi \\
&= b - (b - x_1)/\phi \\
&= b - (b - a)/\phi^2 \\
&= a + (b - a)/\phi \\
&= x_2,
\end{aligned}
$$

i.e. we can re-use a point we already have, we do not need a new calculation to find it, and we don't need a new evaluation of $f(x_1')$, we can re-use $f(x_2)$. Similarly, if we update to $b' = x_2$, then $x_2' = x_1$, and we can re-use that point.

We put this together into the following R function.

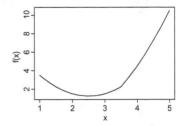

Fig. 8.1   The function
$f(x) = |x - 3.5| + (x - 2)^2$.

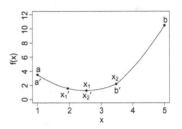

Fig. 8.2   One iteration of the golden section search, applied to the test function
$f(x) = |x - 3.5| + (x - 2)^2$.

```
golden <- function (f, a, b, tol = 0.0000001)
{
    ratio <- 2 / (sqrt(5) + 1)
    x1 <- b - ratio * (b - a)
    x2 <- a + ratio * (b - a)

    f1 <- f(x1)
    f2 <- f(x2)

    while(abs(b - a) > tol) {

        if (f2 > f1) {
            b <- x2
            x2 <- x1
            f2 <- f1
            x1 <- b - ratio * (b - a)
            f1 <- f(x1)
        } else {
            a <- x1
            x1 <- x2
            f1 <- f2
            x2 <- a + ratio * (b - a)
            f2 <- f(x2)
        }
    }
    return((a + b) / 2)
}
```

We test and see that `golden()` works, at least on one function:

```
golden(f, 1, 5)

## [1] 2.5
```

Exercises

1 Apply the golden section minimization technique to the following functions:
   (a) $f(x) = |x - 3.5| + |x - 2| + |x - 1|$,
   (b) $f(x) = |x - 3.2| + |x - 3.5| + |x - 2| + |x - 1|$.
   For the second function, check the graph to see that the minimizer is not unique. Show that the minimizer found by `golden()` depends on the initial interval supplied to the function.

2 For an odd number of data values $x_1, x_2, \ldots, x_n$, the minimizer of the function

$$f(x) = \sum_{i=1}^{n} |x - x_i|$$

   is the sample median of the data values. (Exercise 1.(a) is an example of this.) Verify this result for the data sets

(a) 3, 7, 9, 12, 15 and

(b) 3, 7, 9, 12, 15, 18, 21.

Describe, in words, what happens when the number of observations is even.

3 Write a function which would find the maximizer of a function using the golden section search.

8.2 | Newton–Raphson

If the function to be minimized has two continuous derivatives and we know how to evaluate them, we can make use of this information to give a faster algorithm than the golden section search.

We want to find a minimizer x^* of the function $f(x)$ in the interval $[a, b]$. Provided the minimizer is not at a or b, x^* will satisfy $f'(x^*) = 0$. This is a necessary condition for x^* to be a minimizer of $f(x)$, but it is not sufficient: we must check that x^* actually minimizes $f(x)$. Other solutions of $f'(x^*) = 0$ are maximizers and points of inflection. One sufficient condition to guarantee that our solution is a minimum is to check that $f''(x^*) > 0$.

Now, if we have a guess x_0 at a minimizer, we use the fact that $f''(x)$ is the slope of $f'(x)$ and approximate $f'(x)$ using a Taylor series approximation:

$$f'(x) \approx f'(x_0) + (x - x_0)f''(x_0).$$

Finding a zero of the right-hand side should give us an approximate solution to $f'(x^*) = 0$.

We implement this idea as follows, using the Newton–Raphson algorithm to approximate a solution to $f'(x^*) = 0$. Start with an initial guess x_0, and compute an improved guess using the solution

$$x_1 = x_0 - \frac{f'(x_0)}{f''(x_0)}.$$

This gives a new guess at the minimizer. Then use x_1 in place of x_0, to obtain a new update x_2. Continue with iterations of the form

$$x_{n+1} = x_n - \frac{f'(x_n)}{f''(x_n)}.$$

This iteration stops when $f'(x_n)$ is close enough to 0. Usually, we set a tolerance ε and stop when $|f'(x_n)| < \varepsilon$.

It can be shown that the Newton–Raphson method is guaranteed to converge to a local minimizer, provided the starting value x_0 is close enough to the minimizer and enough continuous derivatives exist. As with other numerical optimization techniques, where there are multiple minimizers, Newton–Raphson won't necessarily find the best one. However, when $f''(x) > 0$ everywhere, there will be only one minimizer.

In actual practice, implementation of Newton–Raphson can be tricky. We may have $f''(x_n) = 0$, in which case the function looks locally like a straight line, with no solution to the Taylor series approximation to

$f'(x^*) = 0$. In this case a simple strategy is to move a small step in the direction which decreases the function value, based only on $f'(x_n)$.

In other cases where x_n is too far from the true minimizer, the Taylor approximation may be so inaccurate that $f(x_{n+1})$ is actually larger than $f(x_n)$. When this happens one may replace x_{n+1} with $(x_{n+1} + x_n)/2$ (or some other value between x_n and x_{n+1}) in the hope that a smaller step will produce better results.

Finally, there is always the possibility that the code to calculate $f'(x)$ or $f''(x)$ may contain bugs: it is usually worthwhile to do careful checks to make sure this is not the case.

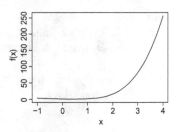

Fig. 8.3 The function $f(x) = e^{-x} + x^4$.

Example 8.1

We wish to find the minimizer of $f(x) = e^{-x} + x^4$. By inspection, we can guess that the minimizer is somewhere to the right of zero, because e^{-x} is a decreasing function, and x^4 has a minimum at zero. We start by plotting the function to find an initial guess (Figure 8.3).

```
f <- function(x) exp(-x) + x^4
curve(f, from = -1, to = 4)
```

From the figure, we can see that the minimizer is somewhere near $x_0 = 0.5$; we will use that as our starting value. Because of the difficulties mentioned above, we will not attempt to write a general Newton–Raphson implementation. Instead, we will simply evaluate several updates to see whether it converges or not.

```
f <- function(x) exp(-x) + x^4
fprime <- function(x) -exp(-x) + 4 * x^3
fprimeprime <- function(x) exp(-x) + 12 * x^2

x <- c(0.5, rep(NA, 6))
fval <- rep(NA, 7)
fprimeval <- rep(NA, 7)
fprimeprimeval <- rep(NA, 7)
for (i in 1:6) {
    fval[i] <- f(x[i])
    fprimeval[i] <- fprime(x[i])
    fprimeprimeval[i] <- fprimeprime(x[i])
    x[i + 1] <- x[i] - fprimeval[i]/fprimeprimeval[i]
}
data.frame(x, fval, fprimeval, fprimeprimeval)
##            x       fval      fprimeval fprimeprimeval
## 1 0.5000000 0.6690307 -1.065307e-01       3.606531
## 2 0.5295383 0.6675070  5.076129e-03       3.953806
## 3 0.5282544 0.6675038  9.980020e-06       3.938266
## 4 0.5282519 0.6675038  3.881429e-11       3.938235
## 5 0.5282519 0.6675038  0.000000e+00       3.938235
## 6 0.5282519 0.6675038  0.000000e+00       3.938235
## 7 0.5282519        NA            NA             NA
```

We see that convergence was very rapid, with the derivative numerically equal to zero by the fourth update. The second derivative is positive there, confirming that this is a local minimum. In fact, since $f''(x) = e^{-x} + 12x^2$, the second derivative is positive everywhere, and we can be sure that this is a global minimum.

8.3 | The Nelder–Mead simplex method

In the previous sections, we have talked about two different methods for optimizing a function of one variable. However, when a function depends on multiple inputs, optimization becomes much harder. It is hard even to visualize the function once it depends on more than two inputs.

The Nelder–Mead simplex algorithm is one method for optimization of a function of several variables. In p dimensions, it starts with $p + 1$ points $x_1, \ldots, x_{p+1}$, arranged so that when considered as vertices of a p-dimensional solid (a "simplex"), they enclose a non-zero volume. For example, in two dimensions the three points would not be allowed to all lie on one line so they would form a triangle, and in three dimensions the four points would form a proper tetrahedron.

The points are labeled in order from smallest to largest values of $f(x_i)$, so that $f(x_1) \leq f(x_2) \leq \cdots \leq f(x_{p+1})$. The idea is that to minimize $f(x)$, we would like to drop x_{p+1} and replace it with a point that gives a smaller value. We do this by calculating several proposed points z_i from the existing points. There are four kinds of proposals, illustrated in Figure 8.4 in two dimensions. The first three refer to the midpoint of $x_1, \ldots, x_p$ which we calculate as $x_{mid} = (x_1 + \cdots + x_p)/p$.

1. Reflection: reflect x_{p+1} through x_{mid} to z_1.
2. Reflection and expansion: reflect x_{p+1} through x_{mid}, and double its distance, giving z_2.
3. Contraction 1: contract x_{p+1} halfway towards x_{mid} to give z_3.
4. Contraction 2: contract all points halfway towards x_1, giving $z_4, \ldots, z_{p+3}$.

We consider each of these choices of simplex in order, based on the values of $f(z_i)$. It is helpful to consider the line shown in Figure 8.5 as you read through the following pseudocode outline of the decision process for one update of the simplex:

```
Initialization:
    Place the initial points in a matrix x, so that point i is in
      x[i,]
    For i in 1:(p + 1) calculate f(x[i,])
    Relabel the points so that
      f(x[1,]) <= f(x[2,]) <= ... <= f(x[p + 1,])
    Calculate the midpoint xmid = (x[1,] + x[2,] + ... + x[p,]) / p
```

Reflection

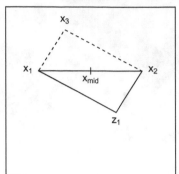

Reflection and Expansion

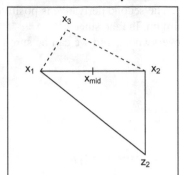

Fig. 8.4 The four types of proposals of the Nelder–Mead algorithm, illustrated in two dimensions.

Contraction 1

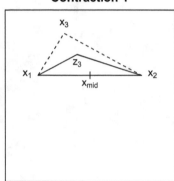

Contraction 2

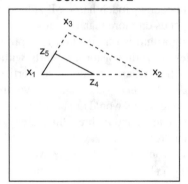

```
Trials:
    Calculate z1 by reflection:  z1 <- xmid - (x[p + 1,] - xmid)
    If f(z1) < f(x[1,]) {                     # Region A
        Calculate z2 by reflection and expansion:
           z2 <- xmid - 2 * (x[p + 1,] - xmid)
        If f(z2) < f(z1) return(z2)
        else return(z1)
    } else {
        If f(z1) < f(x[p,]) return(z1)        # Region B
        If f(z1) < f(x[p + 1,]) {
            Swap z1 with x[p + 1,]            # Region C
        }
    }

    At this point we know f(z1) is in region D.
    Try contraction 1, giving z3.
    If f(z3) < f(x[p + 1,]) return(z3)        # Region A, B, or C

    At this point nothing has worked, so we use contraction 2 to move
      everything towards x[1,]
```

Fig. 8.5 $f(z_1)$ will fall in region A, B, C, or D in the Nelder–Mead algorithm.

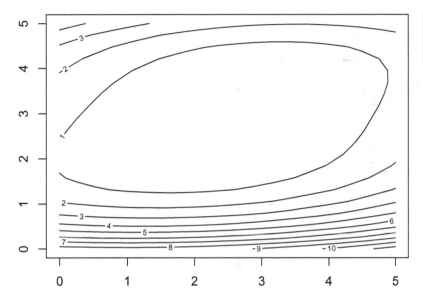

Fig. 8.6 Contour plot of $f(x,y) = [(x - y)^2 + (x - 2)^2 + (y - 3)^4]/10$.

Example 8.2

In this example we try to minimize the function

```
f <- function(x, y) ((x - y)^2 + (x - 2)^2 + (y - 3)^4) / 10
```

using the Nelder–Mead algorithm. We start by drawing a contour plot of the function, in order to get approximate starting values. After some experimentation, we obtain the plot shown in Figure 8.6 using the following code.

```
x <- seq(0, 5, len = 20)
y <- seq(0, 5, len = 20)
z <- outer(x, y, f)
contour(x, y, z)
```

We implemented the Nelder–Mead update algorithm in an R function with header neldermead(x, f), where x is our matrix in the pseudocode, and f is the function[1] . The output of neldermead(x, f) is an updated copy of the matrix x. The following log shows the output of nine Nelder–Mead updates. Figure 8.7 shows the steps the algorithm took in this demonstration.

```
x <- matrix(c(0, 0, 2, 0, 2, 0), 3, 2)
polygon(x)
```

[1] The source to neldermead is available on the www.statprogr.science website.

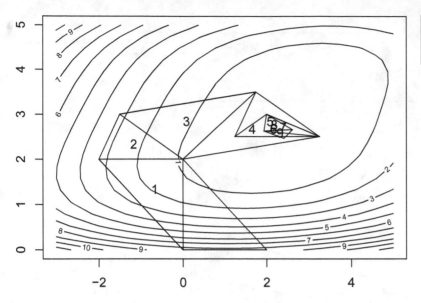

Fig. 8.7 Nine Nelder–Mead updates for $f(x, y) = [(x-y)^2 + (x-2)^2 + (y-3)^4]/10$.

```
for (i in 1:9) {
  cat(i,":")
  x <- neldermead(x,f)
  polygon(x)
  text(rbind(apply(x, 2, mean)), labels = i)
}
```

```
## 1 :Accepted reflection, f(z1) = 3.3
## 2 :Swap z1 and x3
## Accepted contraction 1, f(z3) = 3.25
## 3 :Accepted reflection and expansion, f(z2) = 0.31875
## 4 :Accepted reflection, f(z1) = 0.21875
## 5 :Accepted contraction 1, f(z3) = 0.21875
## 6 :Accepted contraction 1, f(z3) = 0.1
## 7 :Accepted contraction 1, f(z3) = 0.04963379
## 8 :Accepted contraction 1, f(z3) = 0.03874979
## 9 :Swap z1 and x3
## Accepted contraction 1, f(z3) = 0.02552485

x

##              [,1]      [,2]
## [1,]  2.609375  2.656250
## [2,]  1.937500  2.625000
## [3,]  2.410156  2.460938
```

At the end of these nine steps, we see that x should be around 1.9–2.6, and y should be around 2.4–2.7. A further 50 updates narrows these down to the true minimum at $(x, y) = (2.25, 2.5)$.

8.4 | Built-in functions

There are several general purpose optimization functions in R.

For one-dimensional optimization, the `optimize()` function performs a variation on the golden section search we described earlier. There are also multi-dimensional optimizers. The first of these is the `optim()` function. `optim()` is a general purpose wrapper for several different optimization methods, including Nelder–Mead, variations on Newton–Raphson, and others that we haven't discussed.

Syntax

```
optim(par, fn, ...)
```

The `par` parameter to `optim()` gives starting values for the parameters. Besides telling `optim()` where to begin, these indicate how many parameters will vary in its calls to `fn`, the second parameter. `fn` is an R function which evaluates the function to be minimized. Its first argument should be a vector of the same length as `par`; `optim()` will call it repeatedly, varying the value of this parameter, in order to find the minimum. It should return a scalar value. The `optim()` function has a number of optional parameters described on its help page. Besides those, the optional parameters in the ... list could include additional parameters to pass to `fn`.

There are other functions in R for general function optimization: `nlm()` and `nlminb()`. In most cases `optim()` is preferred because it offers more flexibility, but there may be instances where one of the others performs better. The `constrOptim()` function is aimed at cases where there are linear inequalities expressing constraints on the parameters.

Exercises

1 Use the `optimize()` function to minimize the following functions:
  (a) $f(x) = |x - 3.5| + |x - 2| + |x - 1|$,
  (b) $f(x) = |x - 3.2| + |x - 3.5| + |x - 2| + |x - 1|$.
2 Use `nlm()` and `optim()` to minimize the function

$$f(a, b) = (a - 1) + 3.2/b + 3\log(\Gamma(a)) + 3a\log(b).$$

Note that $\Gamma(a)$ is the gamma function which can be evaluated in R using `gamma(a)`.
3 Re-do the previous exercise using `nlminb()`, noting that a and b should be restricted to being nonnegative.

8.5 | Linear programming

We often need to minimize (or maximize) a function subject to constraints. When the function is linear and the constraints can be expressed as linear equations or inequalities, the problem is called a *linear programming* problem.

The so-called standard form for the minimization problem in linear programming is

$$\min_{x_1, x_2, \ldots, x_k} C(x) = c_1 x_1 + \cdots c_k x_k$$

subject to the *constraints*

$$a_{11} x_1 + \cdots + a_{1k} x_k \geq b_1,$$

$$a_{21} x_1 + \cdots + a_{2k} x_k \geq b_2,$$

$$\ldots$$

$$a_{m1} x_1 + \cdots + a_{mk} x_k \geq b_m$$

and the *nonnegativity conditions* $x_1 \geq 0, \ldots, x_k \geq 0$.

The idea is to find values of the *decision variables* $x_1, x_2, \ldots, x_n$ which minimize the *objective function* $C(x)$, subject to the constraints and nonnegativity conditions.

Example 8.3

A company has developed two procedures for reducing sulfur dioxide and carbon dioxide emissions from its factory. The first procedure reduces equal amounts of each gas at a per unit cost of $5. The second procedure reduces the same amount of sulfur dioxide as the first method, but reduces twice as much carbon dioxide gas; the per unit cost of this method is $8.

The company is required to reduce sulfur dioxide emissions by 2 million units and carbon dioxide emissions by 3 million units. What combination of the two emission procedures will meet this requirement at minimum cost?

Let x_1 denote the amount of the first procedure to be used, and let x_2 denote the amount of the second procedure to be used. For convenience, we will let these amounts be expressed in millions of units.

Then the cost (in millions of dollars) can be expressed as

$$C = 5x_1 + 8x_2.$$

Since both methods reduce sulfur dioxide emissions at the same rate, the number of units of sulfur dioxide reduced will then be

$$x_1 + x_2.$$

Noting that there is a requirement to reduce the sulfur dioxide amount by 2 million units, we have the constraint

$$x_1 + x_2 \geq 2.$$

The carbon dioxide reduction requirement is 3 million units, and the second method reduces carbon dioxide twice as fast as the first method, so we have the second constraint

$$x_1 + 2x_2 \geq 3.$$

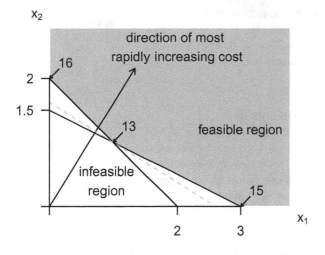

Fig. 8.8 A graphical interpretation of the pollution emission linear programming example. The grey region corresponds to values of x_1 and x_2 which satisfy all of the constraints. The dashed grey line corresponds to values of x_1 and x_2 which give the minimum cost (13); note that this line intersects the feasible region at exactly one point—the optimal solution to the problem $(1, 1)$.

Finally, we note that x_1 and x_2 must be nonnegative, since we cannot use negative amounts of either procedure. Thus, we obtain the linear programming problem:

$$\min C = 5x_1 + 8x_2$$

subject to the constraints

$$x_1 + x_2 \geq 2,$$

$$x_1 + 2x_2 \geq 3,$$

and

$$x_1, x_2 \geq 0.$$

These relations are graphed in Figure 8.8. The region shaded in grey is the *feasible region*; this is the set of all possible (x_1, x_2) combinations which satisfy the constraints. The unshaded area contains those combinations of values where the constraints are violated.

The gradient of the function $C(x)$ is $(5, 8)$, so this vector gives the direction of most rapid increase for that function. The level sets or contours of this function are perpendicular to this vector. One of the level sets is indicated as a dashed line in Figure 8.8. The solution of the minimization problem lies at the intersection of the first contour which intersects the feasible region. If this happens at a single point, we have a *unique* minimizer. In this example, this intersection is located at the point $(1, 1)$.

It can be shown that the only possible minimizers for such linear programming problems must be at the intersections of the constraint boundaries, as in the above example. The points of intersection of the constraints are called *basic solutions*. If these intersection points lie in the feasible region, they are called *basic feasible solutions*. If there is at least one basic feasible solution, then one of them will be an *optimal solution*. In the above example, the point $(1, 1)$ is the optimal solution.

8.5.1 Solving linear programming problems in R

There is more than one linear programming function available in R, but we believe the `lp()` function in the `lpSolve` package may be the most stable version currently available. It is based on the *revised simplex method*; this method intelligently tests a number of extreme points of the feasible region to see whether they are optimal. As usual, we load the package as follows

```
library(lpSolve)
```

The `lp()` function has a number of parameters; the following are needed to solve minimization problems like the one in the earlier example.

- `objective.in`—the vector of coefficients of the objective function.
- `const.mat`—a matrix containing the coefficients of the decision variables in the left-hand side of the constraints; each row corresponds to a constraint.
- `const.dir`—a character vector indicating the direction of the constraint inequalities; some of the possible entries are `>=`, `==` and `<=`.
- `const.rhs`—a vector containing the constants given on the right-hand side of the constraints.

Example 8.4

To solve the minimization problem set out in Example 8.3, type

```
eg.lp <- lp(objective.in = c(5, 8), const.mat = matrix(c(1, 1, 1, 2),
            nrow = 2), const.rhs = c(2, 3), const.dir = c(">=", ">="))
eg.lp

## Success: the objective function is 13

eg.lp$solution

## [1] 1 1
```

The output tells us that the minimizer is at $x_1 = 1$, $x_2 = 1$, and the minimum value of the objective function is 13.

8.5.2 Maximization and other kinds of constraints

The `lp()` function can handle maximization problems with the use of the `direction = "max"` parameter. The `const.dir` parameter allows for different types of inequalities.

Example 8.5
We will solve the problem:

$$\max C = 5x_1 + 8x_2,$$

subject to the constraints

$$x_1 + x_2 \leq 2,$$

$$x_1 + 2x_2 = 3,$$

and

$$x_1, x_2 \geq 0.$$

In R, this can be coded as

```
eg.lp <- lp(objective.in = c(5, 8),
            const.mat = matrix(c(1, 1, 1, 2), nrow = 2),
            const.rhs = c(2, 3),
            const.dir = c("<=", "="), direction = "max")
eg.lp$solution

## [1] 1 1
```

The solution is $(1, 1)$, giving a maximum value of 13.

8.5.3 Special situations

Multiple optima

It sometimes happens that there are multiple solutions for a linear programming problem.

Example 8.6
A slight modification of the pollution emission example (Example 8.3) is

$$\min C = 4x_1 + 8x_2,$$

subject to the constraints

$$x_1 + x_2 \geq 2,$$

$$x_1 + 2x_2 \geq 3,$$

and

$$x_1, x_2 \geq 0.$$

This problem has a solution at $(1, 1)$ as well as at $(3, 0)$. All points on the line joining these two points are solutions as well. Figure 8.9 shows this graphically.

The `lp()` function does not alert the user to the existence of multiple minima. In fact, the output from this function for the modified pollution emission example is the solution $x_1 = 3, x_2 = 0$.

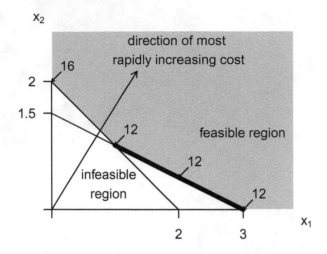

Fig. 8.9 A plot of the gradient of the objective function and the constraint boundaries for Example 8.6. The points on the heavy black segment are all optimal for this problem.

Degeneracy

For a problem with m decision variables, degeneracy arises when more than m constraint boundaries intersect at a single point. This situation is quite rare, but it has potential to cause difficulties for the simplex method, so it is important to be aware of this condition. In very rare circumstances, degeneracy can prevent the method from converging to the optimal solution; most of the time, however, there is little to worry about.

Example 8.7

The following problem has a point of degeneracy which is not at the optimum; however, the `lp()` function still finds the optimum without difficulty.

$$\min C = 3x_1 + x_2,$$

subject to the constraints

$$x_1 + x_2 \geq 2,$$

$$x_1 + 2x_2 \geq 3,$$

$$x_1 + 3x_2 \geq 4,$$

$$4x_1 + x_2 \geq 4,$$

and

$$x_1, x_2 \geq 0.$$

The constraint boundaries are plotted in Figure 8.10.

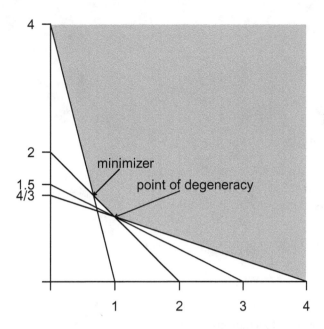

Fig. 8.10 A plot of four constraint boundaries, one of which is redundant, leading to degeneracy. The feasible region is shaded.

This problem can be solved easily:

```
degen.lp <- lp(objective.in = c(3, 1),
            const.mat = matrix(c(1, 1, 1, 4, 1, 2, 3, 1), nrow = 4),
            const.rhs = c(2, 3, 4, 4), const.dir = rep(">=", 4))
degen.lp

## Success: the objective function is 3.333333

degen.lp$solution

## [1] 0.6666667 1.3333333
```

Infeasibility

Infeasibility is a more common problem. When the constraints cannot simultaneously be satisfied there is no feasible region. Then no feasible solution exists.

Example 8.8
In the following example, it is obvious that the constraints cannot simultaneously be satisfied.

$$\min C = 5x_1 + 8x_2,$$

subject to the constraints

$$x_1 + x_2 \geq 2,$$

$$x_1 + x_2 \leq 1,$$

and

$$x_1, x_2 \geq 0.$$

Here is the output from the `lp()` function:

```
eg.lp <- lp(objective.in = c(5, 8),
            const.mat = matrix(c(1, 1, 1, 1), nrow = 2),
            const.rhs = c(2, 1), const.dir = c(">=", "<="))
eg.lp

## Error: no feasible solution found
```

Unboundedness

In rare instances, the constraints and objective function give rise to an unbounded solution.

Example 8.9

A trivial example of unboundedness arises when solving the problem

$$\max C = 5x_1 + 8x_2,$$

subject to the constraints

$$x_1 + x_2 \geq 2,$$

$$x_1 + 2x_2 \geq 3,$$

and

$$x_1, x_2 \geq 0.$$

The feasible region for this problem is the same as for Example 8.3 and is plotted in Figure 8.8. However, instead of trying to minimize the objective function, we are now maximizing, so we follow the direction of increasing the objective function this time. We can make the objective function as large as we wish, by taking x_1 and x_2 arbitrarily large.

Here is what happens when `lp()` is applied to this problem:

```
eg.lp <- lp(objective.in = c(5, 8),
            const.mat = matrix(c(1, 1, 1, 2), nrow = 2),
            const.rhs = c(2, 3), const.dir = c(">=", ">="),
            direction = "max")
eg.lp

## Error: status 3
```

The condition of unboundedness will most often arise when constraints and/or the objective function have not been formulated correctly.

8.5.4 Unrestricted variables

Sometimes a decision variable is not restricted to be nonnegative. The $lp()$ function is not set up to handle this case directly. However, a simple device gets around this difficulty.

If x is unrestricted in sign, then x can be written as $x_1 - x_2$, where $x_1 \geq 0$ and $x_2 \geq 0$. This means that every unrestricted variable in a linear programming problem can be replaced by the difference of two nonnegative variables.

Example 8.10
We will solve the problem:

$$\min C = x_1 + 10x_2,$$

subject to the constraints

$$x_1 + x_2 \geq 2,$$

$$x_1 - x_2 \leq 3,$$

and

$$x_1 \geq 0.$$

Noting that x_2 is unrestricted in sign, we set $x_2 = x_3 - x_4$ for nonnegative x_3 and x_4. Plugging these new variables into the problem gives

$$\min C = x_1 + 10x_3 - 10x_4,$$

subject to the constraints

$$x_1 + x_3 - x_4 \geq 2,$$

$$x_1 - x_3 + x_4 \leq 3,$$

and

$$x_1 \geq 0, x_3 \geq 0, x_4 \geq 0.$$

Converting this to R code, we have

```
unres.lp <- lp(objective.in = c(1, 10, -10),
        const.mat = matrix(c(1, 1, 1, -1, -1, 1), nrow = 2),
        const.rhs = c(2, 3), const.dir = c(">=", "<="))
unres.lp

## Success: the objective function is -2.5

unres.lp$solution

## [1] 2.5 0.0 0.5
```

The solution is given by $x_1 = 2.5$ and $x_2 = x_3 - x_4 = -0.5$.

8.5.5 Integer programming

Decision variables are often restricted to be integers. For example, we might want to minimize the cost of shipping a product by using one, two, or three different trucks. It is not possible to use a fractional number of trucks, so the number of trucks must be integer-valued.

Problems involving integer-valued decision variables are called *integer programming* problems. Simple rounding of a non-integer solution to the nearest integer is *not* good practice; the result of such rounding can be a solution which is quite far from the optimal solution.

The lp() function has a facility to handle integer-valued variables using a technique called the *branch and bound algorithm*. The int.vec argument can be used to indicate which variables have integer values.

Example 8.11
Find nonnegative x_1, x_2, x_3, and x_4 to minimize

$$C(x) = 2x_1 + 3x_2 + 4x_3 - x_4,$$

subject to the constraints

$$x_1 + 2x_2 \geq 9,$$

$$3x_2 + x_3 \geq 9,$$

and

$$x_2 + x_4 \leq 10.$$

Furthermore, x_2 and x_4 can only take integer values. To set up and solve this problem in R, type

```
integ.lp <- lp(objective.in = c(2, 3, 4, -1),
   const.mat = matrix(c(1, 0, 0, 2, 3, 1, 0, 1, 0, 0, 0, 1), nrow = 3),
   const.dir = c(">=", ">=", "<="), const.rhs = c(9, 9, 10),
   int.vec = c(2, 4))
integ.lp

## Success: the objective function is 8

integ.lp$solution

## [1] 1 4 0 6
```

Thus, the best solution when x_2 and x_4 are integer-valued is $x_1 = 1$, $x_2 = 4$, $x_3 = 0$, and $x_4 = 6$.

Here is what happens when the integer variables are ignored:

```
wrong.lp <- lp(objective.in = c(2, 3, 4, -1),
   const.mat = matrix(c(1, 0, 0, 2, 3, 1, 0, 1, 0, 0, 0, 1), nrow = 3),
   const.dir = c(">=", ">=", "<="), const.rhs = c(9, 9, 10))
wrong.lp
```

```
## Success: the objective function is 8

wrong.lp$solution

## [1] 0.0 4.5 0.0 5.5
```

Rounding the solution to the nearest integer will lead to a violation of the first constraint (if x_2 is taken to be 4) or to a minimum value of the objective function that is larger than 8 (if $x_2 = 5$).

8.5.6 Alternatives to `lp()`

The `lp()` function provides an interface to code written in C. There is another function in the `linprog` package called `solveLP()` which is written entirely in R; this latter function solves large problems much more slowly than the `lp()` function, but it provides more detailed output. We note also the function `simplex()` in the `boot` package.

It should also be noted that, for very large problems, the simplex method might not converge quickly enough; other procedures, based on *interior point methods*, often perform better. See the *Optimization and Mathematical Programming* task view for the latest packages.

8.5.7 Quadratic programming

Linear programming problems are a special case of optimization problems in which a possibly nonlinear function is minimized subject to constraints. Such problems are typically more difficult to solve and are beyond the scope of this text; an exception is the case where the objective function is quadratic and the constraints are linear. This is a problem in *quadratic programming*.

A quadratic programming problem with k constraints is often of the form

$$\min_{\beta} \frac{1}{2}\beta^T D\beta - d^T\beta,$$

subject to constraints $A^T\beta \geq b$. Here β is a vector of p unknowns, D is a positive definite $p \times p$ matrix, d is vector of length p, A is a $p \times k$ matrix, and b is a vector of length k.

Example 8.12

Consider the following 20 pairs of observations on the variables x and y. A scatterplot is displayed in Figure 8.11.

```
x <- c(0.45,   0.08, -1.08,   0.92,   1.65,   0.53, 0.52, -2.15, -2.20,
      -0.32, -1.87, -0.16, -0.19, -0.98, -0.20, 0.67,   0.08,   0.38,
       0.76, -0.78,  1.80,  2.09)
y <- c(1.26,   0.58, -1.00,   1.07,   1.28, -0.33, 0.68, -2.22, -1.82,
```

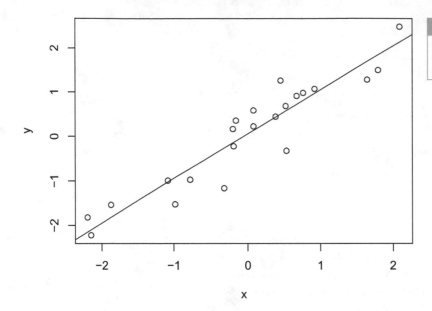

Fig. 8.11 A scatterplot of the 20 observations with a line of slope 1 and intercept 0.05 overlaid.

-1.17, -1.54, 0.35, -0.23, -1.53, 0.16, 0.91, 0.22, 0.44, 0.98, -0.98, 1.50, 2.49)

Our problem is to pass a line of "best fit" through these data. We seek a line of the form

$$y = \beta_0 + \beta_1 x,$$

where β_0 is the y-intercept and β_1 is the slope. However, we have additional background information about these data that indicate that the slope β_1 of the required line is at least 1.

The line we want is the one that minimizes the sum of the squared vertical distances between the observed points and the line itself:

$$\min_{\beta_0, \beta_1} \sum_{i=1}^{20} (y_i - \beta_0 - \beta_1 x_i)^2.$$

Our extra information about the slope tells us that this minimization is subject to the constraint $\beta_1 \geq 1$.

This is an example of a restricted least-squares problem and is equivalent to

$$\min_{\beta} \beta^T X^T X \beta - 2y^T X \beta,$$

subject to

$$A^T \beta \geq b,$$

where $A = [0 \ 1]^T$, $\beta = [\beta_0 \ \beta_1]^T$, y is a column vector consisting of the 22 y measurements, and X is a matrix consisting of two columns, where the first column contains only 1's and the second column contains the 22 x observations:

$$X = \begin{bmatrix} 1 & x_1 \\ 1 & x_2 \\ \dots & \dots \\ 1 & x_n \end{bmatrix} = \begin{bmatrix} 1 & 0.45 \\ 1 & 0.08 \\ \dots & \dots \\ 1 & 2.09 \end{bmatrix}.$$

We then have

$$X^T X = \begin{bmatrix} n & \sum_{i=1}^{n} x_i \\ \sum_{i=1}^{n} x_i & \sum_{i=1}^{n} x_i^2 \end{bmatrix} = \begin{bmatrix} 22 & 0 \\ 0 & 29.0132 \end{bmatrix}$$

and

$$y^T X = [\sum_{i=1}^{n} y_i \quad \sum_{i=1}^{n} x_i y_i] = [1.1 \quad 28.6626].$$

This is a quadratic programming problem with $D = X^T X$ and $d = X^T y$.

Linear programming methods have been adapted to handle quadratic programming problems. The `solve.QP()` function is in the `quadprog` package. It solves minimization problems, and the following are parameters which are required:

- `Dmat`—a matrix containing the elements of the matrix (D) of the quadratic form in the objective function.
- `dvec`—a vector containing the coefficients of the decision variables in the objective function.
- `Amat`—a matrix containing the coefficients of the decision variables in the constraints; each row of the matrix corresponds to a constraint.
- `bvec`—a vector containing the constants given on the right-hand side of the constraints.
- `mvec`—a number indicating the number of equality constraints. By default, this is 0. If it is not 0, the equality constraints should be listed ahead of the inequality constraints.

The output from this function is a list whose first two elements are the vector that minimizes the function and the minimum value of the function.

Example 8.13
For the restricted least squares problem of Example 8.12, we must first set up the matrices D and A as well as the vectors b and d. Here, $D = X^T X$ and $d = X^T y$.

```
library(quadprog)   # load quadprog package
```

```
X <- cbind(1, x)
XX <- t(X) %*% X
Xy <- t(X) %*% y
A <- matrix(c(0, 1), ncol = 1)
b <- 1
```

```
solve.QP(Dmat = XX, dvec = Xy, Amat = A, bvec = b)

## $solution
## [1]  0.05 1.00
##
## $value
## [1]  -14.1835
##
## $unconstrained.solution
## [1]  0.0500000 0.9879158
##
## $iterations
## [1]  2 0
##
## $Lagrangian
## [1]  0.3506
##
## $iact
## [1]  1
```

From the output, we see that the required line is

$$\hat{y} = 0.05 + x.$$

The rest of the output is indicating that the constraint is active. If the unconstrained problem had yielded a slope larger than 1, the constraint would have been inactive, and the solution to the unconstrained problem would be the same as the solution to the constrained problem.

Note that the decision variables in the above example were not restricted in sign. If needed, nonnegativity conditions must be explicitly set when using the `solve.QP()` function. Also, it should be noted that inequality constraints are all of the form >=. If your problem contains some inequality constraints with <=, then the constraints should be multiplied through by −1 to convert them to the required form.

It should be noted that there are more efficient ways to solve restricted least squares problems in other computing environments. The matrix D in the preceding example is a diagonal matrix, and this special structure can be used to reduce the computational burden. The following example involves a full matrix. This example also places a restriction on the sign of the decision variables.

Example 8.14
Quadratic programming can be applied to the problem of finding an optimal portfolio for an investor who is choosing how much money to invest in each of a set of n stocks. A simple model for this problem boils down to maximizing

$$x^T \beta - \frac{k}{2} \beta^T D \beta,$$

subject to the constraints $\sum_{i=1}^{n} \beta_i = 1$, and $\beta_i \geq 0$ for $i = 1, \ldots, n$.

The ith component of the β vector represents the fraction of the investor's fortune that should be invested in the ith stock. Note that each element of this vector must be nonnegative, since the investor cannot allocate a negative fraction of her portfolio to a stock.[2] The vector x contains the average daily returns for each stock; the daily return value for a stock is the difference in closing price for the stock from one day to the next. Therefore, $x^T \beta$ represents the average daily return for the investor.

Most investors do not want to take large risks; the second term in the objective function takes this fact into account. The factor k quantifies the investor's tolerance for risk. If the investor's goal is purely to maximize the average daily return without regard for the risk, then $k = 0$. The value of k is larger for an investor who is concerned about taking risks. The D matrix quantifies the underlying variability in the returns; it is called a covariance matrix. The diagonal elements of the D matrix are the variances of the returns for each of the stocks. An off-diagonal element (i, j) is the covariance between returns of the ith and jth stocks; this is a simple measure of relation between the two returns.

For a specific example, we consider three stocks and set $k = 2$ and

$$D = \begin{bmatrix} 0.010 & 0.002 & 0.002 \\ 0.002 & 0.010 & 0.002 \\ 0.002 & 0.002 & 0.010 \end{bmatrix}.$$

We assume the mean daily returns for the three stocks are 0.002, 0.005, and 0.01, respectively, so $x^T = [0.002\ 0.005\ 0.01]$.

The requirement that $\beta_1 + \beta_2 + \beta_3 = 1$ and the nonnegativity restrictions on the β variables can be written as

$$\begin{bmatrix} 1 & 1 & 1 \\ 1 & 0 & 0 \\ 0 & 1 & 0 \\ 0 & 0 & 1 \end{bmatrix} \begin{bmatrix} \beta_1 \\ \beta_2 \\ \beta_3 \end{bmatrix} \begin{matrix} = \\ \geq \\ \geq \\ \geq \end{matrix} \begin{bmatrix} 1 \\ 0 \\ 0 \\ 0 \end{bmatrix}.$$

Therefore, we take

$$A^T = \begin{bmatrix} 1 & 1 & 1 \\ 1 & 0 & 0 \\ 0 & 1 & 0 \\ 0 & 0 & 1 \end{bmatrix}.$$

To set this up in R, we note first that the maximization problem is equivalent to minimizing the negative of the objective function, subject to the same constraints. This fact enables us to employ `solve.QP()`.

```
A <- cbind(rep(1, 3), diag(rep(1, 3)))
D <- matrix(c(0.01, 0.002, 0.002, 0.002, 0.01, 0.002, 0.002, 0.002, 0.01),
            nrow = 3)
x <- c(0.002, 0.005, 0.01)
```

[2] Such behavior is called *shorting* a stock, and we do not allow it here.

```
b <- c(1, 0, 0, 0)

# meq specifies the number of equality constraints;
# these are listed before the inequality constraints
solve.QP(2 * D, x, A, b, meq = 1)

## $solution
## [1] 0.1041667 0.2916667 0.6041667
##
## $value
## [1] -0.002020833
##
## $unconstrained.solution
## [1] -0.02678571  0.16071429  0.47321429
##
## $iterations
## [1] 2 0
##
## $Lagrangian
## [1] 0.003666667 0.000000000 0.000000000 0.000000000
##
## $iact
## [1] 1
```

The optimal investment strategy (for this investor) is to put 10.4% of her fortune into the first stock, 29.2% into the second stock, and 60.4% into the third stock.

The optimal value of the portfolio is 0.0020 (from $value above). (Recall that the negative sign appears in the output, because we were minimizing the negative of the objective function.)

Exercises

1 (a) Find nonnegative x_1, x_2, x_3 and x_4 to minimize

$$C(x) = x_1 + 3x_2 + 4x_3 + x_4,$$

subject to the constraints

$$x_1 - 2x_2 \geq 9,$$

$$3x_2 + x_3 \geq 9,$$

and

$$x_2 + x_4 \geq 10.$$

(b) Will the solution change if there is a requirement that any of the variables should be integers? Explain.

(c) Suppose the objective function is changed to

$$C(x) = x_1 - 3x_2 + 4x_3 + x_4.$$

What happens to the solution now?

2 Find nonnegative x_1, x_2, x_3, and x_4 to maximize

$$C(x) = x_1 + 3x_2 + 4x_3 + x_4,$$

subject to the constraints

$$x_1 - 2x_2 \le 9,$$

$$3x_2 + x_3 \le 9,$$

and

$$x_2 + x_4 \le 10.$$

Chapter exercises

1 Consider the data of Example 8.12. Calculate the slope and intercept for a line of "best fit" for these data for which the intercept is at least as large as the slope.

2 Re-do the calculation in the portfolio allocation example using $k = 1$. How does being less risk-averse affect the investor's behavior?

3 Often, there are upper bounds on the proportion that can be invested in a particular stock. Re-do the portfolio allocation problem with the requirement that no more than 50% of the investor's fortune can be tied up in any one stock.

4 Duncan's Donuts Inc. (DDI) and John's Jeans Ltd. (JJL) are two stocks with mean daily returns of 0.005 and 0.010, respectively. What is the optimal portfolio for a completely risk-loving investor (i.e. risk tolerance constant $k = 0$) who invests only in these two stocks? (Hint: this question does not require any computations.)

5 Suppose the daily returns for DDI and JJL are independent, but $\sigma_{DDL}^2 = 0.01$ and $\sigma_{JJL}^2 = 0.04$. What is the optimal allocation for an investor with a risk tolerance constant (a) $k = 1$? (b) $k = 2$?

You can use the fact that

$$D = \begin{bmatrix} 0.01 & 0 \\ 0 & 0.04 \end{bmatrix}.$$

6 Repeat the preceding question under the assumption that the covariance between the returns for DDI and JJL is 0.01. You can use the fact that

$$D = \begin{bmatrix} 0.01 & 0.01 \\ 0.01 & 0.04 \end{bmatrix}.$$

Appendix A

Review of random variables and distributions

When an experiment is conducted in which a number of different outcomes are possible, each outcome will have a certain probability of occurrence.

Consider a cancer treatment that will be tested on 10 patients. The number of patients who show an increase in their white-blood cell count at the end of 5 weeks of treatment cannot be predicted exactly at the beginning of the trial, so this number, which we might label N, is thought of as a *random variable*. N is an example of a *discrete* random variable since it only takes values from a discrete set, i.e. $\{0, 1, 2, \ldots, 10\}$. The time, T, until death could also be measured for one of the patients; again, T cannot be predicted exactly in advance, so it is also an example of a random variable; since it can take a continuum of possible values, it is referred to as a *continuous* random variable.

A random variable is characterized by its distribution. This specifies the probability that the variable will take one or more values. If X denotes the number of heads obtained in two independent tosses of a fair coin, we might write

$$P(X \leq 1) = 0.75$$

to indicate that the probability of 0 or 1 head in two tosses is 0.75. In general, the function

$$F(x) = P(X \leq x)$$

is called the distribution function of the random variable X. If $F(x)$ has a derivative, we can define the probability density function of X as

$$f(x) = F'(x).$$

This is often possible with continuous random variables X. Note that, in this case,

$$F(y) = \int_{-\infty}^{y} f(x)dx.$$

Among other things, note that the area under the curve specified by $f(x)$ is 1.

The expected value of a random variable is also an important concept. For continuous random variables, we can write

$$E[X] = \int_{-\infty}^{\infty} xf(x)dx.$$

This is the mean value of the density function $f(x)$. It is often denoted by the symbol μ. We also can take expectations of functions of random variables using the formula

$$E[g(X)] = \int_{-\infty}^{\infty} g(x)f(x)dx.$$

An important example of this is the variance. The variance of a random variable gives an indication of the unpredictability in a random variable. Its formula is

$$\text{Var}(X) = E[(X - \mu)^2] = \int_{-\infty}^{\infty} (x - \mu)^2 f(x)dx.$$

Another important concept is that of *quantile*: this is the value of x for which $F(x)$ takes on a particular value. When the inverse function $F^{-1}(y)$ is defined, the α quantile of X is given by $F^{-1}(\alpha)$. For example, the 0.95 quantile is the value of x for which $F(x) = 0.95$; in other words, x is the 95th percentile of the distribution. Frequently used quantiles are the median $\tilde{x}$ which satisfies $F(\tilde{x}) = 0.5$, and the upper and lower quartiles which satisfy $F(x) = 0.75$ and $F(x) = 0.25$, respectively. When the distribution of the random variable is discrete, $F(x)$ will have jumps, and $F^{-1}(\alpha)$ may not exist. In this case by convention we choose the smallest x with $F(x) \geq \alpha$, so quantiles always exist.

The following tables summarize properties of some commonly used univariate distributions; see also Tables 6.1 and 6.2.

Distribution name	$f(x)$	$F(x)$	$E[X]$	$\text{Var}(X)$
Uniform(a,b)	$\frac{1}{b-a}$, $a < x < b$	$\frac{x-a}{b-a}$	$\frac{a+b}{2}$	$\frac{(b-a)^2}{12}$
Exponential(λ)	$\lambda e^{-\lambda x}$, $x > 0$	$1 - e^{-\lambda x}$	$\frac{1}{\lambda}$	$\frac{1}{\lambda^2}$
Normal(μ, σ^2)	$\frac{1}{\sigma\sqrt{2\pi}} e^{-\frac{(x-\mu)^2}{2\sigma^2}}$	$\int_{-\infty}^{x} \frac{1}{\sigma\sqrt{2\pi}} e^{-\frac{(y-\mu)^2}{2\sigma^2}} dy$	μ	σ^2

Distribution name	$P(X = x)$	$E[X]$	$\text{Var}(X)$
Binomial(n,p)	$\binom{n}{x} p^x (1-p)^{n-x}$	np	$np(1-p)$
Poisson(λ)	$\frac{\lambda^x e^{-\lambda}}{x!}$	λ	λ

We conclude this review with some brief comments about bivariate distributions. In particular, suppose X and Y are continuous random variables having joint probability density $f(x,y)$. We can define expectations using double integrals:

$$E[g(X,Y)] = \int_{-\infty}^{\infty} \int_{-\infty}^{\infty} g(x,y)f(x,y)dxdy$$

for functions $g(x,y)$. In particular, setting $g(X,Y) = I(X \leq u)I(Y \leq v)$ gives

$$E[I(X \leq u)I(Y \leq v)] = \int_{-\infty}^{u} \int_{-\infty}^{v} f(x,y)dxdy,$$

which implies that for any u and v,

$$P(X \leq u, Y \leq v) = \int_{-\infty}^{u} \int_{-\infty}^{v} f(x,y)dxdy.$$

Here, $I()$ denotes the indicator function which takes on the value 1 when its argument is true, and 0 when its argument is false.

The marginal density of X is obtained by integrating over all values of y:

$$f_X(x) = \int_{-\infty}^{\infty} f(x,y)dy,$$

and similarly, the marginal density of Y is obtained by integrating over all values of x:

$$f_Y(y) = \int_{-\infty}^{\infty} f(x,y)dx.$$

X and Y are stochastically independent if

$$f(x,y) = f_X(x)f_Y(y).$$

Among other things, this implies that for independent variables $P(X \leq u, Y \leq v) = P(X \leq u)P(Y \leq v)$, and by the definition of *conditional probability*,

$$P(X \leq u | Y \leq v) = \frac{P(X \leq u, Y \leq v)}{P(Y \leq v)} = P(X \leq u).$$

The term on the left denotes the conditional probability that $X \leq u$, given that $Y \leq v$. Intuitively, the above statement means that knowledge of the value of Y does not give us any additional information with which to predict the value of X.

Appendix B

Base graphics details

In this appendix we describe some low-level details of the base graphics system from Section 3.1.

We will start with a description of how R views the page it is drawing on, then we customize the look of a plot, and finish by showing how some of the common graphics settings are changed.

B.1 | The plotting region and margins

Base graphics in R divides up the display into several regions. The plot region is where data will be drawn. Within the plot region R maintains a coordinate system based on the data. The axes show this coordinate system. Outside the plot region are the margins, numbered clockwise from 1 to 4, starting at the bottom. Normally text and labels are plotted in the margins, and R positions objects based on a count of lines out from the plot region. Figure B.1 illustrates this. (We give the code that produced this plot in Example B.1.) We can see from the figure that R chose to draw the tick mark labels on line 1. We drew the margin titles on line 3.

One may also wish to annotate graphs outside the plot region. Several functions exist to do this:

```
title(main, sub, xlab, ylab, ...)  # adds a main title, a subtitle,
                                    # an x-axis label and/or a y-axis label
mtext(text, side, line, ...)        # draws text in the margins
axis(side, at, labels, ...)         # adds an axis to the plot
box(...)                            # adds a box around the plot region
```

Example B.1
Figure B.1 was drawn using the following code:

```
par(mar = c(5, 5, 5, 5) + 0.1)
plot(c(1, 9), c(0, 50), type = 'n', xlab = "", ylab = "")
text(6, 40, "Plot region")
```

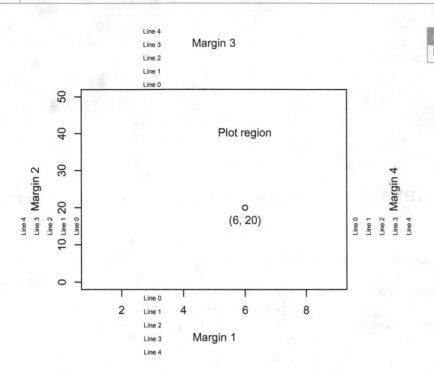

Fig. B.1   The plotting region in base graphics.

```
points(6, 20)
text(6, 20, "(6, 20)", adj = c(0.5, 2))
mtext(paste("Margin", 1:4), side = 1:4, line = 3)
mtext(paste("Line", 0:4), side = 1, line = 0:4, at = 3, cex = 0.6)
mtext(paste("Line", 0:4), side = 2, line = 0:4, at = 15, cex = 0.6)
mtext(paste("Line", 0:4), side = 3, line = 0:4, at = 3, cex = 0.6)
mtext(paste("Line", 0:4), side = 4, line = 0:4, at = 15, cex = 0.6)
```

Understanding the code

The `mar` parameter sets the numbers of lines of margin on sides 2, 3, and 4, so that they are all the same width as the bottom margin (side 1). The `type = 'n'` plot is empty but specifies the scope of the plotting region, essentially from 1 through 9 on the horizontal axis and from 0 through 50 on the vertical axis. The `text()` and `mtext()` functions tell R where to place the given text, such as "Plot region," and so on. Using `paste("Line", 0:4)` avoids typing `c("Line 0", "Line 1", "Line 2", "Line 3", "Line 4")`.

B.2 | Adjusting axis tick labels

In Figure 3.6, a histogram of the `islands` data set was plotted on the base 10 log scale. Although the axis tick labels are displayed accurately, most

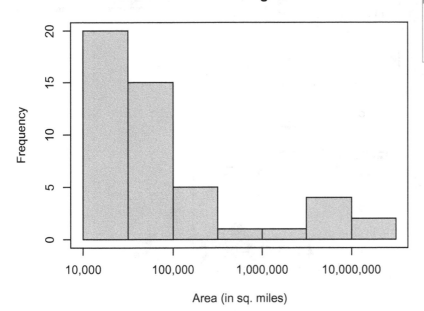

Areas of the World's Largest Landmasses

Fig. B.2 Histogram of landmass areas on the base 10 log scale, with axis labels that are easily readable by a non-technical audience.

individuals who look at such a histogram would need time to process this information in order to answer a simple question such as, "How many of the landmasses have an area exceeding 100,000 square miles?"

In Figure B.2, the axes have been removed initially, using the axes = FALSE argument. This removes the box as well, so it is replaced using the box() function. The horizontal axis is then re-drawn with labels at $4, 5, 6$, and 7, but these correspond to $10^4, 10^5, 10^6$, and 10^7 on the square mile scale. We have explicitly written out the character strings in the labels argument, because scientific notation would have been used with the quicker option labels = 10^(4:7). [1]

[1] The format() function has options to do this automatically.

```
hist(log(1000*islands, 10),  axes = FALSE, xlab = "Area (in sq. miles)",
     main = "Areas of the World's Largest Landmasses")
box()
axis(side = 1, at = 4:7, labels = c("10,000", "100,000", "1,000,000",
     "10,000,000"))
axis(side = 2)
```

Incidentally, it is a quick exercise now to see that exactly 13 of the landmasses exceed 100,000 square miles in area.

Example B.2
Motor vibration (noise) was measured for five samples of motors, each sample using a different brand of bearing. Interest centers on whether there are differences in the mean vibration between brands. The data are stored in a data frame called motor (in the MPV package) as follows:

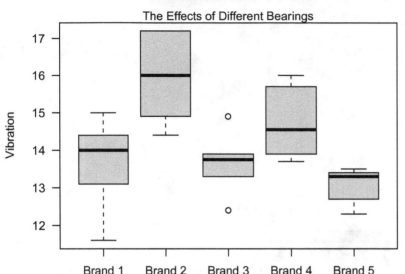

Motor Vibration Data

The Effects of Different Bearings

```
motor

##    Brand 1 Brand 2 Brand 3 Brand 4 Brand 5
## 1    13.1    16.3    13.7    15.7    13.5
## 2    15.0    15.7    13.9    13.7    13.4
## 3    14.0    17.2    12.4    14.4    13.2
## 4    14.4    14.9    13.8    16.0    12.7
## 5    14.0    14.4    14.9    13.9    13.4
## 6    11.6    17.2    13.3    14.7    12.3
```

Our goal is to draw side-by-side boxplots to make the comparison. The default plot (not shown) is produced using the following code.

```
boxplot(motor)
```

Better axis labels and a title are needed than are provided by the default. A subtitle is also helpful for the viewer to see what is being graphed. The result of the following code is pictured in Figure B.3.

```
boxplot(motor, ylab = "Vibration", axes = FALSE)
title("Motor Vibration Data")
mtext("The Effects of Different Bearings", side = 3, line = 0)
box()
axis(side = 2, las = 2)
axis(side = 1, at = 1:5, label = names(motor))
```

Understanding the code

In order to adjust the axis annotation, we have first removed the axes using the `axes = FALSE` argument. The effect is to not only remove the axes but also the box containing the plot. As in the previous example, the box can be re-drawn using the `box()` function. Axes can be re-drawn using the `axis()` function placing tick labels `at` locations and using `labels` of our own choosing. We have also used the `las` parameter to rotate the tick labels on the vertical axis.

B.3 | Setting graphical parameters

When creating a new plot, there are two opportunities to set its overall characteristics. The first is when the plotting device is opened. R normally opens a screen device automatically with default parameters, but a user can open a plotting device explicitly, and set it up exactly as required. Some plotting devices in R that open files for saved output are:

```
pdf(...)        # for PDF output
png(...)        # for PNG bitmap output
jpeg(...)       # for JPEG bitmap output
postscript(...) # for Postscript output
```

You will need to read the help pages for each of these functions to find out the exact details of the available parameters. They control things like the size of the plot, background colors, and so on.

After a device is opened, other graphical parameters may be set using the `par(...)` function. This function controls a very large number of parameters; we will highlight just a few here. For the complete list, see the help page.

```
mfrow = c(m, n)           # draw m rows and n columns of plots, rather than
                          # going to a new page for each plot
mfg = c(i, j)             # draw the next figure in row i and  column j
ask = TRUE                # ask the user before erasing a plot
cex = 1.5                 # expand characters in the plot region
                          #   Use cex.axis, etc. for margin text
mar = c(m1, m2, m3, m4)   # sets size of the margins of the plot
oma = c(m1, m2, m3, m4)   # sets the outer margins (outside the plot array)
usr = c(x1, x2, y1, y2)   # sets the coordinate system within the plot
```

The `par()` function is set up to take arguments in several forms. If you give character strings (e.g. `par("mfrow")`) the function will return the current value of the graphical parameter. If you provide named arguments (e.g. `par(mfrow = c(1, 4))` as in Figure 3.13), you will set the corresponding parameter, and the previous value will be returned in a `list`. You can use a `list` as input to set several parameters at once.

Example B.3
Figure B.4 illustrates the use of a list in the `par()` function to set different graphical parameter values. In this case, a 3×2 layout of plots is obtained, with margin widths set smaller than the default values, allowing the

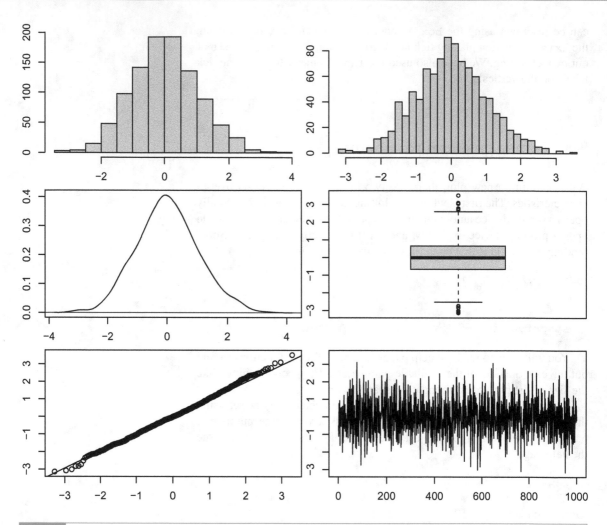

Fig. B.4 Illustrating the use of a list when setting graphical parameters, while providing six different views of a simulated normally distributed random sample.

individual plots to be bigger. In particular, the top and right margins are set to 0.1, allowing very little space in those margins for material, such as titles, and so on. The lower margin is set to 2.5 and the left margin is set to 2.1, values which are large enough for axis tick labels to be drawn, but default axis labels do not fit into such small margins. Code for Figure B.4 is as follows.

```
par(list = list(mfrow = c(3, 2), mar = c(2.5,2.1,0.1,0.1)))
Z <- rnorm(1000)
hist(Z, main = "")
hist(Z, breaks = "Freedman-Diaconis", main = "")
plot(density(Z), main = "")
boxplot(Z)
qqnorm(Z, main = ""); qqline(Z)
ts.plot(Z)
```

Index